The Orient Express

The Orient Express

The Fiction that Brought the East to the West

RANDY ROSENTHAL

CASCADE *Books* · Eugene, Oregon

THE ORIENT EXPRESS
The Fiction that Brought the East to the West

Copyright © 2024 Randy Rosenthal. All rights reserved. Except for brief quotations in critical publications or reviews, no part of this book may be reproduced in any manner without prior written permission from the publisher. Write: Permissions, Wipf and Stock Publishers, 199 W. 8th Ave., Suite 3, Eugene, OR 97401.

Cascade Books
An Imprint of Wipf and Stock Publishers
199 W. 8th Ave., Suite 3
Eugene, OR 97401

www.wipfandstock.com

PAPERBACK ISBN: 978-1-6667-7527-3
HARDCOVER ISBN: 978-1-6667-7528-0
EBOOK ISBN: 978-1-6667-7529-7

Cataloguing-in-Publication data:

Names: Rosenthal, Randy, author.

Title: The orient express : the fiction that brought the east to the west / Randy Rosenthal.

Description: Eugene, OR : Cascade Books, 2024 | Includes bibliographical references.

Identifiers: ISBN 978-1-6667-7527-3 (paperback) | ISBN 978-1-6667-7528-0 (hardcover) | ISBN 978-1-6667-7529-7 (ebook)

Subjects: LCSH: Maugham, W. Somerset (William Somerset), 1874–1965. Razor's edge. | Hesse, Hermann, 1877–1962. Siddhartha. | Salinger, J. D. (Jerome David), 1919–2010. Franny and Zooey. | Kerouac, Jack, 1922–1969. The dharma bums.

Classification: PN49 .R68 2024 (paperback) | PN49 .R68 (ebook)

01/29/24

This book is dedicated to my parents, Sue and Michael, who gave me the freedom to find my own way to the East.

For the artist or intellectual, who happens to also be interested in reality and desirous of liberation, the way out would seem to lie, as usual, along a knife-edge.

ALDOUS HUXLEY, *TIME MUST HAVE A STOP*

Contents

	Permissions	ix
	Author's Note	xi
	Introduction	xiii
1	The Razor's Edge	1
2	Siddhartha	38
3	Franny and Zooey	86
4	The Dharma Bums	117
	Postscript	167
	Sources	173
	Acknowledgments	179
	About the Author	181

Permissions

Grateful acknowledgment is made to the following for permission to reprint previously published material:

© Bhikkhu Bodhi 2005. *In the Buddha's Words: An Anthology of Discourses from the Pali Canon*. Reprinted by arrangement with Wisdom Publications, Inc., wisdompubs.org.

Excerpt(s) from THE DHAMMAPADA: VERSES ON THE WAY by Buddha, translated by Glenn Wallis, copyright © 2004 by Penguin Random House LLC. Used by permission of Modern Library, an imprint of Random House, a division of Penguin Random House LLC. All rights reserved.

THERIGATHA: POEMS OF THE FIRST BUDDHIST WOMEN, translated by Charles Hallisey, Murty Classical Library of India Volume 3, Cambridge, Mass.: Harvard University Press, Copyright © 2015 by the President and Fellows of Harvard College. Used by permission. All rights reserved.

Excerpts from SIDDHARTHA by Hermann Hesse, translated by Hilda Rosner, copyright ©1951 by New Directions Publishing Corp. Reprinted by permission of New Directions Publishing Corp.

Excerpt(s) from THE DHARMA BUMS by Jack Kerouac, copyright © 1958 by Jack Kerouac; copyright renewed © 1986 by Stella Kerouac and Jan Kerouac. Used by permission of Viking Books, an imprint of Penguin Publishing Group, a division of Penguin Random House LLC. All rights reserved.

Excerpts from THE RAZOR'S EDGE by Somerset Maugham reproduced by permission of United Agents Ltd (www.unitedagents.co.uk) on behalf of The Royal Literary Fund (Copyright © The Royal Literary Fund), and by permission of Paradigm Talent Agency on behalf of International Literary Properties (Copyright © International Literary Properties).

Author's Note

THOUGH THIS BOOK IS a work of scholarship, I wrote it for a general audience. Accordingly, I omitted footnotes, endnotes, and diacritics. I hope these absences make the book more accessible.

I also omitted postmodern critical theories commonly used to deconstruct Western narratives about Eastern religion. That is, you won't find condemnations of cultural appropriation, orientalism, or lack of diversity. By now, these critiques are obvious, and I chose to put them aside.

After all, my purpose is not to tear down but to build up—to clarify and help share the wonderful philosophies and practices of Eastern spirituality presented in these four works of fiction, which I believe still hold wisdom that can be greatly beneficial in our troubled times.

Introduction

WHILE WANDERING ALONE THROUGH the streets of Capri, a young Somerset Maugham asked himself: "What is the meaning of life? Has it any object or end? Is there such a thing as morality? How ought one to conduct oneself in life? What guide is there? Is there one road better than another?" Being a reader and writer, he naturally found his answers in books, and he later shared what he found in a book of his own.

As a child, Susan Sontag referred to her books as "household deities." She understood the acts of reading and writing to be spiritual practices, and like her, there are many people who claim literature as their religion. Studying Scripture has long been considered an act of religious devotion, but reading modern fiction, too, can feel like a spiritual practice. For me, reading the fiction of Jorge Luis Borges is a transcendent experience. The same goes for Bruno Schulz, Clarice Lispector, John Banville, and Elena Ferrante—their prose is so beautiful, insightful, and masterfully composed that reading them produces contemplative mental states akin to meditation or prayer. The mundane becomes sacred, and we look at the world anew.

The acts of reading and writing fiction may inspire a spiritual feeling, but fiction that deals directly with spirituality is another matter. We're skeptical of it. It's all good if fiction has meaning, but we don't want it to have a message. Writing with a message is a form of literature we've designated to the self-help shelf. It's pigeonholed as "inspirational." For Western intellectuals, this inherent skepticism is especially the case if the fiction deals with Eastern religions and spiritual practices. We'll dismiss it faster than we can say "airy-fairy."

But in an age when yoga studios are ubiquitous and meditation apps are on millions of smartphones, we forget that things weren't always this way, and that what is now considered cliché was once unknown. So how did the wisdom of the East come to so thoroughly permeate the culture of the West?

Answering that question is what this book is about.

Western intellectuals weren't able to get their hands on translations of Eastern religious texts until the nineteenth century. One of the earliest was Arthur Schopenhauer, who was deeply influenced by the 1802 Latin translations of the Upanishads, which he called "the production of the highest human wisdom," saying it was "the consolation of my life, and will be the solace of my death." Later, he was so impressed by Buddhist scriptures that he claimed Buddhism is "the best of all possible religions." Like the German Romantics, the American Transcendentalists would hardly have been so transcendental if they were not influenced by Indian religions. They read what they could of the Vedas, particularly the Upanishads and the *Bhagavad Gita*, which are frequently referenced in the writings of both Ralph Waldo Emerson and Henry David Thoreau. In *Walden*, Thoreau writes:

> In the morning I bathe my intellect in the stupendous and cosmogonal philosophy of the Bhagavat Geeta, since whose composition years of the gods have elapsed, and in comparison with which our modern world and its literature seem puny and trivial; and I doubt if that philosophy is not to be referred to a previous state of existence, so remote is its sublimity from our conceptions. I lay down the book and go to my well for water, and lo! there I meet the servant of the Brahmin, priest of Brahma, and Vishnu and Indra, who still sits in his temple on the Ganges reading the Vedas, or dwells at the root of a tree with his crust and water-jug. I meet his servant come to draw water for his master, and our buckets as it were grate together in the same well. The pure Walden water is mingled with the sacred water of the Ganges.

Published in 1854, this must have come off as incomprehensible for most readers of the time—not to mentions ours. For many, these references to Hinduism often escape the memory of reading *Walden*, which is more often associated with New England ponds and bean fields. Even so, Thoreau planted some spiritual seeds back then. Seeds that sprouted a century later.

Toward the end of his life, Tolstoy famously became a devout Christian, but he also studied Eastern religions; his late essays reference Lao-Tse, Confucius, and "Hindu wisdom" as often as they do Schopenhauer, Seneca, and Ruskin. Many people know that Nietzsche wrote extensively about religion, but not that he had a particular fondness for Buddhism, which he used as a foil to Christianity. "Buddhism is a hundred times more realistic than Christianity," Nietzsche wrote in *The Antichrist* (1895). Emphasizing the fundamental difference between the two religions, he writes: "Buddhism does not promise but fulfills; Christianity promises everything but fulfills nothing." To us today, this might be stating the obvious, but in the late nineteenth century such sentences would do more than raise a reader's eyebrows. A few hundred years earlier and it would have gotten him burned at the stake.

For these nineteenth-century thinkers, the ideas found in Eastern religion were profound. But these ideas were novel, the translations fresh, and so these Westerners did not fully grasp the concepts they were writing about. Even so, a door was open then. And by opening that door to the East, a question was asked. The question wasn't about the existence of God, or heaven and hell, or any of those old dualisms of belief or unbelief, of faith or atheism. Rather, the question was: *Isn't there something more? Isn't there a deeper, more fulfilling way to live life?*

Our greatest thinkers believed the answer—the solution—was in Eastern religion. Why? Because Western culture teaches us to value the material and the quantifiable. Not only a house, cars, and money, but marriage, children, and status. We're taught that without such things, we can't possibly be happy. But even with them—sometime *because* of them—many of us still aren't happy. We have full bellies and bank accounts, but we're spiritually empty. This spiritual emptiness is what turned the Romantics, the Transcendentalists, the Beats, and the Beatles to the East, and what turns many of us to the East today.

Since Schopenhauer, there have been hundreds of translators, scholars, swamis, lamas, and gurus who've come to the West to enlighten us moderns on the ancient wisdom of Eastern religions. With the ease of international flights, many of us have traveled to Asia to experience these religions firsthand, joining ashrams, communes, and monasteries—all of which are now found at home. Buddha statues and Shinto shrines are as common in American yards as monsoon frogs are in India. Once exotic terms like karma, zen, and nirvana have entered into everyday English. It's normal to find the *Tao Te Ching* or the *Dhammapada* on coffee tables and nightstands. Business consultants have appropriated the meditational terms "mindfulness" and "equanimity." And yet, while there are countless books on meditation and Buddhism, there still seems to be an unspoken taboo about mixing Eastern spirituality and fiction.

This taboo reminds me of Stendhal's famous line: "Politics in a literary work is like a gunshot in the middle of a concert, something vulgar, and however, something impossible to ignore." Writers of fiction usually avoid such vulgarity. Only the most talented are able to incorporate politics in a way that seamlessly blends with their story, so that it doesn't stick out as preachy. Think of Gabriel Garcia Marquez's use of the Banana Company in *One Hundred Years of Solitude*—his generality makes the politics universal, not only tolerable but powerful. Something specific, however, not only makes a work dated, but also insipid. For what's politically important in one era may be passé in another.

While political issues come and go, the spiritual is perennial. So it would seem safe for literary authors to infuse their fiction with spiritual wisdom. Or even to write about specific practices and philosophies. After all, yoga and meditation have been around for thousands of years—they're not going anywhere.

Yet the opposite appears to be the case. It's just not acceptable to write explicitly about matters of the spirit. At least not in literary fiction. Such things may have passed during the Romantic era, but since then it's become critically unfashionable. Anything deep is dismissed as pretentious. Not only can reputations be damaged, careers can be ruined. And yet, ignoring the taboo, there have been a handful of well-respected authors who have written explicitly about Eastern spirituality in their fiction, and who have done so successfully.

Though there may be others, the four works of spiritual fiction I find most influential in bringing Eastern religion to the Western mainstream are *The Razor's Edge* by W. Somerset Maugham, *Siddhartha* by Herman Hesse, *Franny and Zooey* by J. D. Salinger, and *The Dharma Bums* by Jack Kerouac. Through the lives of their characters, these authors present the spiritual practices and philosophies not only of yoga and Buddhism but Hindu Vedanta, Brahmanism, Taoism, and the *hesychast* prayer tradition of Eastern Orthodox Christianity. They also explore what motivates someone to seek a spiritual practice in the first place, the existential questions that inspire the search—those questions Somerset Maugham asked during his visit to Capri: "What is the meaning of life? Has it any object or end? Is there such a thing as morality? How ought one to conduct oneself in life? What guide is there? Is there one road better than another?" Being artists, these authors don't necessarily provide answers to these questions, but through their stories they indicate paths on which answers can be found.

Far from being minor works or embarrassing experiments, these books are among the authors' best. And because of their popularity, they have often served as gateways to Eastern religion, inspiring many readers to go beyond the page and actually experiment with such spiritual practices for themselves. In fact, whenever I ask a Western Buddhist monk, Buddhist studies professor, yogi, or meditator what initially got them interested in Eastern spirituality, they usually mention one or more of these books. In other words, these four writers brought us to the East—and they did so through their fiction.

The Orient Express takes us on this journey.

1

The Razor's Edge

SOMERSET MAUGHAM WROTE *THE Razor's Edge* in seven months, but he'd been developing its characters and plot for over twenty-five years. He had tried to write the story in two of his early works, the short story "The Fall of Edward Barnard" and an unpublished play called *The Road Uphill*. Both are about an amiable young man from Chicago who drops out of society after his experience as an aviator in World War I. Yet these pieces are missing the very thing that gives *The Razor's Edge* its soul: Eastern spirituality. It wasn't until 1942—after Maugham had visited India and was pushing seventy— that he was finally able to return to this character and write his book of spiritual fiction. By then Maugham was said to be the highest paid writer in the business, and so he could afford to make such a gamble. But it took him a while to get there.

A symbol of English glamour and sophistication, William Somerset Maugham was actually born in Paris in 1874. After a happy Parisian childhood, he was orphaned at age ten, and never recovered from his mother's death. The distraught boy was brought back to his family's native England, and lived in a vicarage with his aunt and uncle, the vicar of Whitstable. After completing high school at the once prestigious King's School in Canterbury, Maugham declined to follow his older brothers' footsteps to Cambridge. Instead, he spent a year studying German in Heidelberg, and then became a medical student at St. Thomas's Hospital in London. But he had secretly decided to become a writer.

Ambitious to write for the theater, Maugham first wrote several plays, all of which were rejected. While training in midwifery, he got an idea for a novel, and in 1897 he published *Liza of Lambeth*, a work of straightforward realism that exposed the squalor of London's slums, which Maugham had witnessed while working as an obstetric clerk. Flush with confidence, the twenty-three-year-old abandoned a medical career in order to make a living as a writer. It was a decision he later called "absolutely idiotic," since he "could just well have written at night and avoided the desperate financial struggle."

For the following decade, Maugham all but failed. A closeted bisexual, handsome but self-conscious of his short stature and stammer, Maugham had the expensive habits of a socialite and dandy, and spent his late twenties and early thirties in classy poverty, writing flop after flop, receiving rejection after rejection. He wrote several novels that were either dismissed due to their "improper" sexual content or published to tepid reception. Influenced by Ibsen, Maugham turned back to his first love of playwriting, only to meet equal frustration. His sole income was from the occasional short story sold to a magazine, which earned him respect among the literary intelligentsia but hardly paid the bills. He was in a rut, and saw no future for himself in London. So Maugham moved to Paris, where he befriended artists and lived the bohemian life.

He came close to giving up, and resigned to return to his abandoned medical career. Then in October 1907, Maugham scored his first major success with the play *Lady Frederick*, which had previously been rejected by seventeen management companies. A light but shocking society comedy about a charming, titled widow trying to maintain her status and integrity, the play became the talk of the town. After years of struggle, Maugham never had to worry about money again. Within a year, he had four plays running simultaneously in London's West End. His name plastered all over the press, Maugham was interviewed, photographed, and talked about. And unlike the other authors in this book, he "thoroughly enjoyed" being famous. At age thirty-five, he was so successful a playwright he declared that he would never write another novel. He even told his literary agent as much, requesting to sever their association.

But in 1911, after four busy years in the theater, Maugham became absorbed with the idea of a novel, feeling a compulsion to write something different and more honest than he had ever written before. Retreating from everything except his numerous love affairs, including one with a Russian princess and another that ended in a rejected proposal, Maugham wrote steadily. And in 1915, he published *Of Human Bondage*, a long and autobiographical novel about a medical student's destructive sexual obsession with a callous waitress. It is the book that established Maugham's reputation as a great literary artist—though not immediately; war was occupying Europe, and nearly everyone was swept up in patriotism.

Too old to enlist at age forty, he volunteered for the Red Cross and put his medical skills to use on the battlefields of France. Then he served as a spy for the British Intelligence Service, first in Geneva and then in St. Petersburg, just before the Bolshevik Revolution. Between assignments, he reluctantly entered into a miserable marriage with a woman who'd given birth to his daughter. He then traveled to the South Pacific with Gerald Haxton, a much younger American man who'd been in Maugham's Red Cross ambulance unit and would become his companion for the next thirty years. From these adventures, Maugham contracted tuberculosis, the disease that killed his mother, and had to recuperate at a sanatorium in Scotland. But the fiction he wrote based on his experiences made him fabulously rich, especially *Ashenden*, the spy stories that established the espionage genre; *The Moon and Six Pence*, the Tahitian novel based on the life of Paul Gauguin; and "Rain," a story about a hypocritical missionary that alone earned Maugham over a million dollars in royalties.

During the two decades following the war, he and Haxton traveled extensively. On various trips, they journeyed through China and nearly all of Southeast Asia, where Maugham was immersed in Buddhist culture, got a bad case of malaria, and mined material for his colonial Far East stories, for which he was most well-known during his lifetime. The couple spent time in Hollywood—there were numerous film adaptations of Maugham's work—and also traveled throughout Europe and parts of Central America. But it was in India where Maugham came under the influence of Eastern religion, particularly the Hindu philosophy known as Vedanta, which he learned from the revered Indian sage Sri Ramana Maharshi.

In between trips, Maugham continued to churn out the words. He wrote fourteen more plays (before retiring from the theater in 1933), a dozen short story collections, and half as many novels, including *Cakes and Ale*, the scathing *roman à clef* that Maugham ranked the favorite of his novels, and which made him the top novelist of the day. Though that's not to say he was considered a great literary artist, either by critics or himself: "I know just where I stand," he admitted, "in the very front row of the second rate." As the writer Glenway Wescott put it, Maugham was "the mahatma of middlebrow culture."

Since 1926, Maugham had been living on his nine-acre villa in the French Riviera, halfway between Nice and Monte Carlo. But the Nazi invasion forced him to evacuate, first to England and then to America, where he rode out most of World War II in the South Carolina country home of his publisher, Nelson Doubleday. Offering himself as a tool for propaganda, Maugham again went to work for the British government, writing articles and giving speeches on behalf of the war effort. By then, he was the wealthiest and most famous living writer in the world. With nothing to lose, he was free to break the rules. He could experiment with taking literary fiction further than its acceptable limits. Without concern for critics or sales, he could write a novel espousing a subject that was of tremendous personal importance to him: Vedanta, the philosophical foundation of Hinduism.

The result was *The Razor's Edge*. Published in 1944, it is essentially a story of a spiritual quest, with the ultimate purpose of disseminating a religious truth. And so Maugham was understandably surprised when the book immediately sold out of its first print run. But spirituality was apparently what a war-weary audience wanted, and Maugham found the book's reception greatly satisfying. Praised by such diverse figures as Gandhi and Orson Welles, *The Razor's Edge* sold half a million copies within the first month in the US alone, and went on to be made into two Hollywood films (both flopped). Maugham published a dozen more books before dying in 1965, at age ninety-one, yet he never again reached the level of impact he achieved with *The Razor's Edge*.

In the introduction to a book of Maugham's traveling writings, *The Skeptical Romancer*, Pico Iyer writes that *The Razor's Edge* might be "the first hippie novel ever written." But readers in the late 1960s and seventies found Maugham's conventional stories of late colonial days irrelevant for the rapidly changing times, and instead they turned to innovative authors like Hermann Hesse and Jack Kerouac. Over the decades following his death, Maugham's work was all but ignored. And so perhaps that's why I never heard of *The Razor's Edge* until I was thirty-two and living in New York, teaching English and editing a literary magazine called *The Coffin Factory*. Several issues of the magazine featured the work of photographer Bill Hayward, who kindly invited me to his studio to participate in his ongoing series, *The Human Bible, portraits of the collaborative self*. Before shooting portraits, Bill tries to make his subjects comfortable by casually chatting. As the conversation unfolds, he asks questions that open up their deeper self, the unhindered self he wants to see in his photographs. At some point, he gives his subject paper, paint, and permission to create whatever they feel like. Then he photographs them in front of their creation.

As it turned out, I didn't make a good subject for a portrait. But during our pre-shoot conversation, I mentioned my time in India, where I'd gone five years earlier, after a pilgrimage to Burma. And among other anecdotes, I told Bill how I'd taken a weekend off from managing a meditation center in Dharamsala to hike high into the Himalayas and sleep in a cave next to a glacier. I had no idea what I was doing, and nearly froze to death that night. In many ways it was a revelatory experience—it revealed that I wasn't the kind of person who should be hiking alone and sleeping in caves. Bill laughed and said my story reminded him of *The Razor's Edge*. And that's how I first heard of the book that later inspired me to write this one.

The narrator of *The Razor's Edge* is named Somerset Maugham. On the first page, he claims to have written a novel called *The Moon and Sixpence*. In previous novels, Maugham called his alter ego "Willie Ashenden," but here he uses his own name and biography for the first time, as if he's writing a memoir. He also opens with a disclaimer, saying the book is only called "a novel" because he doesn't know what else to call it, especially as it "ends neither with a death nor marriage." It's about people who actually exist, he explains, and claims he's "invented nothing." Of course, this is a lie. The author is simply trying to make his readers believe the "little story" he's about to tell is true.

Actually an ambitious story, *The Razor's Edge* focuses on four blue-blooded Americans, but is really about one of them: Larry Darrell. In the opening pages, the narrator—who I'll refer to as Somerset, in order to avoid confusing with the author—explains he's writing a book about Larry because "it may be that the life he has chosen for himself and the peculiar strength and sweetness of his character may have an ever-growing influence over his fellow men so that, long after his death perhaps, it may be realized that there lived in this age a very remarkable creature."

Some readers might wonder what makes Larry so remarkable. After all, he doesn't become rich or create great works of art. He isn't powerful and he doesn't own any property. He doesn't invent anything and never earns a degree. He isn't good at sports, and he isn't charismatic. He never marries, has no children, and doesn't even have much sex. Basically, he doesn't do anything that remarkable people usually do. On paper, Larry Darrell appears to be the very opposite of what our society values in a person.

Somerset first meets Larry at a dinner party in Chicago in 1919, when Larry is only twenty. Somerset is on his way to the Far East and Larry had recently returned from World War I, in which he fought as an aviator in the Canadian air corps. (Canadian because he was only seventeen and the US wouldn't accept him; he lied to the Canadians.) But readers don't meet Larry in the flesh until twenty pages in, after being thoroughly introduced to the character Elliott Templeton, who has been friends with Somerset for fifteen years.

Originally from Virginia, Templeton is a discreet art dealer who lives in Paris, sometimes London, and later in the Riviera. He's a social climber obsessed with the parties and balls of the elite, hobnobbing with European royalty his *raison d'etre*. Pretentious, vain, and a "colossal snob," valuing connections and invitations over dignity and integrity, Elliott even converts to Catholicism in order to open social doors that were previously closed. Distancing himself from his American roots as far as possible, Elliott believes he descends from royalty himself, and later has a count's crown embroidered on his bed sheets and dressing gowns. Wearing the right clothes, drinking the right wine, and being invited to the right parties are Elliott's definitions of success. Somerset doubts "whether it was possible for Elliott Templeton to be a friend" because "he took no interest in people apart from their social position." He only befriended the lowly writer after Somerset had several successful plays and became a celebrity, which would add to Elliott's social credibility.

The reason Maugham introduces Elliott at length is so his values can later serve as a foil to Larry's. But in fact, the author has split himself between these three characters. Both Maugham and Elliott are "old queens," as Maugham's biographer Selina Hastings puts it, and Maugham "did love dining with a duke; he was impressed by titles and by the old established aristocracy, discreetly thrilled when in the presence of royalty." But unlike Elliott, Maugham wasn't so snobby as to rate people by their social status. Elliott represents the author's most vain and superficial self, just as Larry represents his deepest and most spiritual self. Larry is who Maugham would like to be, and Elliott is who he fears becoming. And the narrator Somerset, coolly detached and moderate, curious and guarded, most reflects who Maugham actually was.

But in a way, each of the four main characters in *The Razor's Edge* represents a certain type of person, if not a particular philosophy. Isabel Bradley is Elliott's "sparkling and vivacious" niece. "Comely though on the fat side," Isabel grew up with Larry and has always loved him. After he returns from war, they become engaged. But Larry's in no hurry to get married. Unlike his peers, he doesn't want go to college. He also doesn't want to get a job. Orphaned, Larry receives three thousand dollars a year from government bonds, and that's enough for him. (It's an amount roughly equivalent to today's median individual income.)

His best friend is Gray Maturin, who's also at the dinner party. Somerset is impressed by Gray's "virility," and notes the large young man is "obviously very powerful." Gray is later described as "the quintessence of the Regular Guy," a man who speaks in clichés, and whose sense of self derives from his job. He's also in love with Isabel. So in love "he can't see straight." He actually proposed to her while Larry was away at war. But Isabel delayed giving an answer until Larry returned home, when she turned Gray down flat.

Somerset learns this from the girl he's sitting next to at the Chicago party, Sophie Macdonald, who is a peripheral character but plays a crucial role later in the book. Sophie calls Gray "high-principled," and due to his sense of honor, Gray not only bows out of courting Isabel, he convinces his millionaire father to offer Larry a job in his investment brokerage business, where Gray has just begun to work. But Larry refuses the job offer. When asked what he wants to do, Larry says he wants "to loaf." This is all very disconcerting to Isabel and her family, who don't want her to marry "an idler." As Isabel's mother says, "If he loves you, he ought to be prepared to work for you."

Later during the dinner party, after the young people leave, the adults discuss Larry. Elliott's opinion is that America is about to embark on "a period of prosperity such as it had never known," and says Larry had "a chance of getting in on the ground floor, and if he kept his nose to the grindstone he might well be many times a millionaire by the time he was forty." They don't understand what his problem is. Larry's guardian, Dr. Nelson, thinks, "The war did something to Larry. He didn't come back the same person that he went. It's not only that he's older. Something happened that changed his personality." They believe he's "suffering from delayed shock," or what we today might label PTSD. Larry hasn't yet spoken about his war experiences with anyone, and no one really knows what he does all day.

Early the following morning, Somerset goes to a club library to find "hard to come by" university magazines. When he arrives, he's surprised to find Larry reading *The Principles of Psychology* by William James, the philosopher and psychologist who developed pragmatism and radical empiricism—the two doctrines that just so happened to dominate twentieth century American philosophy. They chat a bit and Somerset notes the melodiousness of Larry's voice, which he describes as persuasive and "like balm." He's also struck by the young man's engaging smile, which "lit his face with an inner light," and the "expressiveness of his very black eyes." Larry's irises are so dark they blend with his pupils, which give his eyes a "peculiar intensity." Soon, Somerset goes to find his *Yale Quarterly*. Hours later, he's leaving the library and sees Larry in the same position, immersed in his book as if he hadn't moved. Somerset is stuck by Larry's "evident power of concentration." Later in the evening, out of curiosity, Somerset again drops by the library. And Larry is in the same chair, intent on the same book. Somerset understands that by "loafing" Larry means reading. And because he's reading *The Principles of Psychology*, the book that solidified psychology's credibility as a science and introduced revolutionary theories about the mind, Larry is clearly trying to figure it all out. Somerset sees this, but everyone else thinks of Larry as "a washout" and "a joke." They say he'll "never amount to anything."

A few days after the dinner party, Isabel invites Larry for a picnic to openly discuss their future, once and for all. They head out to the country and when Isabel brings up his job offer, Larry says he knows people expect him to be normal, that he should "follow the beaten path" and "be like everybody else." He admits he could be refusing the job only because he's a "conceited prig." But then he gives the real reason: "Money just doesn't happen to interest me." His fixed income is enough for a bachelor to live on, but nowhere near the amount Isabel expects her husband to earn. She wants diamond rings and fancy dresses, and she can't very well buy them for herself. She wants to entertain and be entertained, and she needs the proper house in order to do so. "It's a matter of self-respect," she says, and because Larry refuses to "be sensible" and take a job that makes a lot of money, she accuses him of making her "miserable."

After a few moments of silent thought, Larry abruptly says, "The dead look so terribly dead when they're dead." Disturbed by the non sequitur, Isabel complains that Larry is "so different" from who he was before he went to France. But of course he's different, he says, and then reveals, "My greatest friend in the air corps was killed saving my life." They were in a dogfight, and his friend risked himself to get an enemy off Larry's tail. When they landed, Larry watched his friend die. He doesn't want to talk much about it, but he adds, "You think of a fellow who an hour before was full of life and fun, and he's lying dead; it's all so cruel and meaningless. It's hard not to ask yourself what life is all about and whether there's any sense to it or whether it's all a tragic blunder of blind fate." Now we have an idea of what changed Larry, and why he tells Isabel, "I want to do more with my life than sell bonds." It often takes the sight of the dead for people to realize they're alive. It's death that motivates people to find the best way to live their life. And while Larry isn't yet sure about the best way to live, he knows there's more to life than making money.

When Isabel relates this conversation to Somerset a few days later, the narrator sympathizes—not with Isabel but with Larry. During the war, Somerset once saw a pile of dead French soldiers heaped upon one another. He tells Isabel they looked "like the marionettes in a bankrupt puppet show that had been cast pell-mell into a dusty corner because they were of no use any more." At the time, Somerset thought just what Larry said: "the dead look so awfully dead." He understands what happened to Larry. He knows that the moment you realize you're going to die is the moment you begin to live real life. It's the epiphany that starts the spiritual quest. Hesse's, Salinger's, and Kerouac's characters have already passed this point by the time we meet them, but Maugham has Larry start at the beginning.

In order to ease the situation with Isabel and her family, Larry decides to move to Paris, where he can "loaf" without interference. Her family finds this to be a tolerable idea, and Elliott promises to introduce Larry to all "the right people." Even Elliott can't blame Larry for wanting to live "in the only city in the world fit for a civilized man to live in." If Larry doesn't find what he's looking for within two years, he'll return to Chicago, take any work he can find, and marry Isabel.

And so off to Paris he goes.

Why does Maugham have Larry go to Paris? For starters, many Americans lived in Paris after the First World War. Along with Ernest Hemingway, F. Scott Fitzgerald, T. S. Elliot, John Dos Passos, Henry Miller, and James Joyce, Larry Durrell is a member of the lost generation. Paris was cheap at the time, and unlike the States, which had just passed the Volstead Act, alcohol was flowing freely. You could eat and drink in cafés every day and every night and hardly run down your bank account. In other words, living in Paris was a practical thing for a bohemian to do. As Hemingway wrote in *A Moveable Feast*, Paris in the 1920s was a place to be "very poor and very happy."

Perhaps more significantly, Paris is a symbolic step on the journey to self-knowledge. The City of Light, the heart of the Enlightenment, Paris represents the peak of Western thought. Montesquieu and Diderot, Voltaire and Rousseau. The Cult of Reason, the Encyclopedia, and The Declaration of the Rights of Man and Citizen. The universal humanist philosophy still dominating Western political thought was born and raised in Paris. One goes to Rome to study Catholicism, to Cairo or Baghdad to study Islam, to Vienna to study music, and to New York or London to make money. But Paris is where you go for philosophy.

To find answers to his existential questions, Larry naturally must live and study in Paris.

Nearly a year after the Chicago dinner party, Somerset is passing through Paris, and learns that Larry has snubbed Elliott's invitations to dinner parties and luncheons, giving lame excuses that he "hadn't brought any evening clothes" and "never ate luncheon." Exasperated, Elliott quickly got the hint and left Larry alone. He doesn't know what Larry has been doing, and thinks his niece shouldn't marry the "thoroughly undesirable young man."

Several days after arriving, Somerset runs into Larry at a café in the bohemian neighborhood of Montparnasse, where Larry rents a "scrubby little room in a hotel." (And where Maugham lived himself, two decades earlier.) Larry invites Somerset to lunch, and they meet again the next day. When Larry orders, Maugham observes that he speaks fluent French, with the proper accent. Asked what he does with himself, Larry reticently answers, "I loaf." He admits he reads, but doesn't say much more. He's curious to know about Somerset's journey to China, and listens attentively. Then Larry abruptly pays the bill and says he must be off. Somerset is pleased but baffled: "I was forced to the conclusion that he had asked me to lunch with him merely to enjoy my company."

The next time he hears of Larry is from Isabel. That spring, Isabel and her mother stay at Elliott's grand apartment on the Rive Gauche, in the fashionable Rue St Guillaume. Larry meets them at the train station, and he appears genuinely happy to see his fiancée. He now accepts all of Elliott's invitations to luncheons and dinners, where he and Isabel behave as if they're still very much in love. But Larry doesn't mention going back to Chicago, or the status of their engagement.

After a month of frustration, Isabel invites herself to Larry's room, which she calls "awfully squalid." She asks what he's been up to, and Larry says he's been reading "eight or ten hours a day." He's learning Greek, and can read in both French and Latin. He mentions Spinoza and the Flemish mystic Ruysbroeck. All this doesn't mean a thing to Isabel. She wants to know when he's coming back to Chicago. With American pragmatism, she asks where all this studying is "going to lead." When Larry replies, "The acquisition of knowledge," she responds, "It doesn't sound very practical." Practical would be moving back to Chicago and getting a job so they can get married.

But Larry can't go back to Chicago, not when he's "on the threshold." What threshold? He sees "vast lands of the spirit" stretching ahead and wants to travel them in order to find answers to his questions. What questions? "I want to make up my mind whether God is or God is not. I want to find out why evil exists. I want to know whether I have an immortal soul or whether when I die it's the end." This sort of talk makes Isabel uncomfortable. She accuses him of shirking his responsibilities as an American. To her, such questions are "adolescent." They're "things sophomores get excited about" and then forget when "they have to earn a living."

Larry reminds her that money "doesn't mean a thing" to him, since his fixed income gives him enough to live on. He says he wants to study as passionately as Gray wants to make pots of money. And he doesn't see anything wrong in spending a few years educating himself. She interprets this to mean he doesn't care about her. But to Isabel's surprise, Larry asks her to marry him, as soon as possible. On his three thousand a year, they could live the bohemian life in Paris, hanging out with painters, writers, and students, honeymooning in Greece and traveling through Italy.

Isabel is disgusted by his suggestion. She can't see past her privileged American perspective of how life is supposed to be. "I want to do all the things that people do," she says. "I want to go to parties. I want to go to dances, I want to play golf and ride horseback. I want to wear nice clothes. Can't you imagine what it means to a girl not to be as well dressed as the rest of her crowd?" Girl wants the bling. Despite her shallow values, Larry speaks patiently, with smiles and a calm voice, trying to persuade Isabel the life he's offering is much fuller than anything she can conceive of: "I wish I can make you see how exciting the life of the spirit is and how rich in experience. You feel such a sense of exhilaration that you wouldn't exchange it for all the power and glory in the world."

But she can't get past the fact that Larry doesn't have a job, and doesn't want one. "It's so wrong," she says. "A man ought to work. That's what he's here for." When Larry continues to try convincing her, she punches below the belt: "Be a man, Larry, and do a man's work." Isabel is an American through and through, and to her life is about one thing: making money. Those who make it are successful, and those who don't are losers. It never occurs to her that intellectual work is a higher form of work than money-making, and that spiritual work is higher still—that it is the highest form of work there is.

She finally threatens him, saying she won't want to marry him if he doesn't come back to Chicago. Larry says returning to Chicago and getting a job would be the betrayal of his soul. Understandably, Larry and Isabel agree to call off their engagement. They remain on amiable terms for the rest of her stay.

Somerset learns all of this a few days later, from Isabel herself, who by then has taken the narrator into her confidence as "a disinterested observer." She is looking for his approval. ("Any writer will tell you," Somerset explains, "people do tell a writer things that they don't tell others.") He tries to help Isabel understand the nature of Larry's quest, explaining that the desire for knowledge is neither selfish nor ignoble. After hearing he's been reading Ruysbroeck, "the Ecstatic teacher," Somerset suggests that Larry's searching "for God." But Isabel has a different sense of the word, a literal one, and she laughs dismissively. To her, if you want to find God you read the Bible and go to church on Sundays. And anyway, Protestants aren't really supposed to be finding God, but fearing him. By "God" Somerset doesn't mean the father figure in the sky, but what Larry later calls "the Infinite." The word "God" is a euphemism for the unknown—what science has yet to understand. It's the same symbolic use of the term that Einstein meant when he said, "God does not play dice." Isabel is no dope, but she just doesn't get it. As Somerset explains, she had "been brought up in a certain way and she accepted the principles that had been instilled into her." That is, she's blinded by American materialism. To Isabel, Larry's search is simply a waste of time.

By now it should be clear that through these conversations Maugham is making a not-so-subtle point. Through his lovers, he's staked out two opposing philosophical viewpoints. Isabel values the material, and Larry values the spiritual. Isabel values the quantitative, and Larry values the qualitative. Isabel is practical, and Larry is idealistic. Isabel is pragmatic, and Larry is Romantic. Isabel thinks with her head, and Larry thinks with his heart. Isabel accepts the values of her society, and Larry creates his own values. In creating this dualistic argument, Maugham implicitly asks his readers: Who are *you*? What do *you* value? Which kind of person will *you* be? What do *you* think life is about?

A few days after her conversation with Somerset, Isabel returns to America. She soon marries Larry's friend Gray Maturin, who's already making fifty thousand a year and is well on his way to becoming a millionaire.

Somerset doesn't see Isabel or Larry for another ten years. By then, the stock market has crashed and Gray is ruined.

After Isabel and Gray married, Gray's father bought the newlyweds a house on Astor Street and spent a hundred grand decorating it. (With subtle sarcasm, Maugham writes that their library was inspired by a room in the Amalienburg Palace in Munich and "except that there was no place in it for books it was perfect.") They have two daughters, Joan and Priscilla. When the first was born, Gray gave Isabel a square-cut diamond ring. For the birth of the second, he gave her a sable coat. For years "they entertained lavishly and were lavishly entertained," just as Isabel wanted. And then they lost everything.

Misjudging the depth of the crash, Gray's father uses his own money to back his clients' losses. When his entire fortune melts, he has a heart attack and dies, leaving Gray to deal with the situation. Unable to meet his firm's large debts, Gray declares bankruptcy. They lose their house and their credit. Gray cannot find work, not even as a clerk. Isabel's mother also dies, with her affairs "being in some disorder." They sell her house, but it's not enough. Isabel must sell her own jewelry. Anxious and humiliated, Gray has a nervous breakdown. He develops incapacitating headaches that leave him "as limp as a wet rag," and which we'd now label migraines. At this point, Isabel feels "that life wasn't worth living any more." She's "absolutely miserable," and can't face her future, which "was too black."

Somerset first learns of Gray's ruin from Elliott, who claims he received a tip of the impending crash from the Vatican. He sold out before October 29th, and came out the other side all the better.ABiding in the Riviera, he invites Isabel and her family to live in his spacious apartment in Paris, even providing them "a staff." Despite his vanity and snobbishness, Elliott turns out to be kind and generous when it counts, literally saving Isabel and Gray from certain poverty.

Months after the Maturins cross the Atlantic and settle in the Left Bank, Somerset comes to Paris. He visits Isabel and notices she's slimmed, and has become more beautiful and chic; he finds her ravishing, and isn't ashamed to say he frequently visits their apartment because he likes looking at her. Almost immediately, she mentions Larry. In an ironic turn of events, Isabel admits: "Gray hasn't a penny and I have almost exactly the income Larry had when he wanted me to marry him and I wouldn't because I thought we couldn't possibly live on it and now I've got two children besides." She tells Somerset that with Gray's headaches and shot nerves, he couldn't work even if he was offered a job. He's sunk into depression. Echoing Isabel's previous idea, Gray "feels it's a man's business to work and if he can't work he may just as well be dead." The loss of self-esteem shows through physical decay; Somerset observes that Gray is balding, has a puffy red face, and a double chin. He's now a heavy drinker and nearing obesity. His eyes show a "sort of puzzled dismay." Gray is simply not the man he once was. Without wealth and position to define him, he's nothing at all.

Nervous breakdowns, anxiety, headaches, depression, insomnia, physical decline. Through Gray and Isabel's situation, Maugham is implicitly making a point about the inevitable vicissitudes of life, and the trap of material values. There is no such thing as security, he's saying. If you trade love for money, you can lose both. What goes up, usually comes down. In a capitalist system, it's always boom and then bust. So whatever possessions we acquire are ultimately worthless—even if we don't lose them in our lifetime, we can't take them with us after we die. On the other hand, you can't lose knowledge. Wisdom is what cannot be taken away. Your mind is the only thing that's truly yours. It's our only possession. Larry seems to have known this intuitively. If he had gone to work for Gray's father, he'd also have been ruined. He'd have sacrificed his intellectual and spiritual quest for nothing. And speaking of Larry, everyone's wondering where he is. But nobody knows.

Then one day about two weeks later, Somerset is having a drink at the Dôme when a ragged looking man approaches him and says hello. The man is hatless, has "a mop of hair that badly needed cutting," and is heavily bearded. He's wearing a frayed shirt, shabby slacks, and a threadbare coat. Somerset has no idea who the man is. He thinks he's a bum pretending to be an acquaintance in order to get a handout. But it's Larry.

Judging by Larry's appearance, Somerset assumes he was hit hard by the crash, lost his fixed income, and was down and out. "What makes you think that?" Larry asks. When Somerset gestures to his clothes, Larry looks down and asks, "Are they as bad as all that? I never thought about it." Another foil, this time in reference to Elliott, who's obsessed with clothes, and also to Isabel, who previously expressed her greatest fear was not dressing as well as her peers. When asked where he's been, Larry replies with characteristic reticence, "India." Somerset then tells him about Isabel and Gray's situation. Larry "listened with his eyes fixed on my face in a meditative, unblinking gaze that suggested to me, I don't know why, that he was listening not with his ears, but with some inner more sensitive organ of hearing." The look makes Somerset feel uncomfortable. It's the first indication that Larry has been changed by his experience in India.

A few days later, Larry visits the Maturins at Elliot's apartment. He's now well-groomed and wearing a new suit. Somerset observes that Larry is "completely self possessed" when greeting Isabel and Gray for the first time in ten years. His "composure" calms his friends. While he's cordial and charming, he also has a "remoteness" about him, an "awareness or a sensibility or a force, that remained strangely aloof." Gray offers him a drink, but Larry has tea. Maugham is dropping hints.

Larry tells them he's been in India for the previous five years—we only find out later what he did for the five years before that. Somerset's curiosity is piqued. He rather abruptly asks, "Is it true that the Yogis acquire powers that would seem to us supernatural?"

Yogis? How many in the English-speaking world knew this word in 1944? For many, *The Razor's Edge* introduced them to the term. But it had been around for a while. The first person to bring yoga to the West was Swami Vivekananda, the chief disciple of India's Ramakrishna Paramahansa, whose image is found in many yoga studios today (or at least the donation-based studio I used to attend in Park Slope, Brooklyn). Vivekananda visited the UK and the US in the 1890s, when he established the Vedanta Society. But then he returned to India. The first yogi who spent the majority of his life in the West was Paramahansa Yogananda, author of *Autobiography of a Yogi*, who came to Boston in 1920 to lecture about Kriya Yoga, which he described as "the science of God-realization through meditation." In 1925,

Yogananda moved to California and opened the Self Realization Center in Los Angeles.

Throughout the 1920s, Americans displayed an eager interest in the philosophy of yoga. With Einstein's revolution of science and the soul seeking that followed the First World War, the timing was ripe. Yogananda gave lectures to packed auditoriums all over the country, and was even invited to the White House by President Coolidge. But by the end of the decade, the media launched an anti-yoga attack, painting spiritual centers as nothing more than "love cults." This was due to a combination of racism and yellow journalism, and fueled by the jealous husbands of female devotees. Its reputation tarnished, yoga again went underground. Yet its ideas had been introduced into Western culture, and soon found their way from the lecture halls and spiritual centers into fiction.

In *Lost Horizon*, which was published in 1933, James Hilton writes of "certain mystical practices that the Indian calls *yoga*, and which are based upon various methods of breathing." (He also mentions the Tibetan Om Mani Padme Hum prayer.) This might have been the literary introduction of the term yoga, but *Lost Horizon* was a popular novel, the first mass-market paperback, and it did not treat the subject seriously. Hilton's Shangri-La was a magical utopian monastery where lamas mysteriously cultivated longevity, and not a realistic presentation of any Indian religion. Rather than impart actual spiritual practices and philosophies, as Somerset Maugham did with *The Razor's Edge*, Hilton helped create a fanciful, false image of Eastern spirituality, which is why I did not include a chapter on *Lost Horizon* in this book. Aldous Huxley made a more serious approach in his novel *Time Must Have a Stop*, which was published the same year as *The Razor's Edge*, 1944. In that novel, Huxley mentions "Brahmanism" and "Mr. Buddha," the Bhagavatam and "the Tao Teh Ching," "a Law or Dharma," and "a Tao or Way." But the plot features spiritualism, not spirituality, and the book offers nothing explicit about specific Eastern religious practices or philosophies. And so it, too, was omitted.

So, getting back to the drawing room, Somerset asks, "Is it true that the Yogis acquire powers that would seem to us supernatural?" Larry answers he wouldn't know, adding that the wisest think such powers "are apt to hinder spiritual progress."

Spiritual progress? What can that phrase possibly mean for a Protestant? Or even a Catholic? For a Christian, you pray and you follow God's rules. Then you get to live in heaven with Jesus forever. Or you don't. That's it. There's no progress. You simply believe, and then you are saved. Jesus does the work for you. The idea that you actually have to do the work yourself brings the entire crux of Christian faith into question. Because if we have to do our own work, what do we need a Savior for?

Gray shifts in his seat, clearly uncomfortable. He again offers Larry a drink, and again Larry refuses. So Gray makes one for himself. But now Isabel is curious. She asks Larry if he knew any of the yogis intimately. "As intimately as you can know persons who pass the best part of their time in the Infinite," he answers. "I spent two years in the Ashrama of one."

The Infinite? Ashrama? What's an Ashrama? they ask, along with, I assume, most readers of the time. Larry explains it's like a hermitage. Isabel has no idea how he could stand such a place for two years. She asks what he did with himself while he was there. As usual, Larry read. But he also says, "I meditated," adding: "Meditation is very hard work; after two or three hours of it you're exhausted as if you've driven a car five hundred miles, and all you want to do is rest."

The word "meditation" has long been used in the West as a synonym for contemplation. We use "meditating" interchangeably with "thinking." For example, the *Meditations* of Marcus Aurelius, or "go ahead and meditate on that." But here Maugham introduces the Eastern use of the word to his audience. Meditation is not contemplation, but a spiritual practice used to train the mind to clear itself of thought. That is to say, meditation is the very opposite of thinking. There are hundreds of techniques of meditation, but in general its purpose is to establish some control over the mind. Left to its own devices, the mind jumps from one thought to the next, like a monkey grasping branch after branch. Such relentlessness prevents us from being internally calm and at peace. The mind always wants something or doesn't want something, oscillating between craving and aversion, creating dissatisfaction. Because the mind is always occupied with the past or the future, it prevents us from experiencing the present moment. We plan for a vacation, but while it's happening we talk about the next one, and take photos to post online or show people when we get back. The mind has to be trained to be aware of the present. To be calm and quiet. To not be swayed by cravings and aversions. This is why meditation is necessary like exercise and a good diet are necessary: You can live without it, but you can't live healthily and happily. And Maugham explicitly lets his readers know that meditation isn't easy—Larry has never before, nor will he after, say anything else is "very hard work."

I was twenty when I found this out, after I first sat for a decent stretch of meditation. It was on a Sunday morning at the Zen Center in Los Angeles, in the fall of 2000. By then I had read Shunryu Suzuki's *Zen Mind, Beginner's Mind* and Alan Watts's *The Way of Zen*, tried meditating a few times and wanted to give it a serious go. So I looked up the Zen Center's address in the Yellow Pages, called to find out when I could come for an introductory session, and somehow made it from Westwood to Koreatown by 8 AM. After listening to a speech from a bald white monk dressed in a black robe, we went into the zendo and sat for an hour of *zazen*, the Zen practice of sitting meditation. Along with the sound of wood knocking against wood, I remember being surprised at how badly my back hurt halfway through the session. I was grateful for the break of fast-walking meditation, despite how silly I felt doing it. Meditation, I learned then, is indeed very hard work.

But that was nothing. In the introductory ten-day courses of Vipassana as taught by S. N. Goenka—the type of meditation I began practicing in 2003—a student has to meditate for over ten hours a day. They cannot speak to other students, read, write, or eat dinner. They have to wake at four in the morning and go to bed at nine. They must abstain from killing any being, lying, stealing, having sex, and using any intoxicants. Before someone takes their first course, they're usually most worried about the noble silence—how can you not talk for *ten days*? Or maybe someone is concerned about not having their evening glass of wine, or not being able to use their phone. But after the course is over, nearly everyone says the most difficult part is the sitting itself, which is not only physically exhausting but painful. Backs, knees, and ankles ache from day one through the end. People pile up cushions in order to ease the discomfort, but to no avail. There's no avoiding the pain. Moreover, it's so difficult to concentrate the mind and keep it focused, that the mental anguish arising from frustration exacerbates the physical pain. Most people experience bodily function issues during a course: constipation, diarrhea, and insomnia are common. Many people break down in tears. Some experience convulsions. This is all a part of the process of purification, and while it's not the place here to describe the theory behind the practice of Vipassana, it's enough to know that Maugham must have experienced some sort of serious meditation, something akin to my first hour of *zazen*, because he knows how difficult it is to meditate. And here he wants to let his readers know that meditation isn't just sitting on your butt.

It's also at this point in the conversation when Isabel finally understands that the Larry she knew before is not the same man standing in front of her now. She frowns and seems not only puzzled but frightened. She doesn't want to hear anymore. But Somerset's curiosity only increases. He wants to know what attracted Larry to his yogi. "Saintliness," Larry answers. Somerset is disconcerted by the reply; in that room of luxury, he writes, the word saintliness "fell like a plop of water that has seeped through the ceiling from an overflowing bath." He asks what Larry gained from his experience. "Peace," Larry answers. Then he leaves.

When Larry returns the following day, Gray is incapacitated by one of his headaches. Rather than go out with Somerset alone, as Isabel suggests, Larry displays "an exhibition of his unexpected power." He goes into the study, where Gray is reclining on a chair. Larry gives him an old Greek coin, and asks Gray to hold it tightly in his hand. Then he says before he can count to twenty, Gray's hand will open and the coin will drop. And that's what happens. Gray is perplexed. Larry tells Gray to again hold the coin, and says that in sixty seconds Gray will fall asleep. He'll sleep for six minutes, and when he awakes he'll have no more pain. Again, exactly that happens. Through the power of suggestion, or what we might call hypnosis, Larry cures Gray of his headache—though Larry is modest and says, "I merely put an idea in old Gray's head and he did the rest himself." After a few more of these sessions, Gray's headaches completely vanish. He soon regains his confidence, and becomes his old self again.

Initially, we might assume Larry gained this "unexpected power" from his Yogi or through his meditation. If so, it would mean Larry's spiritual journey has resulted in him becoming some sort of hypnotist. It would mean that the goal of meditation is to acquire spiritual powers and be able to perform such parlor tricks. But we later learn that's not the case. It was "just something he picked up" along his journey, when he was suffering from insomnia and someone used the same power of suggestion on him. "There's nothing to it really," Larry explains; "it only means putting the idea into the sufferer's mind." He tried the method out on others, and found he was able to "relieve people not only of pain but of fear." Not phobias, he clarifies, but "fear of death and, what's worse, fear of life," which is what Gray was suffering from.

Larry tells this to Somerset after the two randomly meet again, years after the above incident, when Larry finally opens up and speaks at length about his experience in India. But before we get there, Maugham wants to show a more mundane result of Larry's spiritual progress, and so Sophie Macdonald comes back into the story.

Sophie's story is another example of the vicissitudes of life, like that which struck Gray and Isabel. Though Sophie's story is more heartbreaking and dramatic, showing that it's not only money that can be lost, but also those we love. Sophie married one of "the best-looking boys" in Chicago. They were so crazy about each other, they hardly came around to parties. Even after they were married for a few years and had a baby, they still had their arms around each other like young lovers. Then one night they were driving and a drunk driver going eighty miles an hour crashed into them head-on. Sophie suffered only a concussion and a couple of broken ribs, but her husband and baby were instantaneously killed. Sophie nearly went crazy when she was told. She tried to jump out the window of the hospital, and afterward was put in a sanatorium. After being released, she becomes a drunk and goes "to bed with anyone who asked her."

When later relating the story to Somerset, Isabel says she tried to help, but Sophie was impossible. Gray expresses sympathy for Sophie, but Isabel says "a normal person recovers from something like that," and that if Sophie "went to pieces it's because there was a rotten streak in her." This is the first we see of a rotten streak in Isabel herself. Abandoned by her friends and in-laws, Sophie is offered an allowance if she'll live abroad and save everyone the scandal of having to deal with her. So she disappears to Paris. And on a night when Isabel felt like slum-diving through the "tough joints" of the city, the friends run into Sophie. She spits and curses like a sailor, "looked more like a slut than any woman there," and Somerset has the suspicion that "she was not only drunk but doped." He's right; Sophie has become addicted to opium. She also seems to have a pimp for a boyfriend, and Gray nearly gets in a fight to prevent the swarthy man from smacking her around. Isabel is disgusted at the scene and the slum-divers leave.

On the way home, they stop for a postmidnight meal and Larry reveals that Sophie used to share her poetry with him when they were teenagers. Back then she was concerned about the working classes and wanted to become a social worker. When he goes on to say Sophie gave "one the impression of a lovely purity and a strange loftiness of the soul," Isabel can't stand it anymore and says she wants to go home. Where Isabel sees a disgraceful fallen woman, Larry sees a wounded spiritual being. That's the end of the conversation, and Isabel would've been happy if that was the last she heard of Sophie Macdonald. But Larry not only finds Sophie in the phone book, he decides to become her savior.

The tragedy of Sophie reminds me of a story about one of the Buddha's disciples, a woman named Patacara. In a single day, Patacara's husband was killed by a snake, her son drowned in a river, her newborn baby was killed by a hawk, and her mother, father, and brother died when their home collapsed during a storm. Unable to accept such loss, Patacara lost her reason, tearing off her clothes and running about naked, weeping and wailing in the streets. People called her filthy names, and threw trash and stones at her to keep her away. Fortunately, Patacara came to the monastery in Savatthi where the Buddha was residing. Seeing her at the entrance, he motioned for her to come to him. And simply by being in the Buddha's serene presence, she calmed enough to realize she was naked. Someone covered her with a cloak, and she told the Buddha what had happened to her family. With patience and compassion, the Buddha listened and then told her, "It is not only today that you have met with calamity and disaster, but throughout this beginningless round of existence, weeping over the loss of sons and others dear to you, you have shed more tears than the waters of the four oceans." Loss and death are intrinsic parts of life, and there is no use weeping about what must come to everyone. The Buddha's words penetrated her so deeply that she experienced sharp insight into the impermanence of all things and the universality of suffering, so much so that by the time the Buddha finished speaking, Patacara was no longer a lamenting madwoman. She immediately took the going forth and became a nun.

Now, Larry is not the Buddha, but with his presence, with the wisdom he learned in India, he wants to help Sophie like how the Buddha helped Patacara. Because if we can't help one another, then what's the point of acquiring spiritual wisdom?

Three months later, Somerset is again in Paris. When he arrives, he receives a telegram from Isabel that reads: "Come round the moment you get in. Something terrible has happened. Don't bring Uncle Elliott. For God's sake come as soon as you can." Somerset comes immediately and asks what happened. Isabel lets him know that Larry is going to marry "that drunken slut" Sophie Macdonald.

Furious, Isabel is determined to prevent the marriage. She says she didn't sacrifice herself "to let Larry fall into the hands of a raging nymphomaniac." She's convinced herself that she gave Larry up because she "didn't want to stand in his way." Unable to indulge her delusion, Somerset tells her bluntly, "Come off it, Isabel. You gave him up for a square-cut diamond and a sable coat." She throws a dish at his head. When she calms down, Somerset explains that Larry is "enthralled by one of the most powerful emotions that can beset the human breast." Isabel can't possibly believe that Larry is in love with Sophie, but Somerset says love would be "trifling in comparison." He doesn't pretend to know what Larry's been seeking all these years, but he suspects whatever it is has led him to feel "an urgent, clamorous need to save the soul of a wanton woman he'd known as an innocent child." After all, there's "no wine so intoxicating, no love so shattering, no vice so compelling" as the call for self-sacrifice.

To sacrifice oneself for another is an act representing the highest form of love and wisdom. As Somerset says, "When he sacrifices himself man for a moment is greater than God." He elaborates using the example of Jesus's temptation in the desert, when the devil offers all the kingdoms of the world. Jesus infamously says, *Get thee behind me, Satan*, and that was the end of it. But for Somerset, the devil later tempted Jesus in a subtler, slyer way: You want to show your love of God? Then sacrifice yourself for the human race. Accept shame and disgrace and a painful death, and you'll become mankind's redeemer. And Jesus fell for it. He couldn't resist the temptation of becoming a savior, because there's no greater display of vanity than self-sacrifice. This sort of talk bores Isabel, who calls it "idiotic and blasphemous." But Somerset is making a point to show that Larry learned more than how to cure headaches. He can be a savior to someone who's been abandoned by everyone else. And it's not the first time he's done so.

Somerset is friends with another wanton woman named Suzanne Rouvier, who lived in sin with painter after painter until she came down with typhoid. Emaciated and no good for a man, she was living on the street. Larry had previously met Suzanne through a mutual acquaintance. Seeing her on the street, he invites her to live with him in the South of France. For months, he takes care of Suzanne and her daughter, asking nothing in return. Sure, Larry sleeps with her after she's regained her strength, but only when Suzanne takes the initiative and enters his bedroom at night. It'd be rude to refuse her, and Larry is never one to be rude. Suzanne is important because it's from her that Somerset learns the story of what happened to Larry during World War I. She's also one of the three women Larry sleeps with in the novel. And all of his sexual experiences are performed in the same passive way, with the woman taking the lead.

In his introduction to the Penguin edition of *The Razor's Edge*, Anthony Curtis writes, "We cannot help but wonder if Larry is homosexual." Curtis rests this assumption on the fact that, after marrying and producing a daughter, Maugham came out late in life as openly gay. But as usual, things are a bit grayer than gay or straight. "I tried to persuade myself," Maugham said about his younger self, "that I was three-quarters normal and that only a quarter of me was queer—whereas it was really the other way around." While he loathed his wife Syrie, in his thirties Maugham was passionately in love with the actress Sue Jones, to whom he proposed, and he had intense sexual relationships with many other women. But as he aged, his tastes did turn solely toward men—very young men, in fact.

Even so, Curtis's insight is rather obtuse. As is the habit of intellectuals, Curtis is latching on to an -ism—in this case, queer theory. Suzanne says that Larry was "a strange lover. Very sweet, affectionate and even tender, virile without being passionate, if you understand what I mean, and absolutely without vice." And so Curtis writes, "This sounds like a description of a gay man making love to a woman." It's clear he doesn't understand the nature of Larry's sexuality, and is merely projecting Maugham's own. (Though Maugham had a voracious sexual appetite; he was so promiscuous that Virginia Woolf advised he be more discreet unless he wanted to get arrested, under England's anti-homosexuality laws.) Curtis probably isn't familiar with the idea of *bramhacharya*, or spiritual celibacy. If he were, he'd know that Larry is not homosexual, or even bisexual—as Curtis also suggests, throwing around both terms as if they're synonyms—but more likely asexual. Larry has the lack of sexual desire naturally felt by those focused on spiritual rather than carnal matters. For many, of course, these fields overlap, especially practitioners of Tantra. But for Larry, and for many other seekers, they don't. He's simply dispassionate. Sex just doesn't interest him.

Getting back to the conversation about Larry and Sophie's marriage, Somerset tells Isabel he believes that Larry has been "seeking for a philosophy, or maybe a religion, and a rule of life that'll satisfy both his head and his heart." Larry must see the fruition of this philosophy in saving Sophie, by making her his wife. She's willing to be saved, and accepts his proposal. Under Larry's influence, Sophie stops drinking and quits opium, going sober for three months. Then, three days before their wedding, Sophie disappears. Larry searches for her everywhere, but she's vanished.

We don't know what happened until later that year, when Somerset sees Sophie at a café in the Mediterranean city of Toulon. Almost immediately, he asks Sophie why she didn't marry Larry. She replies that when it came to the point, she couldn't see herself "being Mary Magdalene to his Jesus Christ." Somerset must have been satisfied that his insight into the situation was spot on, but he doesn't mention it. Instead, he asks what made Sophie change her mind at the last moment. And over afternoon cocktails, Sophie tells him that, before the wedding, Isabel concocted a wicked scheme to cause her to fall off the wagon; Sophie succumbed to the temptation of a drink, and then before she knew it, she was off to Toulon, where "you can get all the opium you want."

About a year after Sophie disappeared from Paris, Somerset runs into Larry, again "by chance." They meet while seeing Racine's *Bérénice* at the Théatre François. After the play, they talk all night in a brasserie on the Avenue de Clichy, and it's here when Larry finally loses his reticence and tells his whole story, about India and everything else.

Mischievously, Maugham opens this chapter with a warning: he has Somerset say the reader may very well skip the chapter without losing the thread of the story he's telling, since for the most part it's nothing more than a conversation he has with Larry. But then he slyly adds that the conversation he's about to recreate is precisely what motivated him to write the book in the first place.

After Isabel broke their engagement eleven years earlier, Larry went off and worked in a coal mine. He was hurt, he tells Somerset, but he wasn't running away. Whenever he got "water-logged spiritually," when he'd absorbed all he could for the time, he went for the experience of manual labor, which he finds spiritually invigorating: "My mind is free when I'm washing a car or tinkering with a carburetor and when the job's done I have the pleasant sensation of having accomplished something." His Greek teacher knew the manager of a mine near Lens, in the north of France, and so Larry packs up and heads there. At the mine he meets a Pole named Kosti. After a few days, Larry learns that Kosti is an educated man, claiming to have been an officer who fled Russia for political reasons. Kosti changes Larry's life.

During the day they perform "back-breaking" work in the mine, and in the evenings they drink at the local bistro. During these nights, Kosti would sometimes grow serious and start talking of mysticism, referencing "Plotinus and Denis the Areopagite and Jacob Boehme and Meister Eckhart." Larry is ignorant of these thinkers, but he enjoys hearing Kosti speak "of the ultimate reality of things and the blessedness of union with God." Larry describes his feelings during these moments as "someone who's lain awake in a darkened room and suddenly a chink of light shoots through the curtains and suddenly he knows he only has to draw them and the country will be spread before him in the glory of dawn." The answers to his questions don't lie in philosophy, he realizes, but in mysticism.

One of the questions that motivated Larry's search was the problem of evil and why it exists. If God created the world, and God is pure goodness, then why did he create evil, too? In Kosti's view, "evil is as direct manifestation of the divine as good." There was no divine creation, Kosti says. Rather, the world is "a manifestation of eternal nature," of which both good and evil—or creation and destruction—share an equal part. It's only after liters of wine that Kosti "would talk in a morbid way of the flight from the Alone to the Alone, of the Dark Night of the Soul and of the final ecstasy in which the creature becomes one with Beloved." Fascinated as he is confused, Larry tries to get Kosti to speak of mysticism while sober, but the Pole gets angry and tells his young friend to shut up.

Here, as with the city of Paris, we have likely symbolism in the character of Kosti. As my former professor Felicia Bonaparte explains in her book *The Poetics of Poesis*, Poland was repeatedly conquered and divided by the Germans, Russians, and Austrians, and so the country came to be symbolic in nineteenth- and early twentieth-century literature. Through its numerous partitions, or "dismemberments," Poland was seen "to embody the myth of Christ crucified for the sins of others." This led literary folk to use Polish characters to signify spirituality, not only in the abstract but also in personal relations. Perhaps Maugham is doing something similar, I'm not certain. But it is clear he knows what he's doing when Kosti takes Larry into Germany, after they finish their stint in the coal mine.

After the storming of the Bastille and the execution of King Louis XVI in 1793, France descended into a century of bloody revolution and counter-revolution, leaving no country for philosophers. The continuing Enlightenment moved across the Rhine, with French thinkers passing the torch to the Germans. There was Kant, Hegel, Schopenhauer, Shelling, Nietzsche, Goethe, Schiller, Holderlin, Rilke, and Marx, but most importantly Schlegel, who spent the later years of his life at the University of Bonn, exclusively devoted to studying Eastern religions, printing Sanskrit and editing translations of the *Bhagavad Gita* and the *Ramayana*. After separating from Kosti, Maugham has Larry settle specifically in Bonn, where he learns German and reads "the great German philosophers." As with living in Paris, going to Germany is a necessary step in Larry's quest.

It's in Bonn that Larry meets Father Ensheim, a Benedictine monk on leave from his monastery while doing research in the university library. Ensheim befriends Larry, reveals that he used to teach philosophy, and they talk of the Greek tragedies. When Ensheim sees Larry is reading Meister Eckhart, he asks about Larry's interest in mysticism. Larry tells his story, and then the monk asks where four years of reading has gotten him. "Nowhere," Larry replies.

Maugham's point may be that we can read until our eyes go blind, but we'll never progress spiritually unless we practice. Philosophy alone won't accomplish anything. It won't give us useful answers, and it won't make us a better person. In Father Ensheim's opinion, Larry needs religion. He needs to make Kierkegaard's leap to faith. Otherwise there's no risk, and if there's no risk there's no reward. Patient and "with radiant benignity," Ensheim tells Larry the distance separating him "from faith is no greater than the thickness of a cigarette paper." He invites Larry to visit his monastery in Alsace, where Larry stays for three months.

Larry tells Somerset he was very happy living a monk's life and attending the daily prayers, especially the predawn Matins. If he were born in the Middle Ages, when faith was a matter of course, he would have entered the order. But ultimately he "couldn't believe in a God who wasn't better than the ordinary decent man." He finds the Christian God vain, negligent, and unworthy of worship. The fathers offered no answers that could satisfy Larry's head or heart, and so he leaves the monastery. Upon departure, Father Ensheim tells Larry he is "a deeply religious man who doesn't believe in God." He adds: "God will seek you out." God does seek Larry out, but it's not the god that Father Ensheim has in mind.

After Germany, Larry goes to Spain. Wondering "if art could point out the way" to him "that religion hadn't," he wants to see the paintings of Velasquez and El Greco. It is in Seville when Larry first attempts to go beyond reading and thinking and into the realm of action by saving his first woman in distress—before he took care of Suzanne Rouvier and tried to save Sophie Macdonald. Out one night with a painter friend from Paris, Larry meets "a cheerful, good-tempered, and affectionate" Andalusian girl of eighteen. She had gotten into "trouble" and had to leave her native village, as is the usual case for unwed women who become pregnant. After the woman gives birth, she leaves the baby with a wet nurse in a nearby village and finds works in a tobacco factory. (When he was twenty-four, Maugham spent eight months in Seville, and during his evening walks he'd watch the gypsy girls, the "cigarreras," stream out of the government-owned cigarette factory, which was famous as the location of *Carmen*.) While she's shunned by others in that conservative society, Larry takes a liking to her, and asks her to live with him. They play house, and as Larry puts it, the girl "looked upon what you delicately call sexual congress as a natural function of the body like any other." Eventually, she leaves him to reunite with the father of her baby, and Larry sets sail as a deckhand on a boat going to the East.

On the ship is an Indian man, well dressed in a natty tweed suit. He takes an interest in Larry, who calls himself "a student." This inspires the man to strongly suggest that Larry should stop off in India, because "the East has more to teach the West than the West conceives." The man says that, in the least, Larry should see the Elephanta Caves when they dock in Bombay. Taking the man's advice, Larry goes to the caves. But he can't make sense of the colossal heads of the Trimurti sculpture. While he's trying to figure it out, he sees the same Indian man—though now the man has lost the tweed suit and is dressed in the long saffron robe of a swami. The man explains the three heads are of Brahma the Creator, Vishnu the Preserver, and Shiva the Destroyer—"the three manifestations of the Ultimate Reality." Like most English-speaking readers at the time, Larry is baffled. He tells Somerset that all he knew "about Brahmanism were those verses of Emerson's." Yet Larry suddenly feels an intense conviction that India had something to give him that he had to have, and so he doesn't get back on the boat. This is how Larry ends up staying in India for five years—by "chance."

Larry accompanies the swami to the ancient holy city of Benares, or Varanasi, where he stays for six months. He's fascinated with the daily dawn prayers on the Ganges. Unlike Christians, the Hindus "believed not half-heartedly, not with reservation or uneasy doubt, but with every fibre of their being." Larry can't get over it. He learns to read "Hindustani" and studies Hindu scripture.

At this point in his story, Larry pauses to ask Somerset if he knows anything about Hinduism. Somerset replies, "Very little," which besides being a lie, is most likely what his readers would answer; they, too, have likely heard of such things only through verses of Emerson, or the writings of Thoreau, or another of the nineteenth-century thinkers mentioned in my introduction. Larry immediately tells Somerset about the Indian conception of the universe, which "has no beginning and no end, but passes everlastingly from growth to equilibrium, from equilibrium to decline, from decline to dissolution, from dissolution to growth, and so to all eternity." Here we go.

The idea of the big bang was first proposed in the 1920s. The theory was not well supported until the discovery of the cosmic microwave background radiation in the 1960s, well after *The Razor's Edge* was written, but people knew about it since the thirties, when Hubble observed the redshift in deep space. Now it's widely accepted. However, the most contemporary cosmological theories have pushed beyond the idea that the big bang was the origin of the universe, settling instead on something much closer to what Larry is talking about: a cyclical rather than linear understanding of the universe. In fact, many scientists and philosophers are now quite sure there's actually "a multiverse." No, the multiverse isn't as portrayed in Marvel films and other popular media, where there are parallel selves in parallel universes and timelines. Rather, it means our universe is just one of many other universes, all folded within and around one another, all expanding and collapsing and expanding again and again.

Indian cosmology has claimed something similar for several thousand years. The length of time it takes for a universe to arise, develop, and perish is called a *kalpa*, which is usually translated as eon. When a disciple asked the Buddha how long a *kalpa* is, the Buddha answered:

> Suppose, monk, there was a great stone mountain a *yojana* [approximately seven miles] long, a *yojana* wide, and a *yojana* high, without holes or crevices, one solid mass of rock. At the end of every hundred years a man would stroke it once with a piece of fine cloth. That great stone mountain might by this effort be worn away and eliminated but the eon would not have come to an end. So long is an eon, monk.

And when a Brahmin asked the Buddha how many *kalpas* have elapsed and gone by, the Buddha answered:

> Imagine, Brahmin, the grains of sand between the point where the river Ganges originates and the point where it enters the great ocean: it is not easy to count these and say there are so

many grains of sand, or so many hundreds of grains, or so many thousands of grains, or so many hundreds of thousands of grains. Brahmin, the eons that have elapsed and gone by are even more numerous than that.

The Buddha ended each of the above exchanges by saying, "this samsara is without discoverable beginning." It's becoming clear that the linear understanding of the big bang—specifically the idea that there was a beginning—arose as an unconscious projection of the Judeo-Christian linear understanding of time. God created the universe, and it would end once the apocalypse comes. Contradicting the Western perspective, Larry tells Somerset, "The Hindus would say there was no beginning. The individual soul, co-existent with the universe, has existed from all eternity and owes its nature to some prior existence."

As if this wasn't already deep enough for a popular novel, they go on to discuss the particulars of what Somerset refers to as "the transmigration of souls," which he understands as the idea that "the soul passes from body to body in an endless course of experience occasioned by the merit or demerit of previous works." Quite apt for someone who claims to know very little about such subjects. (We'll get to Buddhism in the next chapter, but for now I'll note that Buddhists have a different conception of reincarnation, mainly because they don't believe in the concept of the soul. "As everyone knows," Maugham writes in his travel book *The Gentleman in the Parlour*, "the most important point of Buddha's teachings was that there was no such thing as a soul or self." This is the major theoretical difference between Buddhism and Hinduism.) To Larry, the concept of reincarnation explains and justifies the existence of evil. The evils we suffer are a result of the sins we committed in our past lives. We can bear our suffering with resignation, living virtuously so that future lives will be less afflicted. We can pity the evil that befalls others, and we can help alleviate it, but we cannot be indignant. For others, too, must accept what they've created for themselves.

Somerset asks Larry point-blank if he actually believes in reincarnation. Larry wisely answers that he doesn't "think it's possible for us Occidentals to believe in it as implicitly as these Orientals do. It's in their blood and bones. With us it can only be an opinion. I neither believe in it nor disbelieve in it." It is perhaps surprising that Larry doesn't fully believe in reincarnation, because he goes on to describe "a very strange experience" of seeing his past lives.

One night at the Ashrama, he was meditating as he'd been taught, concentrating his attention on the flame of a candle. After a long time, he sees in the flame a long line of figures, one behind the other. First is an elderly lady in "a tight black bodice and a black silk flounced skirt—the sort of clothes, I think, they wore in the seventies." (The 1870s, that is.) Behind the woman he sees a face with a "great hooked nose" and "a yellow skullcap on his thick dark hair," and behind this "tall gaunt Jew" is a ruddy-faced young man dressed in red velvet "whom you couldn't have taken for anything but an Englishman of the sixteenth century." Behind these three is "an endless chain of figures, like a queue outside a movie house." Larry admits that he could simply have "fallen into a doze and dreamt," or that the flame induced him into a "sort of hypnotic condition" that brought up the figures from his subconscious. Then with a smile he adds, "But it may be that they were myself in past lives. It may be that I was not so very long ago an old lady in New England and before that a Levantine Jew and somewhere back, soon after Sebastian Cabot has sailed from Bristol, a gallant at the Court of Henry Prince of Wales."

In his introduction, Anthony Curtis wrote that Larry's description of his possible previous incarnations make "him seem naïve if not wholly absurd." Maugham would certainly disagree; Larry's skepticism regarding his own experience prevents him from being naïve, and only someone without spiritual experience could call Larry absurd. But intellectual folk are often without such experience, and other contemporary critics tore into Larry and the novel's spiritual aspects upon its release. In *The Nation*, for example, Diana Trilling wrote, "Mysticism is bound to be inviting to the person who is afraid of the deep emotions; yet it can never fully win him, any more than humanity can fully win him." Now here is an example of the absurd, both for the statement's complete irrelevance to the work, and for its severe misconception; only people *brave* enough to explore deep emotions find mysticism inviting. That being said, Larry's description does sound implausible. When a meditator experiences past lives, they see past incarnations in their mind—not in the flame of a candle, as if watching a movie screen. They have memories from those lives, from their own point of view, not visions of their own faces.

Patient, yet displaying the healthy skepticism of an intellectual, Somerset moves the conversation away from reincarnation and asks Larry about the goal of the Hindu's spiritual progress. "Liberation from the bondage of rebirth," Larry replies, as if duh. The Sanskrit term for this liberation is *moksha*. Larry goes on to explain that the self, which "the Vedantists call atman and we call the soul, is distinct from the body and its senses, distinct from the mind and its intelligence; it is not part of the Absolute, for the Absolute, being infinite, can have no parts, but the Absolute itself." Aware this must be going over his readers' heads, Somerset asks Larry to explain what the term "Absolute" means to him. "Reality," Larry replies. "It's inexpressible.

The Indians call it Brahman. It's nowhere and everywhere. All things imply and depend on it."

A Western reader might now be thinking, *Ah, he's talking about God.* But he's not. He's talking about something much grander, more incomprehensible than the God of the Bible. Not to be confused with the Hindu creator god Brahma, *Brahman* is "not a person, it's not a thing, it's not a cause. It has no qualities. It transcends permanence and change; whole and part, finite and infinite. It is eternal because its completeness and perfection are unrelated to time. It is truth and freedom." That is to say, Brahman, unlike Yahweh, is not a personal god with human characteristics. Brahman does not speak to prophets or give commandments. Brahman is not concerned with worship or offerings. While Brahman is often explained as the creative principle of the cosmos, or universal law, Brahman is absolutely inconceivable.

Somerset wonders how "a purely intellectual conception" can be a solace to the suffering human race. Here he shows the Western philosophical approach of dismissing something as a mere conception if we haven't experienced it as a reality. Unlike Somerset, Larry has had direct experience of what he's talking about, so for him the Absolute is not simply "an intellectual conception." Brahman is not merely an idea. Brahman is, as he says, reality. By now Larry understands that the three gods he saw in the Elephanta Caves—Brahma, Vishnu, and Shiva—along with all the other "multitudinous gods of India are but expedients to lead to the realization that the self is one with the supreme self." The pantheon of Hindu gods exists because individuals are on different levels of spiritual development and need different ways of accessing the Absolute, but in actuality they are all one. Everything is simply manifestation of Brahman. Brahman is the god that Father Ensheim predicted would seek Larry out.

At this point, Somerset interrupts the narration by beginning a new section with another disclaimer. He wants to make it plain to the reader that he is "not attempting here to give anything in the nature of a description of the philosophical system known as Vedanta." Not only does he "not have the knowledge to do so," he writes, but even if he had "this would not be the proper place for it."

Maugham is acknowledging the taboo about mixing fiction and spirituality. He's aware that he shouldn't be disseminating religious messages in a work of art. "I think it an abuse to use the novel as a pulpit or platform," the author stated more than once. Somerset claims he's only touching on these intricate subjects to provide plausibility to Larry's subsequent line of conduct, in his dealings with Gray and Sophie. That is to say, he's interested in plot, not philosophy.

But as usual, the author is being sly. He knows damn well that he *is* attempting to give a description of the philosophical system known as Vedanta, and that this description is in fact his very point in writing *The Razor's Edge*. It's the meat missing from his earlier attempts at telling the story. What Larry talks about in this chapter is the message Maugham wants to share with his readers—as his alter ego says at the beginning of the chapter, "except for this conversation I should perhaps have not thought it worth while to write this book."

Next Larry talks about his guru, the yogi Shri Ganesha, who is based on the real guru Sri Ramana Maharshi. Ramana's teachings were first introduced to the West when Paul Brunton published *A Search in Secret India* in 1934, which made both of them relatively famous. After many visits to the Far East, Maugham finally traveled to India in January 1938. He stayed for three months. Unlike most British men visiting at the time, his biographer Selina Hastings writes, Maugham did "not come to shoot a tiger, or to sell anything, nor especially to see the Taj Mahal, the Caves of Ajanta or the temple of Madura, but to meet scholars, writers and artists, religious teachers and devotes." In fact, he did visit these tourist sites, and his partner Gerald Haxton did intend to shoot a tiger. (Haxton had to settle for killing a peacock, an experience that deeply disturbed Maugham.) Nevertheless, Maugham's main motivation for "his quest in coming to India," according to Hastings, "was to investigate the vast subject of Hindu religion in the hope of gaining an insight into a spiritual side of life that had always intrigued and at the same time eluded him." At sixty-four years old, he traveled at length through the Native States, interviewing swamis, sadhus, and holy men.

In his essay "India," Maugham describes how he asked one "holy man" how he could "acquire the power of meditation." This yogi was "richly dressed and wore a great scarlet cloak of fine material." Tall and middle-aged, with "a handsome presence" and a "courtly" manner, the yogi gave Maugham instructions:

> He told me to go into a darkened room, sit on the floor cross-legged and fix my eyes on the flame of a candle, emptying my mind of every thought so that it was a complete blank. He said that if I would do that for a quarter of an hour a day I should presently have some extraordinary experiences. "Do it for nine months," he said, "then come back and I will give you another exercise."

That evening Maugham did as he'd been directed. He noted the time before he began, and remembered, "I remained in that state for so long that

I thought I must have by far exceeded the quarter of an hour he had prescribed. I looked at my watch. Three minutes had passed. It has seemed an eternity."

Ultimately Maugham was unimpressed with this guru, as well as the other "Indian thinkers." They all said what he "had heard from others twenty times before." Saying "the same things in the same words," they repeated the usual metaphors, similes, and illustrations "like parrots." Finally, Maugham visited Sri Ramana Maharshi's ashram in Tiruvannamali, a few hours southwest of Chennai (then known as Madras). The visit changed his life.

In "The Saint," an essay published twenty years after the experience, Maugham writes that he fainted soon after arriving at the ashram. Because he was unable to come into the hall where Ramana usually received visitors, the guru visited the author in his hut. For about half an hour, Ramana sat near his bed and meditated. Maugham was too weak to speak, and asked apprehensively if he should say anything. Ramana, who was known for preferring a rule of silence, maintaining it at one time for three years, told Maugham, "Silence is best. Silence is also conversation." He then settled into *samadhi*, which Maugham defines as "a trancelike state of profound absorption in the Infinite Reality, which is Brahman, in which the adept is one with the Absolute, and in spirit enjoys existence, knowledge and bliss." After the guru left the hut, Maugham felt much better. Later that day, he came to the hall and watched Ramana receive visitors and meditate. While the guru was absorbed in *samadhi*, Maugham thought "the silence was intense and impressive" and "felt that something strange was taking place that made you inclined to hold your breath."

The impression Ramana made on Maugham was so deep that he decided to use Ramana as a model for Larry's guru Shri Ganesha. Upon his return to Europe, Maugham read a mass of literature on Ramana Maharshi, whose teachings on Vedanta influenced many other Westerners (including J. D. Salinger, who we'll get to in another chapter). Maugham also studied Sir Charles Eliot's *Hinduism and Buddhism*; S. Radhakrishnan's *History of Indian Philosophy* and *The Principal Upanishads*; Krisnaswami Iyer's *Vedanta, or the Science of Reality*; L. D. Barnett's *Brahma-Knowledge*; and Adi Sankara's *Vivekachudamani*. He then distilled the knowledge he learned from these books into this chapter of *The Razor's Edge*.

Asked about his guru, Larry says Shri Ganesha sought to wean his disciples "from the slavery of selfhood, passion, and sense, and told them that they could acquire liberation by tranquility, restraint, renunciation, resignation, by steadfastness of mind and by an ardent desire for freedom." Ganesha's teaching was simple: We are all greater than we know and wisdom is the means to freedom; it is not essential to salvation to retire from the world, but only to renounce the self; work done with no selfish interest purifies the mind; duties are opportunities afforded to man to sink his separate self and become one with the universal self. All this is unoriginal—it is essentially what Krishna tells Arjuna in the *Bhagavad Gita*. However, it's not the teaching Larry is drawn to, but the person, "the man himself, his benignity, his greatness of soul, his saintliness." Shri Ganesha himself is what Larry was searching for all this time. He decides to stay at the ashram as long as the guru is alive, or until he received "illumination," which he describes as "the state when you have at last burst the bonds of ignorance, and know with a certainty that there is no disputing that you and the Absolute are one."

As Larry is no longer at the ashram, and his guru hasn't died, the inevitable follow-up question is if Larry had, in fact, received illumination. But before Somerset can ask, Larry anticipates the question, and describes an experience he had two years after coming to the ashram. It was his birthday, and he hiked up into the mountains to spend the night in an isolated log cabin. He awoke before dawn and sat under a tree. As he watched light "filter through the darkness, slowly, like a mysterious figure slinking through the trees," he experienced a sensation of "exaltation" and "transcendent joy." He goes on to relate:

> I had a strange sensation, a tingling that arose in my feet and traveled up to my head, and I felt as though I were suddenly released from my body and as pure spirit partook of a loveliness I had never conceived. I had a sense that a knowledge more than human possessed me, so that everything that had been confused was clear and everything that had perplexed me was explained. I was so happy that it was pain and I struggled to release myself from it, for I felt that if it lasted a moment longer I should die and yet it was such rapture that I was ready to die than forgo it. How can I tell you what I felt? No words can tell the ecstasy of my bliss. When I came to myself I was exhausted and trembling.

Larry is reluctant to claim this was a moment of "illumination." In reply, Somerset suggests this experience was nothing more than "a hypnotic condition" resulting from the atmosphere, the dawn, the hike, the solitude. Larry counters that mystics all over the world have described a similar experience in similar terms. It's indeed a textbook description of a mystical experience, or what Freud and his friend (and Nobel laureate) Romain Rolland referred to as an "oceanic feeling," alluding to the moment when a drop of water merges with the ocean, being at once a drop and the ocean itself. The part dissolves into the whole. The ego dissolves into the Absolute. Larry isn't sure if he was "for a moment one with the Absolute or if it was an inrush from the subconscious of an affinity with the universal spirit which is latent in all of us," but he's certain the experience occurred. And while it seems rare, he thinks the experience will be quite common for people in the future. To him, to be able to experience the "oneness with Reality" is a skill cultivated over a long period of time, even lifetimes. He describes it as similar to how humans developed the opposable thumb only through generations of evolution, but which must have begun with only a few primates being able to touch their thumb and forefinger. It's possible that the development of "a sixth sense" will be common to all humans in the far future, so "that they may have as direct a perception of the Absolute as we have now of the objects of sense."

Larry's idea reminds me of a controversial concept known as "morphic resonance," a term coined in 1981 by Rupert Sheldrake to describe the phenomenon in which an entire species acquires certain knowledge or behavior that becomes collective memory, after a tipping point or critical mass of members acquire it individually. For example, to use "the hundredth monkey phenomenon," Japanese monkeys on one island learned to wash sweet potatoes before eating them, and suddenly monkeys of the same species but on another island perform the same trick, even though there was no physical contact between the two groups. Sheldrake proposed this concept for biological purposes, but Larry's saying it applies spiritually, too. The more humans who raise their consciousness and have mystical experiences, the more other humans will be able to have mystical experiences, until all of us can easily experience "oneness with Reality."

But the opposite might be the case. According to Indian cosmology, we're actually in an Age of Darkness, which is dominated by ignorance, vice, and violence. Hindus call it the Kali Yuga, and Buddhists refer to it in a more complicated way—according to Buddhist cosmology, our present time is understood to be toward the end of the first *antarakalpa* (of twenty) of the *Vivartasthayikalpa*, the eon in which the universe exists in a steady state, which comes before the *Samvartakalpa*, the eon in which the universe dissolves. True virtue, morality, and spirituality cannot exist during this Age of Darkness, which is supposed to last for over 400,000 years—and we're only about five thousand years into it. From now on, according to Indian cosmology, things will only get worse. So, unfortunately, Larry might have had it backward. It was in the far *past* when humans had a "sixth sense" and could easily have mystical experiences. Only now are they rare, and in the future they will be absent.

Pressing further, Somerset asks Larry if his idea of the Absolute forces him to see the world as "merely an illusion—the fabric of Maya." And if so, shouldn't he then live as a recluse, denying all worldly pleasure? After all, what's he doing at a café in Paris? But Larry knows truth is not black and white, and that it lies in shades of gray. Maya, he explains, doesn't necessarily mean the world is an illusion. The world is real, but it is not real in the same sense of the Absolute. It's like how it's true that my desk is solid, but a deeper truth is that within that solidity there are subatomic particles arising and passing away so quickly it is anything but solid. Both are true, but one is a deeper truth. There is a material reality, but it arises from a spiritual reality. Just because the "world we know is but an appearance of the world we know not," it doesn't mean we can't appreciate the beauty and pleasure of the world we know. "Nothing in the world is permanent, and we're foolish when we ask anything to last," Larry says, "but we're still more foolish not to take delight in it while we have it." That is, we can eat our cake and have it too. "If all things are transitory," Maugham wrote in *The Gentleman in the Parlour*, "let us find delight in their transitoriness." And so rather than leave the world and retire to a cloister, Larry wants "to live in the world and love the objects of the world, not indeed for themselves, but for the Infinite that is in them." With this understanding, he left India and returned to Paris.

When Somerset asks Larry what he'll do next, he says that in the near future he plans to write a book. Then he'll give away the rest of his money and return to America. When Somerset asks how he plans to live, Larry wittily replies, "With calmness, forbearance, compassion, selflessness, and continence." In other words, it doesn't matter how you make a living, because as long as you live with these traits you will be happy and fulfilled. Somerset first asks about continence, and somehow Anthony Curtis missed Larry's reply: "I am in the fortunate position that sexual indulgence with me has been a pleasure rather than a need. I know by personal experience that in nothing are the wise men of India more dead right than in their contention that chastity intensely enhances the power of the spirit." So there we have it. No need for queer theory.

Next, Somerset strongly advises Larry against giving away his private income, explaining that money provides invaluable independence. Larry has a different idea: "Money to you means freedom; to me it means bondage." Rather than live on unearned income, Larry wants to work as a mechanic in a garage, and then a truck driver, so he can explore his own country. He ultimately plans to move to New York City, mainly for the city's libraries. He'll buy a taxicab, and become a taxi driver. He'll work as much as he needs to support himself, and then be free to do "other work" with the rest of his time. Somerset calls him "crazy as a loon." He points out that income from driving a cab is the same as income from government bonds. Money is money. "No," Larry replies. "My taxi would be merely the instrument of my labour. It would be an equivalent to the staff and begging bowl of the wandering mendicant." This is how Larry proposes to incorporate the wisdom of the East he's learned into the Westerner he is. He'll be a mixture of the Orient and the Occident, not betraying the truth of one for the other.

By this point, morning has arrived. They've been talking all night. They breakfast on fresh croissants and *café au lait*, and then part ways. By the time Somerset makes it to his hotel, it's after 8 AM. "A nice hour for an elderly gentleman to get home," he remarks to a nude lady figurine on his clock.

Six months later, Sophie Macdonald's body is found in the sea off Toulon, nearly naked and with her throat cut from ear to ear. Somerset was in the Riviera and is called to identify the body; the police found an inscribed book of his in Sophie's room. A photograph of Sophie and Larry is also among her possessions, and the police ask Somerset if he knows the man in the photograph. Somerset not only knows Larry, he happens to know that Larry is in nearby Sanary, where Larry planned to reside while writing his own book. Somerset gives the police his address and Larry comes to Toulon. It's the last time they'll see each other.

They don't talk much. Larry says he went through with the plan of getting rid of all his money. He's soon leaving for America. His book is finished, with a small printing intended for friends. Somerset is sent the book soon afterward, but he's called away to Paris before it arrives. He first sees it at Isabel and Gray's apartment, and he's surprised that Larry's book is a collection of essays on several famous historical figures: Sulla, the Roman dictator who achieved absolute power and then resigned it to return to private life; Akbar, the Mogul conqueror who spread the empire throughout India; Ruben, Goethe, and Lord Chesterfield. Somerset is puzzled, until he realizes that each figure had been supremely successful. He thinks that perhaps Larry was curious to see what they thought their success amounted to in the end.

By then, Elliott Templeton has died. On his deathbed, he regrets his life as a socialite, which he finally understood to be vain and empty:

> Oh, it's so unkind. I hate them, I hate them all. They were glad to make a fuss of me when I could entertain them, but now I'm old and sick they have no use for me. Not ten people have called to inquire since I've been laid up, and all this week only one miserable bunch of flowers. I've done everything for them. They've eaten my food and drunk my wine. I've run errands for them. I've made their parties for them. I've turned myself inside out to do them favours. And what have I got out of it? Nothing,

nothing, nothing. There's not one of them who cares if I live or die. Oh, it's so cruel. I wish to God I'd never left America.

Elliott was always so sure of himself, so superior, but at the end his lifetime of social climbing has left him "intolerably pathetic." All that work for nothing. A wasted life.

And what happened to the other characters? Sophie lost her husband and baby, and was unable to recover from her drug addiction. Gray lost his fortune, and was only able to get himself back together with Larry's help. Isabel became a bitter, cruel woman, incapable of love. They've all missed the point. And why? Perhaps Maugham is saying that without the spiritual wisdom that Larry found in the East, without the wisdom he found in himself through meditation, we're missing what life is really about. Even if we safely make it through our days, without catastrophe or tragedy, rarely can we call our days fulfilling. Coffee and work, happy hour and dinner, a show and maybe some sex. A mimosa-filled brunch and sports on the weekend. Tropical vacations and European tours. (And that's the people who know how to enjoy life. Otherwise it's junk food and TV, TV, TV.) Monotony broken by childbirths, graduations, weddings, and funerals. We'll look back on our deathbed and wonder if we wasted our lives. Did we live in the best way possible? Did we do all we could with the great privilege of being human? Of all the characters in *The Razor's Edge*, only Larry can die without regret.

With the money Elliott leaves to Isabel, Gray buys into an oil business in Dallas, and the Maturins return to America. The next time Somerset passes through Paris, other people live in Elliott's apartment. On the last page, again with his tongue firmly in cheek, Somerset says he's unintentionally written a success story. In the end, all his characters got what they wanted: "Elliott social eminence; Isabel an assured position backed by a substantial fortune in an active and cultured community; Gray a steady and lucrative job, with an office to go to from nine till six every day; Suzanne Rouvier security; Sophie death; and Larry happiness."

He's wrapping things up nicely, ending with a death and marriage despite his disclaimer on the first page. But by now we can see through his sarcasm. Yes, everyone got what they wanted, but only Larry got happiness. And that's all that matters. Because what's the purpose of security, status, career, or fortune if it doesn't bring happiness? What's the point of making money if the result isn't happiness? Why study philosophy if not to achieve happiness? No matter your worldview or way of life, happiness is the goal. Not a momentary, fleeting happiness that vanishes when things don't go your way. Not the *idea* of happiness, the conception of oneself as a happy person, but a consistent *sensation* of happiness, a buoyant sense of well-being that remains steadily independent of external factors. And that happiness—true happiness—is rare. In fact, happiness takes work. And only Larry has put in the work. Only he is successful. Yet he has no wife or children, no money, property, or power, and he has no interest in sex. He's the opposite of everything our pop culture says will lead to happiness. And yet he's truly happy.

Afterward, whenever Somerset visits New York, he peers into each taxi, searching the face of the driver. But he never sees Larry Darrell. Even so, Somerset is sure that Larry is there, still working to "set forth whatever life has taught him and the message he has to deliver to his fellow men." He'd like to think that Larry is at work on another book, but concludes Larry is

> without ambition and he has no desire for fame; to become anything of a public figure would be deeply distasteful to him; and so it may be that he is satisfied to lead his chosen life and be no more than himself. He is too modest to set himself up as an example to others; but it may be he thinks that a few uncertain souls, drawn to him like moths to a candle, will be brought in time to share his own glowing belief that ultimate satisfaction can only be found in the life of the spirit and that by himself following with selflessness and renunciation the path of perfection he will serve as well as if he wrote books or addressed multitudes.

Somerset isn't sure if Larry will write books. And since Maugham the author is already very famous and has no qualms being a public figure, he decides to spread Larry's spiritual wisdom through writing his own book: *The Razor's Edge*.

2

Siddhartha

SOMERSET MAUGHAM WAS ONE of the earliest Western authors to present Eastern spirituality through his fiction, but he wasn't the first. Twenty-two years before Maugham published *The Razor's Edge*, Hermann Hesse wrote *Siddhartha*, by the far the "most Eastern" of novels written by a Westerner.

Hesse was born in 1877 in newly unified Germany, and was raised in the Black Forest town of Calw. His grandfather and parents were Pietist missionaries who had lived in India for years, and so Hesse was exposed to Eastern religions at a young age. He was a talented student, but at sixteen he ran away from the theological seminary where he was studying. Due to what his teachers called "a moral insanity," he was unable to finish high school. Rather than attend university, he worked at a bookstore, first in the college town of Tübingen, and then across the border in Basel, Switzerland. As a bookseller, Hesse read voraciously. He spent his nights in bars, developing a lifelong wine-drinking habit. But he also started writing poems, essays, and short pieces of prose, and in 1904 he published his first novel, *Peter Camenzind*. A poetic bildungsroman in the Romantic tradition, *Peter Camenzind* was well received, and spread Hesse's name throughout the German-speaking world.

With moderate literary fame, Hesse quit the bookstore. He married up, settled in the country, had three children, and produced several popular novels: *Beneath the Wheel, Gertrud, Rosshalde,* and *Knulp*. He also wrote a steady stream of feuilletons and book reviews—his lifelong bread and butter. Despite his success, Hesse remained restless and unfulfilled. Around this time, his readings of Schopenhauer, Schlegel, and theosophy rekindled his interest in the East. Longing to connect with the legendary India of his childhood, Hesse took a trip to Asia in the summer of 1911.

He visited Sumatra, Borneo, Malaysia, and the Buddhist countries Sri Lanka and Burma, which were then part of British India. But Hesse never made it to India proper. Hating the heat and squalor, the beggars and the noise, Hesse found Asia physically oppressive and spiritually unfulfilling—perhaps because he got dysentery and was living on "red wine and opium," as he put it in a letter. And so he ended his trip early. Yet the culture and atmosphere made a deep impression that would later surface in his best work.

Moving his family to Bern upon returning to Europe, Hesse was plagued by depression, as well as chronic eyestrain, which caused him severe headaches. When World War I broke out, Hesse was a lone voice of reason and was despised for the perceived anti-nationalism of his articles. In 1916 he suffered "a crisis of nerves," triggered by the war, the sickness of his son, and the death of his father. Aged thirty-eight, Hesse entered a sanatorium near Lucerne, where he was treated with electrotherapy and Jungian psychoanalysis. He was one of the first major writers to be psychoanalyzed, and the experience hammered his mind inward, into the subconscious.

The result was the novel *Demian*, which Hesse published in 1919 under the pen name of its narrator, Emil Sinclair. With its combination of Greek Gnosticism, Nietzschean existentialism, and Jungian psychology, the book explored what Hesse called "the soul of Europe." Thomas Mann later wrote that *Demian* "struck the nerve of the times" and had an "electrifying influence" on "a whole generation." After a year of praise and prizes awarded to the mysterious Sinclair, Hesse publicly admitted he was the author of *Demian* and became famous throughout the continent. But as his career soared, his marriage crumbled. Hesse's wife suffered from episodes of severe psychosis, which culminated in a total nervous collapse. Leaving her in a sanatorium and his children under the care of relatives, Hesse moved to Ticino, the Italian-speaking canton of Switzerland, where he'd live the rest of his life.

Freed from all familial and social obligations, he began working on a book set in India at the time of Gotama the Buddha. After smoothly writing the early sections, he got stuck. For over a year, he couldn't work on it at all. The year "1920," he admitted, "was the most unproductive year of my life." He again became deeply depressed, but after going to Zurich to be treated by Carl Jung himself, Hesse had a breakthrough and was able to start working again. In 1922, at age forty-five, he published *Siddhartha,* a novel that he said "represents the sum of my life and the ideas that I have absorbed over the course of twenty years from India and Chinese traditions." By presenting the ancient East to the modern West, *Siddhartha* turned Hesse from an author into a spiritual leader.

Despite the public image of a wise sage, Hesse's personal life was in shambles. *Siddhartha* was followed by a five-year silence, during which Hesse divorced, remarried, divorced again, and continued to suffer from depression, gout, and eyestrain. He drank heavily in the bars of Zurich, now whiskey rather than wine. He seriously considered suicide, planning to shoot himself on his fiftieth birthday. Yet with more psychotherapy he was again able to achieve catharsis in writing, producing the cynical and surreal *Steppenwolf* (1927), the sensual and medieval *Narcissus and Goldmund* (1930), and the mythical and elusive *Journey to the East* (1932). While drastically dissimilar in style and approach, all three novels explored the Apollonian and the Dionysian duality of human nature—they also secured Hesse's place among the greatest writers of the twentieth century.

Settling into a third marriage while the world descended into another war, Hesse spent over a decade working on his magnum opus, *The Glass-Bead Game*. He finished it in 1943, the very year the Nazis officially banned his books (it had to be published in Sweden). Set several centuries after our own "Age of Wars" in the utopian province of Castalia, where scholarship has been enshrined as sacred and scholar-priests are bound only by the worship of truth, *The Glass-Bead Game* successfully managed to synthesize the intellectual with the spiritual. A fusion of Eastern and Western culture, it earned Hesse the 1946 Nobel Prize. He lived until 1962, but never wrote another novel.

Among his many masterpieces, *Siddhartha* is known as Hesse's most famous novel—or so it says on the cover of my New Directions edition. But it wasn't translated into English and published in the United States until 1951—this is why I chose to place its chapter after *The Razor's Edge*. Championed by Henry Miller and the Beats in the fifties, *Siddhartha* became something of a bible for the hippies during the sixties and seventies, when Hesse's work received an explosion of acclaim far greater than anything he experienced in his lifetime.

Decades later, one of those hippies, my then-girlfriend's mother—whose legal birth name, I kid you not, is Karma—gave me *Siddhartha* for my nineteenth birthday. At the time, I was all about Camus and naively considered myself an atheist and existentialist. I knew nothing about Eastern religion and wasn't interested in it either. I remember reading *Siddhartha*, but don't recall being particularly inspired by it. Yet over the following year, I took my first yoga class, discovered the *Tao Te Ching*, and read a book on Buddhism. That summer, I was sitting on the bank of a Swiss lake, waiting to hang glide, and for the first time I crossed my legs and closed my eyes in meditation. It was for only ten minutes or so, and I had no idea what I was doing. But that brief glimpse inward later led me to the Zen Center, Vipassana, and a pilgrimage to Burma and India. Only with hindsight did I understand that *Siddhartha* was the catalyst for my own journey to the East.

Both *The Razor's Edge* and *Siddhartha* explicitly promote Indian religion and culture. Otherwise, they have little in common. The most immediate difference is style. Maugham's sentences are verbose—quoting him causes my inner editor to cringe. In contrast, Hesse's sentences in *Siddhartha* are succinct, without an extra word. They are poetic and beautiful, simple and easy, yet also dense, forcing a slow read. ("The German" of *Siddhartha*, writes Edwin F. Casebeer in his 1972 biography *Hermann Hesse*, "is easy enough for a second-semester college student to manage.") It's rare to find such perfection of writing, and it's this beautiful simplicity that often makes a small book a masterpiece.

The other major difference is setting. Though the crucial sections of *The Razor's Edge* refer to Larry's experiences in India, most of the book takes place in Paris. *Siddhartha* is completely set in India—not the India of the twentieth century, but India two and half thousand years ago. Ancient India at the time of Gotama the Buddha, who most scholars agree lived between 563 and 483 BCE, though there's no consensus. Finally, whereas it takes Maugham half of his novel before he mentions India or meditation, Hesse jumps right in with spiritual practices and Sanskrit words, unconcerned if his readers know what he's talking about.

On the first page, Hesse writes that his hero Siddhartha "practiced the art of contemplation and meditation." Young Siddhartha already knows how to "pronounce Om silently—this word of words, to say it inwardly with the intake of breath, when breathing it out with all of his soul." That is, he's breathing in a specific pattern while repeating a *mantra*, or religious incantation, with the purpose of inducing a state of deep concentration. The mantra he's using, the syllable *Om*, begins and ends all Brahmin prayers. Actually written AUM, its three letters stand for the three gods Brahma, Vishnu, and Shiva, unifying all of Hinduism in a syllable. Siddhartha also knows "how to recognize Atman within the depth of his being, indestructible, at one with the universe." Atman is the soul, the essence of Brahman, Ultimate Reality, the eternal that each person carries within.

Siddhartha knows all this because he's a Brahmin's son, a member of the priestly class. The Kshatriyas are the ruling military elite, but the Brahmins are the most respected, because they are considered to be the purest.

They are the keepers of sacred knowledge, the performers of ritual and sacrifice. Someone cannot become a Brahmin. They must be born one. As a Brahmin, Siddhartha can read scripture, sing holy songs, and write prayers.

Showing his familiarity with the Hindu religion within the first few pages, Hesse quotes various *Vedas*, the ancient scriptures of Hinduism. In Sanskrit, the word *veda* means "knowledge." Being somewhat similar to the anthology of anthologies that is the Bible, the four *Vedas* collect over a hundred books of legends, philosophy, poetry, and mantras. The more mystical and philosophical last section, the *Upanishads*, provides the doctrine of the *Vedanta* from which most modern Hindu thought has evolved (and which Larry Darrell explained to Maugham that night in Paris).

At the time of the Buddha, however, there was no such religion as "Hinduism." The religion of ancient India is referred to as Brahmanism, which was based on the Vedic scriptures and centered on sacrifice—most often the sacrifice of goats, a ritual still widely practiced on the Indian subcontinent. Like Judaism, the goals of the Brahmanist religion were earthly: sons, cattle, prosperity. What we today consider morality and ethics hardly featured in the religion, if at all. The doctrine of *ahimsa*, or nonviolence, is absent from the early Vedas, and like the Hebrew patriarchs of the Bible, the gods of the Vedas committed adultery, incest, brutal violence.

Yet from Vedic times there was a tradition of ascetics, called *munis*, mendicants who renounced the householder's life, lived in the forests, and survived by begging. These ascetics often had long, matted hair, wore a yellow or orange robe, the skin of deer, or simply smeared their naked body with ashes. They were usually vegetarian, sober, and celibate. Unlike the Brahmins and the rest of Indian society, these *munis* had a pessimistic view of life and sought *moksha*, liberation from the bonds of rebirth. They aimed to achieve *moksha* through means of yogic meditation, fasting, or bodily deprivation. In *Siddhartha*, these ascetics are called *samanas*, which in the Pali language means "seekers." Samanas provided an alternative, unorthodox spiritual path to the conventional ritualism of the Brahmin religion. But they were viewed as the "dropouts" of society, and were traditionally looked down upon. This is a basic view of the religious world in which both Gotama the Buddha and Hesse's Siddhartha were born.

It was also a time of great social change. The lively public debates of the samanas increasingly uprooted the society's traditional religious foundations. The ascetic culture became more mainstream, with more people "dropping out" to search for truth and liberation. There was also the rapid growth of large cities, as the old tribal federations were replaced by powerful monarchies, kingdoms that supported large militaries and oversaw the rise of wealthy merchants. Along the trade routes, new ideas traveled more easily than ever before, and everything was called into question.

A quick note about the term Pali, now that I've introduced it and will reference it throughout the rest of this book: Though Pali was long thought to have been the language spoken in northern India at the time of Gotama the Buddha, the word *pali* properly means "text" and only became a "language" in the codifying of Buddhist scripture. Being a homogenized hybridization of several Prakrit dialects used around the third century BCE, Pali is not exactly identical with any language the Buddha would have spoken. But, as Bhikkhu Bodhi writes in *In the Buddha's Words*, because Pali "belongs to the same broad linguistic family as those he might have used and originates from the same conceptual matrix," its words "capture the subtle nuances of that thought-world without the intrusion of alien influences in even the best and most scrupulous translations," which inevitably "reverberate with the connotations of the words chosen from the target languages." That is, Pali is as close to the Buddha's language as we can get.

Back to the story. Hesse describes young Siddhartha as "intelligent and thirsty for knowledge," and his parents expect him to be "a great learned man, a prince among Brahmins." His best friend is Govinda, which means "cowherd" and is one of the many names of Vishnu and his avatar Krishna. Govinda knows that Siddhartha would "not become an ordinary Brahmin, a lazy sacrificial official, an avaricious dealer in magical sayings, a conceited worthless orator, a wicked sly priest, or just a good stupid sheep amongst a large herd." These charlatan types were common at the time, as they are now, but Siddhartha would be the real thing.

With his father's guidance, Siddhartha performs the ancient cleansing rituals instructed in the *Rig-Veda*. Yet he finds them unfulfilling: "The ablutions were good, but they were water; they did not wash sins away, they did not relieve the distressed heart." In India it was common then, as now, to leave offerings of fruit, sweets, and incense before statues of the gods, and to slay animals in the temples. But Siddhartha understands that offerings and sacrifices are empty gestures. Blasphemously, he wonders, "Were not the gods forms created like me and you, mortal, transient? Was it therefore good and right, was it a sensible and worthy act to offer sacrifices to the gods?" Siddhartha is seeing through the veil of performance that kept the class of Brahmin priests in power. Gotama the Buddha, too, dismissed these Brahmanist rituals as empty and useless for the eradication of suffering. When thousands of his followers did the same, many Brahmins suddenly found themselves without a livelihood—and the Buddha found himself with many enemies.

Siddhartha studies the holy books, particularly the *Upanishads* of *Samaveda*, which says, "Your soul is the whole world." For him, the soul is the focus—Atman, not the gods. Siddhartha reasons that if Atman is to be found inside oneself, shouldn't he be searching for Atman instead of performing useless rituals? Shouldn't he be trying to penetrate the innermost part of his self? But the Brahmins did not know the way to Atman. Their holy books and songs explained the creation of the world, how to properly speak, eat, breathe, and worship. But they "did not know the one important thing, the only important thing." They had knowledge about Atman, but not experience. Among all the wise men Siddhartha knew, not one had "quenched the eternal thirst." And so he concludes he'll never experience Atman by being a Brahmin.

With this realization, Siddhartha decides to join a group of samanas who had recently passed through his village. Hesse describes the samanas as "thin wornout men, neither old nor young, with dusty and bleeding shoulders, practically naked, scorched by the sun, solitary, strange and hostile— lean jackals in the world of men." Siddhartha asks his father's permission to join the ascetics, but his father is displeased. By becoming a wandering mendicant, Siddhartha would give up the privileged social status of his class, a relatively luxurious lifestyle, and the family lineage. He'd be a "dropout." Moreover, he'd be considered dead, a walking corpse. He'd be impure, which is anathema to Brahmins, who are obsessed with purity. A Brahmin would even find the presence of a samana to be polluting. In justifying the hierarchical caste system, Brahmins believed they were the offspring of Brahma's mouth, the *khattiyas* of his arms, the mercantile class (*vessa*) of his belly, the workers (*sudda*) of his legs, and *samanas* the soles of his feet, where impurities are released from the body. (This is why in Asian countries it's rude to point your feet at someone; you're spraying your impurities all over them.) Samanas are the lowest of the low, the dirtiest of the dirty. So it's understandable that Siddhartha's father would initially refuse.

But after stubbornly waiting all night, Siddhartha finally gets his father's approval. "If you find bliss in the forest," his father says, "come back and teach it to me. If you find disillusionment, come back, and we shall again offer sacrifices to the gods together." Joined by his companion Govinda, Siddhartha leaves his family and becomes a samana.

Among the samanas, Siddhartha "traveled along the path of self-denial through pain, through voluntary suffering and conquering of pain, through hunger, thirst and fatigue." He wears only a loincloth. Wandering through the forest, he eats only once a day—and never food that had been cooked. He fasts. He fasts for two weeks. He fasts for four weeks. He becomes emaciated. His beard and fingernails grow long. He looks with contempt at people and the world. When he goes into towns to beg for food, he sees businessmen, prostitutes, doctors, priests, mourners, mothers, and lovers, and he thinks: "Everything lied; stank of lies; they were the illusion of sense, happiness and beauty. All were doomed to decay. The world tasted bitter. Life was pain."

During the years he wrote *Siddhartha*, Hesse was poor and alone. According to his biographer Ralph Freedman, his lifestyle was like "a samana in twentieth century Switzerland." And so this part of the book was easiest for Hesse to write, as it was disguised autobiography. Hiking around the Ticinese Alps, wearing threadbare clothes, living on rice, milk, and macaroni, he could easily see himself as a young Brahmin searching for wisdom. He had experimented with self-deprivation and renunciation. With his eyestrain, headaches, gout, and depression, he experienced life as pain. Trying to live a more moral and meditative existence, Hesse, too, held society in contempt. Viewing his contemporaries as mindless and materialistic, he looked upon them with the haughty disdain of an ascetic. In a letter written just before his second marriage, Hesse told his friend Romain Rolland, "In my heart I am a Samana and belong into [sic] the forest."

This chapter is also where Siddhartha's story most parallels that of Gotama the Buddha. Born near Lumbini in today's southern Nepal, the Buddha's first name was also Siddhattha. ("Siddhartha" is the Sanskrit spelling of the Pali, and the shared name is why many people mistakenly think that *Siddhartha* is a book about the Buddha.) Gotama was his family name, and Sakya his clan. They were a wealthy family, rulers of their province, and Siddhattha Gotama was raised in luxury as a prince. The legend of his youth is well known: sheltered within the palace walls, his life was occupied by music, dancing women, and other sensual entertainment. At age sixteen, he married his cousin, Yasodhara. This may come as a surprise to many, but even after marriage, Siddhattha still kept a harem of at least nine women— or "royal concubines," as Buddhist scholar Charles Hallisey observes in the notes of his *Therigatha: Poems of the First Buddhist Women*—and so we can assume the prince was quite sexually active. But he also studied scripture and practiced meditation, and at a young age mastered difficult absorption meditations, known as *jhanas*. One day he traveled outside the palace walls and saw a sick man, and then a dying man, and then a corpse. Like Larry Darrell, the sight of death changed his life. If suffering and death were inevitably part of life, what was the point of living? Then Siddhattha saw a serene ascetic, and like Hesse's Siddhartha, he decided to become a samana.

By then, the Buddha-to-be was twenty-nine. His wife Yasodhara had just given birth to a son, whom Siddhattha named Rahula, which means "fetter" or "obstacle." He knew that a child would only strengthen the bonds of suffering and ignorance. The time for action had come. At night, Siddhattha took a last look at his sleeping son, and then left his wife and family. The act is referred to as the Great Renunciation. Many people think ill of the Buddha for selfishly abandoning his wife and child. Many others have great admiration for his sacrifice of familial joy and the easy householder's life so that he could achieve liberation and help alleviate suffering for countless others. Using a sword, he cut off his long hair, gave away his royal clothing, and joined a group of samanas in the forest.

As an ascetic he fasted, sometimes eating only one grain of rice a day. Otherwise he took very little food, usually a handful of soup. He became extremely emaciated. As the Buddha recounts in the Longer Discourse to Saccaka:

> because of eating so little my limbs became like jointed segments of vine stems or bamboo stems. Because of eating so little my backside became like a camel's hoof. Because of eating so little the projections on my spine stood forth like corded beads. Because of eating so little my ribs jutted out as gaunt as the crazy rafters of an old roofless barn. Because of eating so little the gleam of my eyes sank far down in their sockets, looking like the gleam of water that has sunk far down in a deep well. Because of eating so little my scalp shriveled and withered as a green bitter gourd shrivels and withers in the wind and sun. Because of eating so little my belly skin adhered to my backbone; thus if I touched my belly skin I encountered my backbone and if I touched my backbone I encountered my belly skin. Because of eating so little, if I defecated or urinated, I fell over on my face there. Because of eating so little, if I tried to ease my body by rubbing my limbs with my hands, the hair, rotted at its roots, fell from my body as I rubbed.

He stood for hours, for days. He slept in cemeteries and charnel grounds, among rotting corpses. He performed other rigorous austerities and mortifications, all with the goal of killing his desires, his passion, his ego, his self.

Hesse's Siddhartha, too, performs austerities in order "to let the Self die." He believes that once all passions and desires were silent, the "innermost of Being that is no longer Self" would awaken. Then he would "experience pure thought." This was his goal. So like the other samanas, Siddhartha "stood in the fierce sun's rays, filled with pain and thirst, and stood until he no longer felt pain and thirst." It may sound dumb, but if we easily become irritable when we're hungry or hot or thirsty, how free can we really be? We're enslaved by discomfort, not just to pain but to the mind's fear of pain. By killing his senses, Siddhartha is trying to free himself from this mental slavery.

In addition to austerities, samanas try to "let the Self die" through yogic meditation. Thus Siddhartha "sat upright and learned to save his breath, to manage with little breathing, to hold his breath." This is the practice of *pranayama*, or "control of breath," an ancient technique of calming the mind. Today, many yoga instructors begin their classes with a form of *pranayama*, such as breathing through alternate nostrils. Siddhartha also "learned, while breathing in, to quiet his heartbeat, learned to lessen his heartbeats, until there were few and hardly any more." It's well known that we consciously use about ten percent of our brain, because most of our bodily functions operate subconsciously. While we sleep, our brain makes sure our lungs breath and our heart beats. It keeps our digestion working and our blood moving. Our liver metabolizes, our kidneys purify, and our glands secrete. All this happens on its own. But through deep meditation, one can consciously use more of the brain and control these normally subconscious bodily functions, as Siddhartha is doing.

Using another meditation technique, Siddhartha shifts his consciousness outside of himself, seeing from the perspective of animals, or even corpses: "He became a dead jackal, lay on the shore, swelled, stank, decayed, was dismembered by hyenas, was picked at by vultures, became a skeleton, became dust, mingled with the atmosphere." Here Hesse was probably influenced by the Charnel-ground Observation section of the *Satipatthana Sutta*, or Discourse of Establishing Awareness, in which the Buddha offers a similar form of meditation for disciples very attached to the sensuality of the body—disciples who were obsessed with women, with sex, and whose mind was therefore too agitated to sit cross-legged and meditate. The Buddha told them to go to the cemetery, the kind where bodies were dumped, not buried. The Buddha said to watch a corpse for one day, two days, three days. Watch it swell, become bloated, turn blue, fester. Understand that your body will also one day swell, become bloated, turn blue, fester. Watch the flesh of the corpse get eaten by crows, hawks, vultures. Watch it get torn apart by jackals and dogs. Watch it get eaten by worms, by maggots. Understand that your body will also get eaten and torn apart by animals and insects. Watch the corpse be reduced to a skeleton, held together by tendons, attached with patches of flesh and blood. Understand that your body is a skeleton, held together by tendons, attached with blood and flesh. Watch the leg bones, arm bones, pelvis, spine, skull come apart, scatter in different directions. Watch the bones become white, bleached by the sun. See the bones rot, break down, turn to dust. Understand the bones of your body will also separate, become white, break down, turn to dust. This is the true nature of the body, the end result for every one of us. Yes, this practice of Charnel-ground Observations is uber morbid, but it breaks our attachment to the body, sensual pleasures, and the idea of a self. Our mind becomes less agitated, and we can sit and meditate.

But no matter how many times Siddhartha manages to escape his Self, he always comes back to it. Eventually he understands the austerities of the samanas to be "a temporary palliative against the pain and folly of life." Just like sex or alcohol, the relief from the self is temporary. After being with the ascetics for three years, he's as far from wisdom as when he joined them. He asks Govinda if they are going in circles. An optimist, Govinda answers that "the path is spiral," and that they "are going upwards." Siddhartha points out that the eldest of their companions is sixty years old, and has not yet attained "nirvana." Siddhartha believes that among all the samanas, probably not even one will attain nirvana. "We find consolations," he says, "we learn tricks with which to deceive ourselves, but the essential thing—the way—we do not find." To Govinda's dismay, Siddhartha expresses a desire to leave the ascetics. The Buddha, too, before he became the Buddha, gave up extreme austerities in favor of what he called the Middle Way. Neither indulgence in luxury, nor indulgence in mortification. Neither fasting nor gluttony. Torturing the body was not the way to eradicate suffering. When he abandoned self-mortification practices, the Buddha lost the respect of his five fellow ascetics—they thought he was a quitter because he ate food—and Hesse's Siddhartha, too, gains the wrath of the samanas when he decides to leave.

But before he and Govinda leave, they hear "a rumor, a report." There is someone, a man, called Gotama, the Buddha. People refer to him as the Illustrious One, the Perfect One. "He had conquered in himself the sorrows of the world and had brought to a standstill the cycle of rebirth," and now he wanders through the country, preaching his teaching, surrounded by a group of ever-growing disciples. People in towns are talking about the Buddha. Brahmins and samanas are talking about the Buddha, some with praise and others with scorn. People say "he remembered his former lives, he had attained nirvana." People say "he had performed wonders, had conquered the devil, had spoken with the gods." Young men all over northern India listened to these reports, feeling "a longing and hope." Everyone wants to hear news of this Gotama, the Buddha. Many have set out to seek him and hear his teaching for themselves.

Siddhartha is not intrigued by these rumors, but Govinda suggests they go and hear the teachings from the lips of the Perfect One. By then, Siddhartha has "become distrustful of teachings" and has "little faith in words that come to us from teachers." But he'll go see Gotama anyway, because at least it gives them a reason to leave the samanas. When Siddhartha declares that he and Govinda are leaving, the eldest samana becomes angry, raising his voice and scolding the friends. Siddhartha then "looked into the old man's eyes and held him with his look, hypnotized him, made him mute, conquered his will, commanded him silently to do as he wished." The old man becomes quiet. His arms hang down limply. He bows several times and gives his blessing. Like Larry Darrell, Siddhartha has apparently learned how to hypnotize. Similarly, he doesn't give it much credit. Yet Govinda is extremely impressed, and says that if they had stayed with the samanas then surely Siddhartha would have learned to walk on water. "I have no desire to walk on water," Siddhartha replies.

By walking on water, Jesus captivated his disciples and impressed millions of gospel readers. It's one of the acts that proved Jesus was not only the Messiah, but the divine Son of God. Yet in several suttas of the Pali Canon—and also the fifth-century Theravada Buddhist manual and scriptural commentary by Buddhaghosa called the *Visuddhimagga*, or *Path of Purification*—it's claimed that many Buddhist monks could "walk on water as if it were earth," as well as "dive into solid ground as if it were water." Once you mastered your mind, you could easily manipulate matter and perform such "miracles." Walking on water was nothing special. Certainly not proof of being divine. And here Hesse is basically telling his Christian audience that the miracle Jesus performed is a waste of time, that walking on water will not help one reach the final goal.

Before moving on, it would be wise to take a closer look at this word Hesse introduced: nirvana. It is the Sanskrit form of the Pali word the Buddha used to describe the final goal of his teaching: *nibbana*. In English, nirvana is usually rendered as "Enlightenment," but this is due to the time period in which the Buddhist texts were first translated into Western languages. In the person of Gotama the Buddha, nineteenth-century Western thinkers saw the epitome of their Enlightenment movement: the perfectly rational, the perfectly self-dependent, the perfectly knowledgeable. The Buddha was *the* Enlightened One.

But the term Enlightenment is misleading and generally misused. *Nibbana* literally means "blowing out," or "extinguished," as in the extinguishing of a fire. So rather than a light going on, it would be more accurate to say that a light goes off. Instead of referring to one who has achieved *nibbana* as "an enlightened person," it is more appropriate to refer to "a liberated person," because they are liberated from the bondage of suffering and ignorance, liberated from the bondage of samsara. This final goal of nibbana, in the words of Bhikkhu Bodhi, "is not achieved abruptly but by passing through a series of stages that transforms an individual from a worlding into an arahant, a liberated one." And each stage is accompanied by a progressively deeper and more purifying *nibannic* experience—"a dip in the nibbanic realm," as S. N. Goenka puts it—until one has finally purified all the mental defilements that cause rebirth.

Okay, but what *is* nibbana? The Buddha was often asked this question. To explain what it is. But he never gave a direct answer. It's impossible to give one, because nibbana is beyond the field of mind and matter. When a person experiences nibbana, all the sense organs stop working. When they return from the nibbanic experience, the sense organs begin working again. Because the nibbanic experience is beyond the sense organs, it cannot be explained or understood with the sense organs. In order to understand what it is, it must be experienced for one self.

The Buddha was also asked to explain what happens after a liberated person dies. Where is he reborn? Or is he not reborn? The Buddha said the terms reborn and not reborn do not apply. Well then, is he both reborn *and* not reborn? Or is he neither reborn nor not reborn? The Buddha answered that these terms also do not apply. To show the irrelevancy of the question, the Buddha in turn asked, "When a fire is extinguished, which direction does it go: to the east, the west, the north, or the south?" It's impossible to say the fire "goes" anywhere. Similarly, what happens to someone who has experienced nibbana is impossible to understand using language, because the very terms we use to refer to an individual and existence no longer apply.

Even so, in order to help people understand nibbana, the Buddha did use synonyms for it. Among them are: the unconditioned, the undisintegrating, the unmanifest, the deathless, the taintless, the destruction of craving, the peaceful, the blissful, the shelter, the destination, purity, and freedom. We can get closer to understanding nibbana through negatives. By what it is not. As the Buddha's foremost disciple Sariputta put it, "the destruction of lust, the destruction of hatred, the destruction of delusion: this, friend, is called nibbana."

After leaving the samanas, Siddhartha and Govinda travel to the city of Savatthi, where "every child knew the name of the illustrious Buddha and every house was ready to fill the alms bowls of Gotama's silently begging disciples." Though they are not wearing the yellow robe of Buddhists, a woman gives food to the friends. Siddhartha asks her where the Buddha dwells, so they can "see the Perfect One and hear his teaching from his own lips." The woman replies that "the Illustrious One sojourns in Jetavana, in the garden of Anathapindika." This answer proves that Hesse has read his Pali scriptures, because many *suttas* begin with the opening lines: "Thus I have heard. On one occasion the Blessed One was dwelling at Savatthi, in Jeta's grove, Anathapindika's park."

At the time of the Buddha, Savatthi was the capital of the kingdom of Kosala, and with a population nearing a million, it was one of the biggest cities in northern India. It was on the Aciravati River, now called the Rupti, in the state of Uttar Pradesh, near the current Nepalese border. Of the forty-five rainy seasons of his life as a teacher, the Buddha spent twenty-five of them in Savatthi, with nineteen of those in Jeta's grove, Anathapindika's park. That is to say, it's the place where the Buddha spent the most time, and gave the most discourses.

Now, who is Anathapindika? His real name was Sudatta, and he was a very wealthy merchant. He was also very generous—Anathapindika means "one who gives alms to the helpless." Once he visited his brother-in-law in Rajagha, a city in the nearby state of Magadha. When Anathapindika arrived, he was surprised to find his brother-in-law's entire household preoccupied with preparing a meal for the Buddha and his followers. That night, Anathapindika met the Buddha and heard his teaching. Afterward, Anathapindika asked if he could build the Buddha a monastery back in Savatthi, his hometown. The Buddha consented, and Anathapindika went home to find suitable property. The site had to be close to the city center, so that it was accessible, but not too close, as to be overrun with people and too noisy to meditate. Eventually, Anathapindika found an ideal forest garden belonging to the son of the king, Prince Jeta—it was called Jetavana, or Jeta's grove. Anathapindika found the prince and asked if he could buy the garden. Jeta was offended, saying that his garden was not for sale. Mockingly, he said he'd only sell his garden for the amount of gold coins it took to completely cover the land. To his surprise, Anathapindika agreed to the deal, and started bringing carts filled with gold coins, spreading millions of them over the garden. He spent millions more on buildings and furnishings, including individual meditation cells, a meeting hall, a dining hall, storerooms, walkways, latrines, wells, and ponds for bathing, as well as a surrounding wall. The forest garden was transformed into a mega monastery, and in honor of its patron, the texts always refer to it as "Jeta's grove, Anathapindika's park." Anathapindika became known as the foremost patron of the *Sangha*, the community of Buddhist monks and nuns.

But that's not why I find his story interesting. Due to bad investments, unpaid debts, and a flash flood that washed his treasury into the sea, Anathapindika lost nearly all of his money. He went from being the richest man in the city to living in poverty. As a good Buddhist, he didn't complain about his situation, accepting it as fruits of past karma. With what money he had, he continued to feed the monks, now with thin rice gruel instead of hearty meals. Soon, he had nothing left to give. But a householder must bring something when visiting a monastery, and dirt from his garden was all he had. So when he came to the monastery at Jetavana, he brought handfuls of soil. He put the soil around the bases of trees, thinking, *May someone become enlightened under the shade of this tree*. Doing such acts with a pure mind helped expedite his negative karma, and once it was exhausted, his debtors paid back his loans, his gold was retrieved from the sea, and Anathapindika again became a rich man. Or so the story goes.

In Hesse's own story, when Siddhartha and Govinda arrive at Anathapindika's monastery at Jetavana, most of the monks are out on their begging rounds. Even Gotama the Buddha is out begging. Siddhartha and Govinda go to find him, and even though the Buddha is dressed like the hundreds of other monks wearing yellow robes, Siddhartha recognizes Gotama immediately, "as if pointed out to him by a god." They follow him and observe that the Buddha's "peaceful countenance was neither happy nor sad. He seemed to be smiling gently inwardly." Every gesture and part of his body "spoke of completeness, sought nothing, imitated nothing, reflected a continuous quiet, an unfading light, an invulnerable peace." Even in "every joint of every finger of his hand there was knowledge; they spoke, breathed, radiated truth." Siddhartha recognizes Gotama "was truly a holy man down to his fingertips."

Upon seeing the Buddha, Govinda becomes excited to hear his teachings. But Siddhartha still "did not think they would teach him anything new." They follow the Buddha back to the monastery and watch him eat an amount that "would not have satisfied a bird." In the evening they hear Gotama talk "about suffering, the origin of suffering, and the way to release from suffering." That is to say, the Four Noble Truths.

The Four Noble Truths are presented like the formula for a medical diagnosis. It states the illness, the cause of the illness, the cure for the illness, and the way to bring about the cure. The first Noble Truth is that *dukkha* exists. *Dukkha* is usually translated as "suffering" or "pain," but more relevantly can be understood as "dissatisfaction" or "discontent," or simply "agitation." The literal meaning of the word is "bad fit," referring to the bad fit of an axle in a wheel. Many people who consider themselves happy would deny their life is suffering, but nobody can deny that life is full of dissatisfaction or agitation, or that it often feels like a bad fit.

But of course, there *is* suffering. We will grow old, become weak, become diseased, decay, and we will die. That is suffering. *Dukkha.* People we love will leave us. They, too, will become old, weak, decay, and they will die. That is *dukkha*. Birth is *dukkha*, old age is *dukkha*, death is *dukkha*. But mosquito bites are also *dukkha*. Heat is *dukkha*. Cold is *dukkha*. Indigestion is *dukkha*. Hunger is *dukkha*. Bickering is *dukkha*. Heartbreak is *dukkha*. Passion is *dukkha*, because passion is agitation. Sex is passion, and so sex is *dukkha*. Love, too, is *dukkha*, for we worry about those we love, and worry is *dukkha*. Even happiness is *dukkha*, because happiness is agitation. And happiness doesn't last—when it leaves, that is *dukkha*. (As Romain Gary writes in *The Life Before Us*, "Happiness is famous for the misery of going without it.") In sum, simply being alive is *dukkha*. Sitting there doing nothing is agitating, because there is so much heat and friction in the body, because deep down everything is constantly changing, arising, and passing away. So yes, in life there is dissatisfaction, discontent, suffering, agitation, *dukkha*. That's the first Noble Truth.

The second Noble Truth is that *dukkha* has a cause. The Buddha was a scientist of the self, and as a scientist, he knew that every effect has its cause. So if there is suffering, then suffering must have a cause. And with great insight, the Buddha observed that *tanha*—craving—is the cause of *dukkha*. Craving is what causes dissatisfaction. Craving is agitation. If craving is too strong a word, then we can use wanting. The mind wants things, and it doesn't want things. It is always craving and wanting. Wanting reality to be other than it is. This is why there is *dukkha*. We are given a physical discomfort, and we make it worse by turning it into mental suffering. If we're cold, we don't have to suffer—it can simply be a sensation of cold. But we don't *want* to be cold, and so we create mental suffering. We create our own suffering by wanting reality to be other than it is. *Dukkha* is caused by craving. That's the second Noble Truth.

The third Noble Truth is that there is a way out of *dukkha*. The Buddha discovered this way, which is why he is the Buddha. The word buddha means "awakened one," and a buddha is someone who discovers the way out of suffering, on their own. If craving ceases, then suffering ceases. If no cause, then no effect. Suffering can be eradicated through the cessation of craving. There is a way out of *dukkha*. That's the third Noble Truth.

The fourth Noble Truth is that there is a way of life that leads to the cessation of *dukkha*, and this way of life is the Noble Eightfold Path. Buddha is a doctor, and the Noble Eightfold Path is his prescription. If followed, it alleviates the disease of suffering by eradicating craving.

For those not familiar with it, as Hesse's readers likely weren't, or anyone needing a refresher, the Noble Eightfold Path is: right view, right intention, right speech, right action, right livelihood, right effort, right mindfulness, and right concentration. And here's my consolidated version of the Buddha's explanation of each part:

Right view is knowledge of suffering, the origin of suffering, the way leading to the cessation of suffering—that is, the acceptance of the Four Noble Truths.

Right intention is intention of renunciation, non-ill will, harmlessness.

Right speech is abstaining from false speech, malicious speech, harsh speech, and idle chatter.

Right action is abstaining from killing living beings, taking what is not given, and sexual misconduct. (Later, after one of his monks embarrassed everyone by getting dead drunk in the street, the Buddha added abstaining from "fermented and distilled beverages that cause heedlessness.")

Right livelihood is abstaining from trading in weapons, living beings, meat, intoxicants, and poison.

Right effort is striving to purify the mind through cultivating wholesome mental states, preventing unwholesome mental states from arising, observing moral conduct, and not being idle.

Right mindfulness is being continuously and ardently alert and aware of the breath, bodily sensations, states of mind, and contents of the mind—that is, the impermanence of all phenomena—and also keeping in mind instructions and intentions that are useful on the path.

Right concentration is one-pointedness of mind, with sustained focus, without distraction; states of meditative absorption called *jhana*.

Despite being called a "path," these are not subsequent steps—as you likely noticed, each depends upon the rest, strengthening each other, like the cords of a rope. Still, it can seem kind of complicated. So to simplify his teaching, the Buddha summarized the Eightfold Path in a way anyone can understand: "Perform wholesome actions, abstain from unwholesome actions, and keep purifying the mind."

So that night in Jeta's grove, Siddhartha and Govinda listen to the Buddha's discourse. Speaking "clearly and quietly," in "a soft but firm voice," and using "examples and repetition," Gotama "taught the four main points, taught the Eightfold Path." Along with hundreds of others, Siddhartha and Govinda hear that "life was pain, the world was full of suffering, but the path to the release from suffering had been found."

After the discourse, many pilgrims step forward and ask to join the Buddha's community, to take the going forth from home into homelessness—as the scriptures say—and enter the *sangha,* the community of monks and nuns. Hearing that "there was salvation for those who went the way of the Buddha," Govinda also steps forward and asks to join the community. The Buddha accepts him, and then withdraws for the night.

Eager and disturbed, Govinda asks Siddhartha why he didn't also ask to join the *sangha*. Why doesn't he want to tread the path of salvation? How can he not do other than swear allegiance to the Buddha? Siddhartha gives Govinda his blessing, but gives no explanation. Govinda understands that he'll now have to separate from his friend, and so he weeps. Siddhartha reminds Govinda that by taking the going forth he has not only renounced home and parents, origin and property, he has also renounced friendship. Confused, Govinda asks if there's a flaw in the Buddha's teachings, something he may have missed. Siddhartha reassures him: "The Illustrious One's teachings are very good. How could I find a flaw in them?"

But Siddhartha does think he found a flaw. And later that night, he finds Gotama to talk about it. First, he tells the Buddha that while Govinda will remain, he will continue on his pilgrimage. Yet he wants to communicate his thoughts before he goes, and he asks if Gotama will listen. Characteristically, the Buddha silently nods his consent. Siddhartha praises the teachings, saying they are "completely clear and proved" and "irrefutably demonstrated." He tells the Buddha: "You show the world as a complete, unbroken chain, an eternal chain, linked together by cause and effect."

He's referring to the law of Dependent Origination, the *Pattica-Samuppada*, which is the Buddha's analysis of the origin and perpetuation of all existence. It explains why there is craving, and why there is the cycle of birth and death. It basically explains everything.

Sitting under that tree the night he achieved *nibbana*, the Buddha looked into himself with great insight. And this is what he discovered: when an external stimulus comes in contact with one of the sense doors, a sensation arises in the body. The word he used is *vedana*. *Vedana* means a physical sensation—or as some translate it, feeling tone. It can be a localized gross sensation, like pain or itching. Or it can be a subtle sensation, one that flows throughout the body, through the chemicals of the bloodstream. Whether gross or subtle, the sensation immediately causes craving. Subconsciously, we crave for more of a pleasant sensation, and we crave for an unpleasant sensation to go away. This was the Buddha's great discovery: we never react to external objects, only to internal sensations.

We don't crave ice cream, for instance, we crave the internal sensation that arises when we taste ice cream. We don't crave to hear music; we crave the sensation that arises when we listen to music. We also crave the sensation of craving itself. When we look closely enough, we find that we don't crave a coffee—we crave the sensation of craving a coffee. We are addicts to the sensation of craving. And all this craving causes relishing, clinging, attachment. Attachment to sensations. Attachment to life itself. It causes such strong attachment that as we are dying, we cling so strongly to life that the clinging causes what is called *bhava*, becoming. The will to live. Becoming causes birth. Birth inevitably causes decay, death, and all the suffering that comes with life. In order to cease the cycle of birth and death, there must be a break in this chain of links. So where can we break the chain?

The Buddha found that the only part of the chain we have any control over is the link between sensation and craving. After all, there is nothing we can do about having senses. And there is nothing we can do about there being external stimuli. When an external stimulus comes in contact with our senses, a sensation will arise. There is nothing we can do about that. But rather than react to the sensation with craving or aversion, we can train the mind to observe the sensation with equanimity. That is, without reacting. The sensation arises and you just observe it, without reacting. You observe as the sensation arises, as it stays for some time, and as it passes away. You observe *annica*, "impermanence" or "change." (More accurately, it's the arising and passing away of subatomic particles millions of times per second.) *Annica*. Wavelengths, vibrations. *Annica*. You observe the sensation with equanimity, without reacting. You experience that the sensation is *annica*. That all sensations are *annica*. When you experience sensations with equanimity, then there is no craving. If there is no craving, there is no clinging, no attachment. If there is no attachment, there is no becoming. If there is no becoming, there is no birth. And if there is no birth, then boom: there is no life, no death, and no suffering. This discovery is why the Buddha is the Buddha. He found that the key to coming out of craving is to observe bodily sensation with equanimity.

But wait. This chain of dependent origination assumes the existence of reincarnation, so a note on that. When Larry Darrell and Somerset Maugham previously discussed "the transmigration of the soul," I mentioned the major difference between Hinduism and Buddhism is the belief in the soul. There are other major differences—for instance, the Buddha found the Indian class system, the gods, and all Brahmanistic ritual and sacrifice to be irrelevant to the spiritual path. Theoretically speaking, however, the biggest difference between the religions is the belief in the soul. In the idea of *atman*. In Hinduism, atman is the part of the self that is eternal, permanent, and unchangeable. In Hinduism, the soul is what reincarnates through the rounds of birth and death. For a Hindu, the goal of liberation is achieved when one experientially realizes atman is the same essence as Brahman. When the soul becomes part of Ultimate Reality. But the Buddha taught something else. He taught *anatta*.

The Pali word for atman is *atta*, and so *anatta* means the opposite of atman. *Anatta* means "not-Self." Self-less. At the time of the Buddha, there was a saying among Brahmins and ascetics: What is *vinyana* is *atta*, what is *atta* is *vinyana*. What is conscious is soul, soul is what is conscious. The Buddha dissected this and found something quite different. He found there is no such thing as a soul. When he peeled back the layers of the body and mind, there was nothing left. He saw that the Self has no essence. He saw that the Self is a conditioned process. That the Self is an illusionary sum of its ever-changing parts. The Self is only a convention, a concept necessary for communication. Otherwise we'd have to address each other as "bundle of vibrations." As everything is *annica*, as everything is impermanent and constantly changing, there can be no essential Self, no permanent soul, no atman. Because nothing is eternal, nothing is unchangeable. And so the soul cannot possibly exist. In Buddhism, there is no atman to discover, and the soul is not what reincarnates. There is no "transmigration of the soul." So what reincarnates? What happens?

"What actually happens," according to Nyanatiloka Mahathera, one of the earliest Westerners to become fully ordained as a Buddhist monk, "is that a psychophysical process, which is cut off at death, continues immediately thereafter somewhere else, in strict conformity to causes and conditions." What reincarnates is called *kamma-vega*, or "kamma-energy." In other words, energy is what reincarnates.

The first law of thermodynamics (and the law of conservation of energy) states that energy cannot be created or destroyed. Energy can only change forms, flowing from one place to another. And what is the mind? It is energy. The mind is an accumulation of energy arising from past mental action. (The literal meaning of *kamma* is "action.") Every time the mind has a thought or intention, an action or reaction, it creates a vibration. These mental vibrations accumulate throughout a lifetime, creating a certain charge. Because energy cannot be created or destroyed, at death the vibration of mental energy moves from one form of embodiment to another, like a train changing tracks as it enters and then leaves a station. Or as Nyanatiloka Mahathera explains: "At the moment of death, a dying individual, with his whole being clinging to life, sends forth karmic energies, like a flash of lightning, that hits a new mother's womb ready for conception."

To understand more clearly, we can think of the mechanics of speech and listening. One person uses their acoustic organ to produce a sound vibration, which then hits another person's auditory organ. No "transmigration of sound" takes place, but simply a transference of energy, air vibrations that are perceived by another person's auditory organ. Or think of lighting one candle with another. The flame does not "transmigrate," but the latter flame is impossible without the former. Or think of how a wave moves through the ocean. There is a continuous rising and falling of ever-new masses of water, each time caused by the transmission of energy. Like a wave through the ocean, so the kamma-energy passes through samsara, the round of birth and death, from one body to another. Not a permanent ego, personality, identity, or soul. But a subconscious life stream, called a *bhavanga-sota*. This subconscious life stream is what carries one's karma from one life to the next.

Because our actions literally create what we are, the karmic seeds sown in one life bear fruit in another. Once, as related in the Shorter Exposition of Kamma, a student named Subha asked the Buddha why people are so different from each other, why some are ugly and others are beautiful, why some are rich and others are poor, why some are healthy and others are sickly, and why some live a long life while others die young. The Buddha answered that if someone is murderous and kills other beings, they will be reborn into a short life. If someone abstains from killing others, they will be reborn into a long life. If someone is violent, they will be reborn sickly. If someone is peaceful, they will be reborn healthy. If someone is angry and irritable, hostile and bitter, they will be reborn ugly. If someone is not angry or irritable, not hostile or bitter, they will be reborn beautiful. If someone is stingy, they will be reborn poor. If someone is generous, they will be reborn wealthy.

They pretty much got it down to a science. And whether we choose to believe in it or not, it makes a lot of sense. As Somerset Maugham wrote in an essay titled "Buddha,"

> my heart can accept the evils that befall me if they are the consequences of actions that I (the I that is not my soul, which perishes, but the result of my deeds in another state of existence) did in past time, and I am resigned to the evils that I see about me, the death of the young (the most bitter of all), the grief of mothers that bore them in anguish, poverty, and sickness and frustrated hopes, if these evils are but the consequences of the sins which those that suffer them once committed.

For Maugham, "the law of Karma" is "the only explanation of the evil of this world that does not outrage the heart."

Despite the logic of the law of Dependent Origination, Hesse's Siddhartha tells the Buddha he has an objection. According to Siddhartha, this unity and logical consequence of all things is broken in one place. "Through a small gap there streams into the world of unity something strange," he says, "something new, something that was not there before and that cannot be demonstrated and proved: that is your doctrine of rising above the world, of salvation." He's referring to nibbana. How can nibbana fit into Dependent Origination? It doesn't make sense. The Buddha admits that Siddhartha has "found a flaw."

But the objection is baffling. And I doubt that the Buddha would admit a flaw in his teaching. He always said it's airtight, nothing to add and nothing to take away. It seems Siddhartha has misunderstood the concept of nibbana. This is understandable, because as I mentioned, nibbana is a state outside of mind and matter, so it's impossible to understand using mind and matter. By definition, it's outside the chain of dependent origination. That's the whole idea. But whatever. Let's put that aside. Because Siddhartha then raises a more valid point. And the point is that it's impossible to find salvation through teachings. He tells the Buddha, "To nobody, O Illustrious One, can you communicate in words and teachings what happened to you in the hour of your enlightenment." It's an experience impossible to express in language. Something that can only be understood through experience. This is why Siddhartha says he's continuing on his own way, "not to seek another and better doctrine, for I know there is none, but to leave all doctrines and all teachers and to reach my goal alone—or die."

In response, Hesse has the Buddha give an uncharacteristic reply: "I hope you are not mistaken in your reasoning." The Buddha wishes Siddhartha well on reaching his goal, but then asks if he thinks it would be better for all the monks "to relinquish the teaching and to return to the life of the world and desires." Siddhartha says the thought never occurred to him. "May they all follow the teachings!" he exclaims. It's not for him to judge the life of others. He must judge for himself. He must choose and reject for himself. He further explains that if he were one of the Buddha's followers, he'd "fear that it would only be on the surface, that I would deceive myself that I was at peace and had attained salvation, while in truth the Self would continue to live and grow, for it would have been transformed into your teachings, into my allegiance and love for you and for the community of monks." It other words, it would appear like his ego would shrink, but in actuality it would grow. Half smiling, with imperturbable brightness and friendliness, the Buddha replies, "You are clever, O Samana, you know how to speak cleverly, my friend. Be on your guard against too much cleverness."

In the scriptures, the Buddha doesn't talk like this. Like never. But, again, whatever. This Gotama Buddha is simply a character in a narrative, not the real Gotama Buddha. (Though the "real" Gotama Buddha is also a character in narratives, which is what scriptures are—after reading *A Critique of Western Buddhism*, in which Buddhist scholar Glenn Wallis refers to the Buddha as "a literary protagonist," I can't help but think of the Buddha as the protagonist of the Pali Canon.) It doesn't matter. Hesse is making a point. It's a point of individualism, of faith in the individual. That one cannot rely on anyone else for salvation. The Buddha would be the first to agree. He stressed that no one should believe him unless they experience the truth of his teachings for themselves. You want a cure for the disease of suffering? Here's the prescription, the Buddha says. You try it and see for yourself. If it doesn't work, don't follow it. If it works, then why not follow it?

But Siddhartha refuses to try the prescription, and sets off to find his own.

Siddhartha's argument in this section makes more sense when we know Hesse's personal feelings about Buddhism at the time of writing *Siddhartha*. "For years," he wrote in a 1921 letter to his friend Lisa Wenger, "I believed in Buddhist doctrine, my sole source of consolation at that point, but gradually my attitude changed, and I'm no longer a Buddhist. I now feel more attracted to the India of the gods and temples, and have just to grasp the deeper meaning of pantheism." That is, he's more attracted to Hinduism, the Brahmanism from which Buddhism arose.

To Hesse, the relationship between Buddhism and Brahmanism resembled that between Protestantism and Catholicism. While he appreciated "the conscientious behavior of the Protestants," he felt "the Protestant church itself has nothing much to offer, and the various Protestantism sects nurtured the cultivation of inferiority complexes. That is also more or less how I view Buddhism." In his letter, he goes on to explain that Buddhism "adopts a rational attitude toward the world without gods, and seeks redemption solely through the intellect. It's a beautiful form of Puritanism, but it is also suffocatingly one-sided, and I have become disenchanted with it."

It's unfortunate that Hesse held these misconceptions, which many people share. Buddhists are usually considered to be atheists, and Buddhism a religion without gods. But that's not at all true. The gods are all over the Pali *suttas*. There are *devas* and *brahmas* galore. While the gods certainly exist within Buddhist cosmology, they are simply irrelevant. There's no reason to worship them. No reason to envy them. In fact, the gods learn from the Buddha. In fact, the *Abhidhamma*, the third section of the Pali Canon, is said to be entirely based on an extremely long lecture the Buddha gave to the gods. More importantly, even though Buddhism is rational and logical, the Buddha repeatedly states that his teaching is not possible to understand "solely through the intellect." He said that the Dhamma he attained is "unattainable by mere reasoning." Though Buddhism is intellectually appealing, it can only be understood experientially.

In another letter that same year, this one to his patron's brother, Hesse wrote about his true faith: "Psychoanalysis is not a creed or philosophy, but an experience. Analysis is only worthwhile when one is prepared to experience it fully, and bring it to bear on one's life. Otherwise, it's nothing but a nice little game." The same can be said about the Buddha's teaching, which remained a "nice little game" for Hesse. Buddhism, too, is not a creed or philosophy, but an experience. Buddhism is also only worthwhile when one experiences it fully, bringing it to bear on one's life. But some part of Hesse knew this, because in a lecture delivered around the time *Siddhartha* was being printed, he said: "Buddha's Way to Salvation has been often criticized and doubted, because it is thought to be wholly grounded in cognition. True, but it's not just intellectual cognition, not just learning and knowing, but spiritual experience that can only be earned through strict discipline in a selfless life."

Even so, like most people, Westerners and Easterners alike, Hesse found the Buddha's teaching easier to study than to practice. "It's not easy to practice the Indian-Buddhist form of meditation," he wrote in another letter to Wenger. "One cannot expect a sudden flash of insight. It's a discipline, an exercise to be repeated constantly, every day." Intellectually, he certainly knew he should meditate. (In Castalia, his idealized province in *The Glass Bead Game*, "the practice of spiritual refreshment by meditation" is intrinsic to the daily life of the scholar-priests. They are dependent on "meditation as a well-spring of energy, as the ever-renewing concord of mind and soul.") But knowing and writing about something is very different than living it. Rather than work to develop such "strict discipline," Hesse rationalized his inability to meditate by telling Wenger, "Given the lives we lead, it's difficult." He was just too busy. His life had too many demands. Still, he admits his problems were due to his lack of practice: "We're suffering because we would like to follow that path, but that is no longer possible. We're being held back, not just by the desires and egotistical cravings of the 'real world,' but also by the duties and responsibilities we have assumed." Perhaps if Hesse meditated regularly, he wouldn't have suffered decades of depression, might have cured his chronic physical ailments, and maybe had better relationships, too. But he preferred to read, write, and drink wine.

After Hesse first moved to Ticino (and just before he started *Siddhartha*), he wrote a lovely little book of essays called *Wandering*. And in the last chapter, he summarizes his personal spiritual philosophy. Someone follows the Buddha's teaching because they want to change themselves. "But," Hesse writes, "it is not my concern to change myself. Only a miracle could do that. And whoever seeks a miracle, whoever grasps at it, whoever tries to assist it, sees it fleeing away. My concern is to hover between many extreme opposites and to be ready when a miracle overtakes me. My concern is to be unsatisfied and to endure restlessness."

Restless and unsatisfied, Siddhartha is about to move from one extreme to another.

After leaving Govinda and the Buddha at Jeta's grove, Siddhartha has an awakening—the title of the chapter itself is "Awakening." But it's not like the Buddha's Awakening, and a line in *The Glass Bead Game* helps clarify what Hesse means by this tricky term:

> Awakening, it seemed, was not so much concerned with truth and cognition, but with experiencing and proving oneself in the real world. When you had such an awakening, you did not penetrate any closer to the core of things, to truth; you grasped, accomplished, or endured only the attitude of your own ego to the momentary situation. You did not find laws, but came to decisions; you did not thrust your way into the center of the world, but into the center of your own individuality.

Like a snake that has shed its old skin, Siddhartha realizes he's shed his youth. Throughout his life, he took for granted the world was *Maya*, an illusion. How things appeared were not as they are. Reality was "on the other side of the visible." The senses were enemies. Pleasure was a distraction. Beauty was a lie. But now that he's an adult, Siddhartha starts to see things differently.

The aim of his spiritual quest was to find his Self. He was seeking Atman—Brahman, the Divine, the Absolute. He wanted to destroy his false self, get away from Siddhartha, and find his true innermost Self. Now he understands he doesn't know anything about himself, because he's been afraid of himself. He was afraid of his senses, afraid of pleasure, afraid of beauty. Afraid of life. By trying to get away from himself, he became lost. With this realization, he decides to no longer escape from himself. He will be Siddhartha, and learn from Siddhartha—from his own thought and senses. He will no longer practice asceticism or meditation. He will no longer study the Vedas or any other teaching. He will no longer devote his thoughts to Atman. He will no longer seek a reality "on the other side." He will no longer see the world as sorrowful, as "the magic of Mara," the Evil One, or as the "fleeting and illusive veil" of Maya, regarded with contempt and distrust.

For the first time, he looks at the world as it is. He looks at the sky and river, the woods and mountains, and he sees blues and yellows and greens. He listens to the singing of birds, the hum of bees, the wind blowing gently across the rice fields. All this had always been there, but he had never seen it. He's been "deaf and stupid" and "was never present." Now he sees things as they are, and he understands that "meaning and reality were not hidden somewhere behind things, they were in them, in all of them." Unlike Larry Darrell, he does not come to love things for the divineness that is behind their forms—"for the Infinite that is in them," as Larry explained—but for the forms themselves. After all, Siddhartha reasons, when someone reads do they despise the letters and punctuation marks, calling them worthless shells, an illusion? No, they love the letters, the punctuation, the words. So if a seeker wishes to read the book of the world, how can they despise the letters and signs of the world?

With this epiphany, Siddhartha feels like a child, like he's just been born. He feels he's awake to reality—he calls himself "Siddhartha, the awakened." He's no longer an ascetic, no longer a Brahmin. He's not his father's son, nor a religious man. He's simply Siddhartha. More himself than ever.

This is what an "inward voice" is telling him. And from now on, he'll be guided by his "inward voice," going only where this voice tells him to go.

Siddhartha continues wandering through the forest and comes to a river. That night, he sleeps in a ferryman's straw hut and has a dream. In the dream, Govinda comes to him and asks, "Why did you leave me?" Then Govinda embraces him, pulling Siddhartha to his breast. Govinda transforms into a woman, and Siddhartha drinks from the woman's breast, intoxicated by the milk that "tasted of woman and man, of sun and forest, of animal and flower, of every fruit, of every pleasure." Getting Freudian, the milk in his dream can symbolize the sensual life he's hitherto denied himself, and now will embrace. On one hand, this desire for sensual pleasure might seem like a regression in spiritual progress. But the Buddha said that before being able to experience nibbana, one must pass through *all* the sensory experiences. You have to go through it to get beyond it.

In the morning, Siddhartha asks the ferryman to take him across the river on a bamboo raft. While they're crossing, Siddhartha comments, "It is a beautiful river," something he wouldn't have previously said. The ferryman agrees, adding: "One can learn much from a river." Once they land on the other side, Siddhartha admits he has no money. The ferryman says he's learned from the river that "everything comes back." He adds that Siddhartha will come back, too, and can make his payment then.

Leaving the river, Siddhartha comes to a town. He's dirty, still with the long, matted hair and beard of a samana, and the town children run away from him. He sees a young woman washing clothes, and calls out to her. Despite his appearance, she approaches him and, by stepping on his foot, indicates she'd like to sleep with him. He recalls his dream and becomes sexually aroused. Leaning over, he kisses "the brown tip of her breast." He has never touched a woman, doesn't really know what to do, and hesitates before going further. Then he hears his inward voice say, "No!"

Immediately, all "the magic" of sexual attraction disappears. This isn't the woman for him. But he knows he needs to find a woman. He knows he needs to have sex. If he doesn't know his own sexuality, how can he know his self? After all, it's during sex, in the throes of passion, that our deepest and truest self emerges from its dark hiding places.

Siddhartha wanders a little more and sees a procession: a woman is being carried on an ornamented sedan chair of red cushions. She has "heaped-up" black hair and a "bright red mouth like a freshly cut fig." She's wearing gold bangles on her wrists, and her eyebrows are painted in a high arch. As she's carried into her garden, she meets Siddhartha's eyes, nods, and smiles. In the town, he asks about the woman and learns her name is Kamala, a well-known (and we assume high-priced) courtesan. Her name is derived from Kama, the Hindu god of love and lust—as in the *Kama Sutra*.

That evening, at the town's temple of Vishnu, Siddhartha befriends a barber by telling stories about Vishnu and his wife Lakshmi, goddess of prosperity and the embodiment of beauty. His scriptural knowledge comes in handy, because in the morning the barber shaves Siddhartha's beard and cuts, combs, and oils his hair, all without charge. After bathing in the river, Siddhartha comes to Kamala's house and tells her servant he'd like to speak with the courtesan. He's brought inside, where Kamala is reclining on a couch. She asks if he's the same dusty-haired, loincloth-wearing samana she saw the previous day. He admits he is, explaining he cleaned himself up because he wants her to be his "friend and teacher," for he's ignorant of the art of which she is master. She laughs, saying she'll be his teacher so long as he has money in his purse. He also needs to bring her presents, and present himself in fine clothes and shoes. Siddhartha says he's achieved much more difficult things than "these trifles." Then he asks where he can obtain these things as quickly as possible. Kamala laughs again, saying many people want to know this. She asks what Siddhartha can do. "I can think, I can wait, I can fast," he replies.

She's not very impressed, and if you put those skills on your résumé most employers wouldn't be either. But they are important skills, and very much lacking in most people today. Instead of thinking for ourselves, we repeat. When we have to wait for five seconds, we become impatient and check our phones. The moment our stomach grumbles, we get cranky. If most of us knew how to think, wait, and fast, the world would be a much more pleasant place. The skills are useful, too. If Siddhartha could not wait, he would have approached Kamala when he was still a dirty samana, repulsing her. If he could not fast, he would have starved the previous night. But because he can fast, he could ward off hunger, and wait patiently. And look at the result: he's now talking with Kamala, which is what he wanted. He says this is what he learned from the samanas: how to achieve his goal. How to control his fate. Fools think fate is determined by magic or demons. But "nothing is caused by demons" and "everyone can perform magic, everyone can reach his goal, if he can think, wait and fast."

Kamala asks if he can do anything else, and Siddhartha says he can also compose poetry. Another résumé winner. This piques her interest. He makes a deal with her: he'll compose a poem, and if she likes it they'll kiss. He does, she does, and they do. And in that kiss she already starts teaching Siddhartha about himself, luring him and then repelling him, mastering him. After the kiss he feels "like a child astonished at the fullness of knowledge and learning which unfolded itself before his eyes." Kamala is also impressed by his kiss, as well as attracted to him. Wanting to help this "handsome man" whose "glance pleases women," she asks if Siddhartha can read and write. Of course he can. He was a Brahmin, after all. But most people cannot, and upon her recommendation, Siddhartha is given an interview to be the assistant of a rich and powerful merchant named Kamaswami.

The next day, Siddhartha impresses the merchant with his literacy, and is hired to read and write sales agreements, letters, and orders. Since he's homeless and without possessions, he's invited to live in Kamaswami's house. The merchant gives Siddhartha clothes, shoes, and a bath. Splendid meals are served twice a day, but Siddhartha eats only once, and does not consume meat or alcohol. He still has a samana's habits, but he appreciates the simplicity of the householder's life. When he was a samana, everything in his life was difficult. He was constantly struggling, wrestling with his mind, mutilating his body, hopelessly working toward an elusive goal. Now things will be simple. He only requires clothes and money, "easy goals which do not disturb one's sleep." This is the householder's life. A life without spiritual striving.

Kamaswami takes Siddhartha under his wing and teaches him the business of trade. He learns many new things, but unlike Kamaswami, who conducts his business with passion, Siddhartha regards it all as a game. He simply wants to learn the rules so he can have money to pay Kamala to be his "friend." He learns how to make a living from Kamaswami, but Kamala will be his true teacher. In her is "the value and meaning of his present life, not in Kamaswami's business." Dressing in fine clothes and shoes, bringing money and presents, he visits Kamala daily, and she teaches him the art of sex. As her pupil, he learns that "one cannot have pleasure without giving it, and that every gesture, every caress, every touch, every glance, every single part of the body has its secret which can give pleasure to one who can understand it." Kamala is impressed by how quickly Siddhartha learns. She soon says he's the best lover she ever had. Similarly, Kamaswami is impressed by Siddhartha's "happy knack" for learning about rice, wool, shipping, and trade, and even more by his "calmness and equanimity, and in the art of listening and making a good impression on strange people."

With these skills, and with "the secret of those people to whom success comes by itself," Siddhartha becomes rich. He buys his own house, complete with servants, and even his own pleasure garden on the outskirts of town. Despite Siddhartha's success, Kamaswami thinks his partner is "no real merchant and will never become one." He observes that Siddhartha "always seems to be playing at business," that he "never fears failure," and "is never worried about a loss." Once, when Kamaswami gets upset and starts scolding, Siddhartha tells him, "Nothing was ever achieved by scolding." Moreover, he adds, "Do not hurt yourself by scolding." It takes insight to see that anger is self-damaging. That we hurt ourselves when we scold others. Unlike Kamaswami, Siddhartha does not hurt either himself "or others through annoyance or hastiness." He's never upset when a transaction goes wrong, and never elated when one goes well. This is quite unlike how a merchant is expected to act. Kamaswami may have taught Siddhartha "how much a basket of fish costs and how much interest one can claim for lending money," but the merchant did not teach him how to think.

Siddhartha also understands that even though he's living "amongst the people," something still separates him from them. From his perspective, people live "in a childish or animal-like way." He sees "them lament over pains at which the Samana laughs, and suffer at deprivations which a Samana does not feel." They are like falling leaves, blown by the wind. People like him are like stars, set on their path. But the thing that most separates Siddhartha from "ordinary people" is love. They are in love with their children, in love with their honor and money, in love with their plans and hopes. Most of all, they are in love with themselves. Siddhartha has always been suspicious of his ego, always looked at himself with detachment. But ordinary people don't think this way, and carry on with a strong sense of self-importance. They are natural narcissists. So Siddhartha feels superior to people, despising them. Yet this capacity to love is what he envies, and hopes to learn.

For years, Siddhartha plays the role of businessman. Yet sometimes he hears "a soft, gentle voice." The voice "reminded him quietly, complained quietly" that while he's playing this game, "real life was flowing past him and did not touch him at all."

This begs the question: What is "real life"? If focusing on external things is not real life, then real life must be the interior life, the life of the mind. For the first few years, the things Siddhartha learned as a samana, from Gotama the Buddha, and from being a Brahmin's son remain with him: "a moderate life, pleasure in thinking, hours of meditation, secret knowledge of the Self, of the eternal Self, that was neither body nor consciousness." At heart, he's still a seeker. But this is only inertia, like how a wheel continues to spin long after it has been spun. Eventually, the wheel stops spinning. Eventually, Siddhartha's inward voice quiets, and then becomes silent. His experience of awakening has passed. His senses were once awakened, but they become dulled.

Initially, he only plays at being a wealthy merchant, but then he truly becomes one, like an actor who completely loses himself in his role. For twenty years, Siddhartha eats gourmet foods, wears fine clothes, orders servants around, exercises power over people, amuses himself with women, is carried in sedan chairs, sleeps on a soft bed, learns to play dice, watches dancers, and drinks wine, "which made him lazy and forgetful." (Hesse knows such consequences well, since he drank wine nearly every day of his adult life.) Inevitably, his spirit becomes subdued, his energy dissipated.

This is why the Buddha prescribed his precepts, because sensual pleasures inevitably deplete spiritual energy. Habits become addictions. Pleasures become bondage. Sensation leads to craving. Craving leads to clinging, attachment. We indulge in our vices because we think they make us feel free and happy. But eventually our vices are what make us feel stuck and dissatisfied.

By the time he's in his forties, Siddhartha understands he's become "caught" by the world. He's become "trapped" by his own possessions and property, by his own need for acquisitiveness. No longer is trade a game. With his mind weakened by vices and luxurious living, Siddhartha becomes like the "ordinary people" he disdains, acquiring their childishness, their anxiety. He rarely laughs or smiles. He becomes impatient with slow-paying debtors. He's no longer kindhearted to beggars. His face takes on the expression "often found among rich people—the expressions of discontent, of sickliness, of displeasure, of idleness, of lovelessness." Slowly, "the soul sickness of the rich crept over him."

The soul sickness of the rich—what an indictment! The whole point of our capitalist society is for everyone to become rich, but look what happens when we do: we're perpetually discontented. We lose our capacity for joy. Our soul becomes sick. If being rich prevents us from being happy and healthy, then why would anyone want to be rich?

On some level, Siddhartha understands what's happening to him. And in order to show his contempt for money and "the false deity of the businessman," he becomes a gambler. Over food, wine, and women, the game of dice becomes his foremost passion. Squandering his "wretched money" becomes his only pleasure. He recklessly stakes huge sums on a throw of the dice, wins thousands, loses thousands, loses jewels, loses his country house, and wins it all back again, only to lose once more. After a great loss, he presses his debtors for payment and pursues his business all the more aggressively, so that he'll again have money to gamble away. He becomes greedy and begins to hoard his wealth. No longer will he give to the poor, but he'll stake ten thousand on a single roll. He loves the anxiety that comes when he rolls the dice, "that terrible and oppressive anxiety." He seeks this thrill, wants to renew and increase it. In doing so, he becomes addicted to gambling, because he becomes addicted to this sensation of anxiety. In this feeling alone does he find "some kind of happiness." But such happiness is fleeting and deceitful. And when Siddhartha sees an old and uglier face in the mirror, when he is overwhelmed by shame, he escapes into sex, into wine, and back to a new game of chance. Because it's only in the suspense of a high-stakes roll that he finds a "heightened living in the midst of his satiated, tepid, insipid existence." It's a "senseless cycle" that wears him out, making him feel old and sick.

Unlike Siddhartha, Hesse was never addicted to gambling. But he certainly had experience with games of chance, and also found happiness in them. He even saw gambling as a religious experience. (Leave it to Hesse.) After writing *Siddhartha*, Hesse vacationed in the mineral bath resort town of Baden, where among other entertainments, he hung around the roulette table. And in his autobiographical essay "A Guest at the Spa," Hesse describes the moment of winning as not only "marvelous" but "godlike." To expect the rolling ball to fall on a certain number, and then to see the ball fall on that very number, gives the gambler a feeling that "a miracle has occurred." The money won is beside the point. Because in retrospect, once the money is gone it is "the beautiful moments of winning" that shine as "a feast of the soul, a confirmation and affirmation and heightening of the innermost, deepest life instinct." The moment is akin to an epiphany, or the lightning-like creative inspiration. And in the ups and downs of gambling, Hesse also sees a copy of life,

> where things go exactly the same way, where inscrutable, unreasoning presentiment gives us control of the strongest magic,

releases the greatest powers, where with the flagging of sound instinct, criticism and intellect take over, get by for a while and try to hold their own, then finally what had to happen happens entirely without us and over our heads.

Thankfully, Hesse does not recommend gambling as a spiritual exercise. He points out that games of chance share the same flaw as alcohol or the cinema. What makes gambling "a vice despite its splendid aspects" is that the pleasant excitement it brings comes from the outside, not the inside, and so it encourages the neglect of one's own spiritual exertion. "If one sets the soul in motion through the purely mechanical means of the roulette wheel instead of by thinking, dreaming, fantasying, or meditating," Hesse observes, "it is about the same as making use of a bath and masseur for one's body but giving up one's own exertions in sport or gymnastics."

This is the stage where we now find Siddhartha, a phase without spiritual exertion. And whether he, too, finds godlike moments in his throws of the dice, or if such throws set his soul in motion, gambling has become his only love, his only happiness, his only reason for living.

Not even making love with Kamala can compete. By then, with gray streaking his own hair, Siddhartha sees "a sad sign" in the courtesan: "fine lines and wrinkles, a sign which gave a reminder of autumn and old age." Weariness is now written on Kamala's beautiful face. She's become weary of her job, weary "from continuing along a long path which has no joyous goal." She's afraid of old age, afraid of death. Now she wants to hear more about "the Illustrious Buddha," a subject she used to mock. She wants to hear about his clear eyes, his gracious smile, and his peaceful manner. She can't hear enough about the Buddha. Siddhartha talks for a long time, and then Kamala says she will one day give away her garden to Gotama's monks, take refuge in his teachings, and become one of his followers.

Kamala's aging and weariness reminds me of other courtesans who became disciples of the Buddha. There are many in the Buddhist tradition, and several wrote verses collected in the *Therigatha*, a section of Pali scripture written solely by Buddhist nuns (*bhikkhunis*). The poems in the *Therigatha* are considered the earliest example of women's writing in the world, and certainly one of the oldest works of feminism. Some of the contributors were the most notorious female teachers at the time of the Buddha, like Patacara and Kisagotami. Nine were once the royal concubines of Prince Siddhattha's harem. Another was Ambapali, a courtesan of great beauty who became a nun later in life. She, like Kamala, contemplated the faded charms of her formerly desired body:

> *The hairs on my head were once curly,*
> *black, like the color of bees,*
> *now because of old age,*
> *they are like jute.*
>
> *Once my breasts were beautiful,*
> *full, round, close together, high*
> *now they sag down,*
> *like empty waterbags made of leather.*
>
> *Once my body was beautiful,*
> *like a polished slab of gold,*
> *now it is covered*
> *with very fine wrinkles.*
>
> *It's just as the Buddha, the speaker of truth, said,*
> *nothing different than that.*

When their beauty begins to fade, many women in the *Therigatha* realize they spent their youth in folly, caring about what is impermanent. With the wisdom of maturity, they turn toward the Buddha's path. Yet of all prostitutes in Buddhist lore, Kamala most reminds me of the story of Sirima—though she's not in the *Therigatha* and didn't write verses.

Sirima was an extremely beautiful and high-priced courtesan in the city of Rajagaha. She was so beautiful, so desired, men paid a thousand pieces of gold just to spend one night with her. One day she had the good fortune to come in contact with the Buddha while he was staying in the city, and upon hearing his words, she immediately quit her profession and became a lay disciple. Afterward, she regularly used her wealth to provide food for the Buddha's monks. One of these young monks was so captivated by Sirima's wonderful beauty, he instantly fell in love with her. Passion arose, overwhelmed him, and he became indifferent to everything else. He went back to his monastery and curled up in a corner, refusing to eat, go on alms rounds, or perform the other duties of a monk.

On that very day, Sirima became afflicted with a disease, and that night she died. The king of the city, who was a lay disciple, informed the Buddha that Sirima died. The Buddha instructed the king to not burn her body, as is custom, but lay it out in the charnel ground, and make sure dogs and crows didn't devour it. For three days, Sirima's body lay there in the open. On the fourth, it began to bloat, and maggots oozed forth from her nine openings. Her whole body looked like "a cracked vessel of boiled rice." Then, according to the Buddha's instructions, the king commanded the entire city to approach and behold Sirima. The Buddha likewise told his followers to go to the charnel ground and do the same.

For these four days, the young monk who had fallen in love with Sirima had been lying in a corner, burning with passion for her, not eating, not meditating, not paying attention to anyone. He didn't know she was dead. And when he heard the Buddha's proclamation and the name Sirima, he jumped to his feet and ran to the burning ground. When all monks and inhabitants of the city were gathered around her rotting corpse, the Buddha said, "Here is the beautiful courtesan Sirima. Who will pay a thousand pieces of gold for one night with her?" No one in the crowd answered. "Who will pay five hundred?" the Buddha asked. Again, everyone was silent. "Two hundred and fifty?" He went lower and lower. One hundred? Fifty? Twenty-five? Ten? Five? A penny? Still, no one made a noise. "Who will have her for nothing?" the Buddha asked. No one answered. The Buddha said, "Men used to pay one thousand for a night with her, and now no one will take her as a gift. Such was her beauty, who now has perished and gone. Behold, bhikkhus, this body diseased and corrupt." Then the Buddha spoke these stanzas, which were later collected in the *Dhammapada*:

> *Look at this beautiful image*
> *Composed of wounds amassed.*
> *Full of sickness, yet desired by many,*
> *It has neither permanence nor constancy.*
> *Worn out is this body,*
> *A frail nest of disease.*
> *This festering mass breaks apart,*
> *For life has death at its end.*
>
> *Like gourds*
> *Cast off in autumn*
> *Are these gray bones.*
> *Seeing them as such—what joy?*
>
> *A fortress built of bones*
> *Plastered with blood and skin,*
> *Wherein are hidden*
> *Death and decay,*
> *Pride and pretense.*

Upon hearing these verses—and seeing the decomposing body of his former passion—the young monk saw through the delusions of beauty and desire. Understanding the decay and death inherent in the body, he achieved dispassion, and with such insight he achieved the first stage of enlightenment.

As Kamala ages, Siddhartha visits her less frequently. He spends most nights at his house, indulging with dancing women and wine. He wakes up with nausea. It's a lesson from Sartre that too much pleasure will only come to nausea. Siddhartha learns this through experience. He becomes nauseated with himself. Nauseated at his flabby skin, his perfumed hair, and the taste of wine in his mouth. He realizes he's miserable. He had thrown away all that "was good and of value in himself." He doesn't think his decision to renounce the spiritual life was wrong, necessarily, but he knows the life he's since lived has been mistaken.

The Greek word "sin" originally meant "to miss," as in "to miss the mark." And in Hebrew, the word sin originates in archery, referring to an arrow missing the center of a target. In both cases, sin means an error, a failure. A mistake. To sin is not to do something evil, but to be mistaken. And Siddhartha understands that he has sinned. He understands that he's "spent his life in a worthless and senseless manner," being "content with small pleasures and yet never really satisfied." He's amassed great wealth, property, and power, but he's "retained nothing vital, nothing in any way precious or worth while." This is the result of the householder's life, of a life without spirituality. He understands the householder's life is "flat and desolate." That it is a "soft, well-upholstered hell." This "game was called Samsara," the cycle of life and rebirth, and he realizes it's "a game for children, a game which was perhaps enjoyable played once, twice, ten times—but was it worth playing continually?" Clearly, he knows it's not. And with this realization, he knows he's finished playing the game.

Without saying goodbye to anyone, without packing a bag, Siddhartha leaves his house, garden, and servants, never to return to the town. For a long time, Kamaswami believes Siddhartha was kidnapped by bandits, and tries to find him. But Kamala doesn't try. She always knew that Siddhartha was a samana at heart, and that one day he would leave. When that day comes, the courtesan closes her house and accepts no more customers.

She's also pregnant.

Still dressed in his fine clothes and shoes, Siddhartha wanders away from the town and into the forest. And he hopes the forest will kill him. That a tiger will eat him. That lightning will strike him down. He feels there's nothing left in the world that can give him pleasure. He's done it all: "Was there any kind of filth with which he had not besmirched himself, any sin and folly which he had not committed, any stain upon his soul for which he alone had not been responsible?" When he comes to a river—the same river he crossed all those years earlier—he wants to fall in and drown. He craves oblivion. Annihilation.

Standing on the riverbank, Siddhartha was "so lost, so confused, so devoid of reason" that he "sought death." He decides to drown himself. He holds onto the branch of a coconut tree, and leans over the water. He's about to let go: "He bent, with eyes closed—toward death." And then he hears a sound. It was one word, one syllable. The ancient beginning and ending of all Brahmin prayers. The sound of "the holy Om." The sound comes from deep within himself, from his past. Upon hearing the Om, "his slumbering soul suddenly awakened." For the first time in years, Siddhartha pronounces Om inwardly, and becomes "conscious of Brahman, of the indestructibleness of life" within himself. In a flash he remembers "all that he had forgotten, all that was divine." It's only for a moment, but it's enough to bring him back from the water's edge. From the desire for death. Murmuring *Om*, Siddhartha lies against the roots of the tree, and falls into a deep sleep.

When he awakes, he feels "happy and curious," like he again died and was reborn. Like he's again experiencing an Awakening. Looking around, he sees a yellow-robed monk sitting next to him, a follower of the Buddha. And though his friend has aged over the years, he recognizes that the monk is Govinda. As Siddhartha is wearing the "clothes of a rich man" and "shoes of a man of fashion," Govinda does not recognize his old friend. He explains he was traveling with his fellow monks when he saw a man sleeping under a tree. As there are many snakes and other dangers in the forest, he thought he'd watch over the sleeping man. Siddhartha slyly thanks the monk by name, and then Govinda realizes he's talking to Siddhartha.

Their reunion is dispassionate, which is appropriate for a Buddhist monk and a man who has just thrown his life away. Siddhartha asks where his friend is going, and Govinda replies he's not really going anywhere. "We monks are always on the way," he explains. Siddhartha says he, too, is not going anywhere, and that he is "only on the way." They're both pilgrims, but of a different sort. They say goodbye without speaking, and Govinda leaves to join his fellow Buddhists. Watching him go, Siddhartha first feels a love for his friend, and then "a joyous love towards everything he saw." He understands that he had been miserable because he loved nothing and nobody.

He feels love, and he also feels hunger. He hasn't eaten for days, and he can no longer fast. He once knew how "to think, to wait, and to fast." These were his possessions. They were "his power and strength." But he's lost them. He "exchanged them for the most wretched things, for the transitory, for the pleasures of the senses, for high living and riches." Now he has nothing. He's completely ordinary. He knows nothing, possesses nothing. He cannot think, he cannot wait, and he cannot fast. And again he feels like a child. He had to sink to the depths of despair, to the verge of suicide, so that he could awaken again. But he understands that the last twenty years were not wasted. They were necessary. He "had to sin in order to live again." He had to go through all those sensory experiences in order to go beyond them. As a child, he learned that worldly pleasures and riches were "not good," not worthy of seeking. But this was merely intellectual knowledge. Now he knows it experientially, not with "my intellect," he thinks, but "with my eyes, my heart, my stomach." He now has what's called in Pali *bhavana-maya panna*, wisdom through direct experience, not merely *suta-maya panna*, knowledge that comes from hearing others and reading books.

When I spent a month hanging around monasteries and meditation centers in Burma, I saw hundreds of child monks—monks who joined monasteries before they had the intellectual capacity to understand the sophisticated teachings of the Buddha. And I thought: A monk who never had sex will always be tempted by sex. His vow of celibacy will be fraudulent, because he's renouncing something he never experienced. His vow of poverty will be fraudulent, because he's renouncing wealth he never had. His vow to abstain from intoxicants will be fraudulent, because he's never experienced intoxication. Unlike those child monks, Siddhartha can now truly renounce the pleasures of the world—that "soft, well-upholstered hell." He's experienced them for himself, and found them ultimately to be empty.

By becoming a drinker, a gambler, a customer of prostitutes, a man of wealth and property, Siddhartha killed the priest and the ascetic in him, the Brahmin and the samana. Holy verses, sacrificial rites, mortifications of the flesh and austerities had inflated his ego, just as earning money and having women inflated his ego. Both ways of life made him arrogant, each in their own way. Now he can leave all that behind. By wanting to drown himself in the river, he drowned all those old Siddharthas. The river was what saved him, and so he feels a deep love for the river. A gratefulness to the flowing water. His reawakened inward voice tells him, "Love this river, stay by it, learn from it." So he decides to remain by the river. The river will be his teacher, his guru, his scripture.

With hunger pangs in his stomach, Siddhartha finds the ferryman who took him across the river all those years ago. Like Govinda, the man doesn't recognize him. Siddhartha is again rowed across the river, and on the way, he asks if the ferryman will accept his clothes as payment, as he doesn't have any money. The ferryman thinks he must be joking. Siddhartha says he's not, and adds he owes the man payment from over twenty years earlier. Then the ferryman remembers. He asks Siddhartha's name, and says his own is Vasudeva—the name of Krishna's father. Siddhartha asks if he could become Vasudeva's apprentice, and the ferryman accepts.

Vasudeva, too, thinks of the river as his guru. "The river knows everything," he says, "one can learn everything from it." But Vasudeva knows a lot himself, and from him Siddhartha learns how to be a ferryman. He learns how to row and how to take care of the boat, how to make oars and make baskets. When there are no customers to ferry, he learns to work in the rice field, gather wood, and pick fruit. But as the days turn into weeks, and the weeks turn into months, he learns more from the river than from Vasudeva.

Many sages of the past have talked about rivers, using them as metaphors to teach wisdom. The twelfth-century Japanese author Kamo no Chomei opens his *Hojoki* with the lines: "The current of the flowing river does not cease, and yet the water is not the same water as before. The foam that floats on the stagnant pools, now vanishing, now forming, never stays the same for long. So, too, it is with the people and dwellings of the world." Around the time of the Buddha, the Greek philosopher Heraclitus said, "You cannot step twice in the same river." The water keeps flowing, and so the river you step in the second time is completely different from the river you stepped in the first time. It looks the same, but it's actually completely different water. *Panta rhei*, Heraclitus said—everything flows. Similarly, the flame of a candle looks to be continuously burning, but in actuality it is constantly renewing itself, flame by flame. Same with the light of an electric bulb. There is a flow of electricity that gives the illusion of a light being "on." In actuality, the light is arising and passing away so quickly the naked eye cannot perceive it. Everything flows.

Taking the metaphor further, the Buddha said you cannot step twice in the same river, not because the river will be different, but because *the person* will be different. Between the first step and the second, the particles of a person's body have arisen and passed away millions of times. It's a completely different person, just like it's a completely different river. A person *is* a river.

One thing Siddhartha learns from the river is that there is no such thing as time. The river is "everywhere at the same time," at its origin in the mountains, its waterfalls, and its mouth merging with the ocean. For the river, there is no past and no future, only the present. It's all one river, existing everywhere at the same time. The same can be said about the universe. The universe exists at its origin, its expansion, its dissolution. It's all there. And time depends on where you are in space. By the time light from a star reaches us, that star could have been dead for millions of years. If you look toward our solar system from another part of the universe, our sun may not yet exist. Or it could have already exploded. We can look deep into space and see supernovas that happened billions of years ago. We can see back to when the first stars were illuminated, to the very origin of the universe. Where you go in space is where you go in time. The universe, too, is like a river.

Siddhartha understands that an individual's life is also like a river. Looking back on his life, he sees that Siddhartha the boy, Siddhartha the mature adult, and Siddhartha the old man are "separated only through shadows, not by reality." He understands that his "previous lives were also not in the past, and his death and return to Brahma are not in the future. Nothing was, nothing will be, everything has reality and presence." This realization makes Siddhartha happy. He understands that all sorrow and all self-torment are in time, and that all difficulties and evil could be conquered when one conquers time.

He's asking to be taught another lesson.

Years pass. Rumors spread that there are "two wise men" who live at the ferry. People go to them, expecting to find "magicians or holy men." Travelers on the ferry confess their troubles and sins, asking for comfort and advice. Other people come to ask questions. But Siddhartha and Vasudeva have nothing to say. Then news spreads that Gotama the Buddha has become ill, that the Illustrious One will soon die his last death.

After eating a dish called *sukara-maddava*, the Buddha died of dysentery on the outskirts of Kushalnagara, a city a little south and east from where he was born in Lumbini. *Sukara-maddava* is translated as "tender succulent pork," because *sukara* means "pig" and *maddava* means "sweet." So most people understand the Buddha's last meal to be the meat of a young pig, or "hog's mincemeat." However, others have written that *sukara-maddava* refers not to pig meat but to what a pig ate, namely truffles or mushrooms. Other interpretations claim *sukara-maddava* means tender bamboo shoots—the bamboo trampled by pigs. There are even medicinal plants with the name of *sukura*, so *sukara-maddava* could have been some sort of elixir. But it's probably a safe bet that the Buddha died of dysentery after eating spoiled pork. For one thing, it's the most direct interpretation. And it fits well within the context. A man named Cunda is the one who offered this meal to the Buddha and his disciples. Knowing the meat was spoiled, the Buddha accepted it on the condition that only he eat it—he said the rest needed to be buried, so the spoiled meat did not contaminate any of the other monks. At the age of eighty, after teaching the Dhamma for forty-five years, he was ready to die his final death.

In Hesse's story, once news spread that the Buddha was dying, people from all over northern India traveled to Kushinagar, to where "the savior of an age was passing into eternity." So the ferrymen are very busy, rowing monks, pilgrims, and lay followers across the river. One of these pilgrims is Kamala, the once beautiful courtesan. By then, she's given her property to the Buddha's monks and taken refuge in his teachings. She's dressed in simple clothes and is traveling with a young boy. The boy wants to rest by the river, and when Kamala crouches to the ground, a snake bites her. Vasudeva hears her cry for help. He takes them in his boat to his hut, where Siddhartha recognizes Kamala immediately. She asks if he recognizes the boy, and he knows the boy is his son. She tells Siddhartha that even though he's grown old, his eyes are still like the young samana who came to her without fine clothes. By staying with Vasudeva and the river, he's remained childlike after his second awakening.

Kamala's wound turns black and her body swells. She loses and regains consciousness. Dying, she asks Siddhartha if he's attained peace. In answer, he smiles. Kamala wanted to see Gotama the Buddha before he died, "to obtain some of his peace." But seeing Siddhartha was "just as good as if she had seen the other." She wants to express this thought to her former lover, but by then she cannot speak, and soon Siddhartha watches "the life fade from her eyes." He stays awake all night, listening to the river. Kamala's death makes him suffer, but in the morning, he tells Vasudeva he isn't sad, because he's been given the gift of his son.

For days following his mother's death, Siddhartha's son sits on the hill where Kamala was buried. The boy is eleven years old and doesn't know his father. Siddhartha respects his son's grief, giving him space. He allows the boy freedom and makes no demands. He doesn't expect his son to love him, but he's disturbed by the boy's behavior. A spoiled mother's boy accustomed to luxurious living, to eating fine food and commanding servants, the boy is arrogant, defiant, and disrespectful. He does no work at all. He robs Vasudeva's fruit trees. He sulks. Siddhartha quickly understands that "happiness and peace had not come to him with his son, only sorrow and trouble." Even so, he loves his son, and he prefers the sorrow and trouble of being a father to the peaceful and pleasurable life he had without the boy. He's learning the paradox of parenthood: happiness within unhappiness.

For many months, Siddhartha treats his son with patience and kindness. He hopes the boy will come to understand that his father loves him, and perhaps love his father in return. He answers the boy's rudeness with smiles, insults with friendliness, naughtiness with kindness. But the boy continues to show defiance and spite. He tells Siddhartha, "I would rather become a thief and a murderer and go to hell than be like you. I hate you; you are not my father even if you have been my mother's lover a dozen times!" Concerned, Vasudeva takes Siddhartha aside to ask if he disciplines the boy, if he punishes or hits him. Siddhartha admits he doesn't, and Vasudeva accuses him of being too soft. Water is stronger than rock and love is stronger than force, Vasudeva says, but Siddhartha is shaming his son with his patient love, with his goodness. He's trying to protect the boy from making the same mistakes he made, but no parent can protect their child from making mistakes, and everyone must follow their own path. To Vasudeva, it's obvious that the spoiled boy will never be happy living in a small hut with "two old banana eaters." Like water being water, youth will be youth. So Vasudeva advises Siddhartha to take his son back to town and leave him with Kamala's servants or a teacher.

But Siddhartha doesn't want to give up. He's become attached and can't let his son go. He had never "lost his heart to anybody so completely" and "had never loved anybody so much, so blindly, so painfully, so hopelessly and yet so happily." What previously kept Siddhartha apart from ordinary people was his inability to love, his inability to lose himself in another person so completely that he forgets himself. But since his son arrived, he's become completely like everyone else, "through sorrow, through loving." He experienced being a Brahmin, ascetic, merchant, and ferryman, but for the first time in his life he's experiencing "the strongest and strangest of passions." He's "madly in love, a fool because of love." This love makes him suffer tremendously. Yet the love is also uplifting, renewing his life and making it richer. Siddhartha knows he's back in the web of *samsara*, tangled in the passion of human emotion. But he also knows it's necessary to experience "this emotion, this pain." One must journey through all sensory experiences before being able to go beyond them. So these "follies" of parental love must also be experienced.

Then one morning, Vasudeva's basket of coins is missing. So is the boy. He's stolen their money, taken their boat, and run away. Thinking his boy will come to harm alone in the forest, Siddhartha starts after him. But Vasudeva advises he let the boy go. The boy is right to go to town, to follow his own path. "I see you are suffering," Vasudeva says, "suffering pain over which one should laugh, over which you will soon laugh yourself." But Siddhartha is unable to detach and laugh at his pain. He's unable to use whatever wisdom he's gained.

Desperate, he follows his son through the forest, all the way to the edge of the town. But when he comes to Kamala's old garden, he stops. He remembers the day he arrived there, as a dirty samana. He understands that everyone must make their own way, and that he cannot save his son from sorrow or pain or disillusionment. And he understands that the boy does not want to be followed. A wound opens then, a wound from the deep love he feels for the boy. A wound from love that is unrequited. Again he becomes depressed, thinking there's no happiness in life, no goal. To lessen the pain of the wound, he whispers the word *Om*, fills himself with *Om*. From the river, he's learned to have patience, to listen. So he sits and waits. Eventually, Vasudeva comes to get him, and together they return to their hut by the river.

Afterward, whenever Siddhartha rows travelers with sons or daughters, his wound flares up and festers. All he wants is his son back. He's jealous of the families. Seeing them makes him depressed. He reasons "childishly and illogically," so much like the "ordinary people" he used to disdain and has now become. He no longer feels superior. People no longer seem alien: "Their vanities, desires and trivialities no longer seemed absurd to him; they had become understandable, lovable and even worthy of respect." He's become humbled through the pain and loss of parenthood. He's conquered his ego not through reading scriptures, or meditating, or practicing austerities, or debasing himself through debauchery, or even living a simple life as a ferryman, but through the selfless love a parent has for their child. This is something Larry Darrell never experienced, and will never know.

Siddhartha now sees Brahman in a mother's blind love, in a father's foolish pride, in the family's desires and needs. And with this insight "there slowly grew and ripened the knowledge of what wisdom really was and the goal of his long seeking." And what is this goal? What is wisdom, really? According to Hesse, wisdom is "nothing but a preparation of the soul, a capacity, a secret art of thinking, feeling and breathing thoughts of unity at every moment of life." This is the goal of the yogi. To feel and breathe unity at all times. And in Vasudeva's old childlike face, Siddhartha sees the reflection of this wisdom; he sees harmony, knowledge of the eternal perfection of the world, and unity.

Despite his knowledge of wisdom, the wound of loss still pains him, like a flame burning his insides. Siddhartha still feels bitterness and yearns to have his son back. But he accepts such pain and bitterness and yearning as part of life. He understands he must have made his own father feel the same way, years ago when he left the Brahmin's life to become a samana. He caused his own parents such pain, just as his son caused him pain. With this understanding, he sees life as "a comedy, a strange and stupid thing, this repetition, this course of events in a fateful circle." Each person advances on their own path, focusing on their own goals and desires, causing pain and sorrow and loneliness for those that love them, everyone suffering. Suffering from the loss of love or the desire for love. Suffering from not being loved enough or from being loved too much.

This suffering is why people take the Buddha's prescription: To untangle themselves from this web of love and sorrow and pain. This is why the Buddha left his family the night his son was born. He knew the sticky emotional web of parental love was what he needed to avoid if he was to find the way to end suffering.

By then, Vasudeva has grown too old to row the ferry. His eyes have become too weak to see, his arms and hands too weak to row. He weaves baskets, and he listens. He listens to Siddhartha talk of his troubled love, his envy, his wound, and his folly. And as he talks, Siddhartha feels that Vasudeva "was absorbing his confessions as a tree absorbs the rain, that this motionless man was the river itself, that he was God Himself, that he was eternity itself." Vasudeva had always been this way, yet Siddhartha only recognizes it now. He sees that Vasudeva is a true "holy man, a saint," someone who "realized the essential the same as Gotama." Suddenly he regards Vasudeva "as the people regarded the gods."

Seeing this change in his friend's gaze, Vasudeva takes Siddhartha to the river. They sit on the bank and listen. "Listen better!" Vasudeva whispers. And as Siddhartha stares into the river and listens, he sees images from his life. Images of his son and Kamala, of Govinda and Gotama. They all flow together, appearing and vanishing, turning from pleasure to sorrow, just as the water of the river "changed to vapor and rose, became rain and came down again, became spring, brook and river, changed anew." His entire life flows together, and in the sound of the river he hears thousands of voices, young and old, laughter and crying, and then the thousands of voices become one, unifying into one word: "Om—perfection."

The *Om* dissolves Siddhartha's pain. It heals his wound. It absorbs his Self. It merges him into unity. Through the sound of *Om* he hears in the river, he penetrates Atman. And from that hour

> there shone in his face the serenity of knowledge, of one who is no longer confronted with conflict of desires, who has found salvation, who is harmony with the stream of events, with the stream of life, full of sympathy and compassion, surrendering himself to the stream, belonging to the unity of all things.

Siddhartha has had several moments of awakening, but now it appears he's truly awakened. Like Vasudeva, he's become a true yogi, unifying the part with the whole in his own being. And in doing so, he's reached his goal.

Seeing that Siddhartha finally understands the river's secret, Vasudeva says farewell. He says farewell to the hut, farewell to the river, and farewell to Siddhartha. He says he's ready to depart "into the unity of all things." And like a cat that knows its time has come, Vasudeva goes off into the woods to die.

After all the years of being a monk and following the Buddha's teaching, Govinda is still restless, his seeking unsatisfied. During the rainy season, he had been staying with fellow Buddhist monks in Kamala's old garden. And in town he hears talk of a sage who lives alone by the river, an old ferryman. So he comes to the ferryman's hut to seek spiritual guidance.

As before, he does not recognize Siddhartha, who quietly rows his old friend across the river. Along the way, Govinda asks the ferryman to share some of his wisdom. "What can I say to you that would be of value," Siddhartha responds, "except that perhaps you seek too much, that as a result of your seeking you cannot find." Govinda is confused. Siddhartha explains: When we seek, we only see what we are looking for. Therefore we miss what is actually there. We can't absorb anything, we can't find anything. Seeking is being obsessed with a goal. But finding is being free, having no goal. In other words, seeking prevents finding.

Siddhartha's response to Govinda reminds me of the story of Ananda, the Buddha's cousin. Ananda and the Buddha were born on the same day, and grew up in the same city of Kapilavatthu. Two years after the Buddha achieved enlightenment and began his ministry, he returned to his home city. Jesus said a prophet is never recognized in his hometown, but the Sakyan clan recognized that their Siddhartha had become a buddha. Afterward, many Sakyans left home to become one of the Buddha's followers, including the aunt who raised him, the wife he left, the son he abandoned, and his cousin Ananda.

At the time, they were both thirty-seven years old. Nearly twenty years later, at the age of fifty-five, the Buddha decided he needed a full-time attendant. He was unsatisfied with his previous attendants, and didn't accept any of the disciples who offered their services—most wanted privileged access to miracles or secret teachings, teachings they assumed the Buddha didn't share publicly. So he chose his cousin, and for the next twenty-five years, Ananda served as the Buddha's *upatthaka*, his personal attendant. Acting as secretary and servant, Ananda made sure Buddha was fed, rested, and sheltered. He arranged Buddha's seat, brought him water, fanned him, massaged his back, washed his feet, swept his cell, and mended his robes. He carried the Buddha's messages and organized meetings for the monks, sorting out disputes that arose. Once, when Devadetta—another of their cousins—set loose a wild elephant in the Buddha's path in attempt to kill him, Ananda put himself between the Buddha and the elephant. Ananda was also responsible for convincing the Buddha to establish a community of nuns and allow women to take the going forth—the Buddha previously allowed only men to be his disciples, as it was too dangerous for women to be traveling roads teeming with rapists, thieves, and murderers. Most importantly, Ananda was by the Buddha's side for twenty-five years, hearing every discourse, every answer the Buddha gave to those who had questions. And fortunately, Ananda was blessed with what we call a photographic memory. It was said he could immediately remember anything, even after hearing it once, like a computer or voice recorder. He could flawlessly repeat the Buddha's discourses without leaving out a syllable. He could recite fifteen thousand of the Buddha's four-line stanzas. He also had a talent for systemizing, and could organize the Buddha's discourses both chronologically and by length. If not for Ananda, we would not know much of what the Buddha taught.

The story goes like this. Soon after the Buddha died, an old monk named Subhadda was happy and basically said, "Now that the Buddha is dead, we don't have to follow his rules anymore. We can do whatever we like." There are 227 precepts that Buddhist monks must observe, and so lazy monks would understandably have liked for the discipline to be more lax. One of the Buddha's foremost disciples, Mahakassapa, heard what Subhadda said and became concerned that over the years people would distort the Buddha's teachings, changing his words and removing some of the essential disciplines. So after the Buddha's funeral pyre had burned, Mahakassapa called a council of five hundred elderly monks who would gather to recite, compile, and authenticate the Buddha's words, so that his teaching would be accurately preserved through posterity. Mahakassapa could have selected only a few monks to accomplish this, but he specifically invited five hundred to ensure that future generations would accept the authenticity of the council. But only *arahants*—fully enlightened monks—could attend.

Ananda was initially invited to the council, but he was not fully enlightened. He'd been so busy assisting the Buddha for the previous twenty-five years, he never had time to seriously meditate and become liberated. Like Govinda, he was still restless, unsatisfied, even after decades of being a disciple of the Buddha. But Ananda was indispensable for the meeting. So Mahakassapa essentially told him, "Ananda, we know you've been with the Blessed One the longest, that you were closest to him, that you can recite everything he said. You need to achieve *nibbana* and come to this meeting in a few days." Ananda goes to sit under a tree and with strong determination, he meditates. For two days, he works vigorously, striving to become enlightened. *I must become enlightened before the council*, he tells himself,

I must become an arahant. But he wasn't making any progress. He worked hard, but he worked incorrectly. He was focused on his ego—*I must*. He was focused on the future, by giving himself a deadline.

The night before the meeting, Mahakassapa came to Ananda and told him, "Look, if you're not an *arahant* by tomorrow, the meeting will start without you. If necessary, we'll take someone else." Ananda doubles down on his efforts. *I must become an arahant. I must become an arahant.* The evening passes, and then most of the night passes, and Ananda is still striving, working hard but without progress. When morning comes, he gives up. "I'm not enlightened," he admits. "I'm not an *arahant*." Exhausted from his effort, he stops striving and starts to lie down. He stops thinking of his ego. He stops thinking about the future. He is simply aware of his sensations in the present moment. And then, *voila*, before his heads hits the ground, he achieves *nibbana*. He's allowed to come to the council. In front of all the monks, Ananda recites the Buddha's discourses, which were committed to memory and then later written down in the Pali Canon. That's why Ananda is known as the Guardian of the Dhamma. The lesson is that you can't try too hard. Seeking prevents finding. If you're too set on your goal, you'll push your goal away. With too much laxity you achieve nothing, but with overexertion the mind becomes imbalanced. The Buddha used the metaphor of a stringed instrument. If it's too slack, the string won't make the right sound. If it's too tight, the string will break. The right balance between striving and relaxation is key to success. The middle path.

Similarly, Siddhartha sees Govinda's problem is that he's been striving too hard. He tells Govinda, "In striving towards your goals, you do not see many things that are under your nose." Astonished, Govinda realizes the ferryman is his old friend Siddhartha. He stays the night in the hut, and in the morning before he leaves, Govinda asks if Siddhartha has "a doctrine, belief or knowledge" that he upholds to help him "live and do right." Siddhartha still distrusts doctrines. If not a doctrine, then how about certain thoughts? It would give Govinda great pleasure to hear his friend's thoughts. "Wisdom is not communicable," Siddhartha answers. "Knowledge can be communicated, but not wisdom." The problem is with language. When you express the truth, it can only be a one-sided truth, and so it is only a half-truth. There is no way to express a complete truth using language. The truth is ineffable. Teachers divide the truth into dualities, because that is the way they must teach. We say that the sinner is on their way to becoming a saint. But that's not the truth, because the saint already exists in the sinner. All small boys are already old men. A stone is already soil, is already plant, animal, or man. Samsara is in nirvana. Similarly, the world is not evolving on a path to perfection—it is already perfect. Siddhartha tells Govinda that during deep meditation, it is possible to dispel time, to see simultaneously all the past, present and future, and then everything is good, everything is perfect, everything is Brahman. Therefore, it seems to me that everything that exists is good—death as well as life, sin as well as holiness, wisdom as well as folly.

Govinda listens silently. He objects only when Siddhartha says, "Samsara and nirvana are only words." To Govinda, "Nirvana is not only a word." Nirvana "is a thought." Siddhartha doesn't differentiate between thoughts and words, attaching no importance to either. He attaches importance to things. One can love things. And to Siddhartha it seems "that love is the most important thing in the world." Many thinkers and seekers despise the world and hate "ordinary people," but wisdom is found in loving everyone and everything. Govinda is under the impression that love is bondage, restriction, which is what he believes the Buddha taught. And indeed, many people who first study Buddhism ask, *Where's the love?* But Siddhartha knows better and asks, "How, indeed, could he not know love, he who has recognized all humanity's vanity and transitoriness, yet loves humanity so much that he has devoted a long life solely to help and teach people?"

Hesse might not have known this, but the Buddha not only spent forty-five years working tirelessly to alleviate people's suffering, he also taught a meditation of loving-kindness: *metta-bhavana*. Unlike vipassana, in which you observe reality as it is, *metta* is a deliberate cultivation of positive energy. To practice *metta*, the meditator first lets go of all hatred, animosity, and other negative feelings by focusing on thoughts of benevolence, peace, and love within oneself. This generates loving vibrations within the meditator's body. Then the meditator spreads those positive vibrations out to the world. When one is practicing *metta*, one thinks: "May all beings be happy. May all beings be peaceful. May all beings be free from suffering. May all beings be liberated." This exercise puts one in a state of mind filled with compassion, empathy, kindness, and love. As a meditator progresses on the path of purification and eradicates mental defilements through meditation, *metta* arises naturally, spontaneously. *Metta* is a meditator's armor, a bubble of protection against the negative vibrations of the world. Often overlooked, it is key to the whole Buddhist practice.

By now, Govinda understands that his childhood friend has become a holy man. Siddhartha's "glance and his hand, his skin and his hair, all radiate a purity, peace, serenity, gentleness and saintliness" that Govinda hasn't seen in anyone besides Gotama. "I can see, my dear friend, that you have found peace." Enveloped by Siddhartha's presence, Govinda experiences an all-encompassing love, a love that unifies all things, just as the river unifies all voices into the sound of *Om*. He sees all the births and deaths of all people who ever existed, all present and past and future forms, all existing at once in the same substance. Just as Siddhartha saw all of this in the river, Govinda sees all of this in the face of Siddhartha.

At the end of the novel, Govinda bows low in veneration, tears trickling down his cheeks, overwhelmed by love, immersed in the radiant presence of his friend whom he perceives to have the same inward smile as Gotama, the Buddha.

After his long and arduous journey, Siddhartha had apparently attained Enlightenment.

Or at least that's what Hesse wants us to think. But if we want to be responsible, if we want to be accurate, as I do, we cannot say that Siddhartha had attained "enlightenment." Due to Hesse's disenchantment with Buddhism, whatever Siddhartha achieved is neither the Buddhist final goal of *nibbana*, nor the Hindu goal of *moshka*. Both cases entail freedom from samsara, the cycle of death and rebirth. And in the same 1921 letter to Lisa Wenger I quoted earlier, Hesse wrote: "When Siddhartha dies, he will not wish for nirvana, but will be content with his reincarnation, with beginning the cycle anew." He has indeed achieved a high state, but not the highest. Because if he'll again experience rebirth, he hasn't achieved enlightenment and gotten out of samsara. So what did Siddhartha attain? The term "self-realization" is clumsy, "illumination" is vague, and "awakening" has already been used at earlier stages of his development. While Jung's goal of "individuation" might have been in Hesse's mind, the word would be out of context, too modern for this ancient setting.

Like Hesse, Siddhartha is essentially a mystic. So we can responsibly say that after his long and arduous journey, Siddhartha attained unity—the unity of all things. He achieved the state of "feeling and breathing thoughts of unity at every moment of life." He had become the Om.

3

Franny and Zooey

Much of J. D. Salinger's work engages with what can be called matters of the spirit, but *Franny and Zooey* does so more explicitly than any other. First published as separate stories, in 1955 and 1957, respectively, and then published together as a book in 1961, "Franny" and "Zooey" introduced readers to spiritual practices and philosophies they'd likely never heard of before, and because of Salinger's innovative style—writing as people talk; capturing the tones, emphasis, inflections, rhythms, and repetitions of postwar American speech—it made otherwise esoteric subjects sound ordinary. That is to say, *Franny and Zooey* is more relatable and realistic than the novels covered so far. After all, no modern person can relate to the experience of living in India at the time of the Buddha, and Maugham's Larry Darrell, too, is inaccessible, for rarely is someone actually that reticent, patient, and detached. Both *The Razor's Edge* and *Siddhartha* are valuable for inspiration, but impractical as guides. Yet in *Franny and Zooey*, Salinger realistically depicts the difficult experience of trying to live a spiritual life in a modern materialistic society. This struggle between the material and the spiritual, between the West and the East, often makes someone, in Zooey's words, "a freak."

A freak himself, Jerome David Salinger was born in 1919 to an Irish-Catholic mother and a Jewish father, a prosperous yet decidedly unkosher importer of meat and cheese. Raised in Manhattan, Salinger spent much of his youth in Central Park, the park zoo, and the Metropolitan Museum of Art, all within close walking distance of his family's posh Park Avenue apartment. He originally wanted to be an actor, and then a theater critic. But he was an undisciplined student, and after he was expelled from a private high school, his parents sent him to Valley Forge Military Academy, where he began writing fiction. After graduating, he studied for two semesters at New York University and then spent a year in Europe, where he witnessed the Nazis take over Vienna. He came home, attended a semester at Ursinus College in rural Pennsylvania, and decided to become a professional writer.

For a year, he took classes in poetry and short-story writing at Columbia University, where he developed grand literary ambitions. From the start, Salinger wanted to be The Most Important Writer of His Generation. Not just the Hemingway but the Shakespeare. And he was dead set on being published in *The New Yorker*. To the young Salinger, a writer hadn't made it otherwise. His career got off to an early start in 1940, when *Story* magazine (run by his professor Whit Burnett) published "The Young Folks," a story satirizing shallow and petty upper-class college students. The twenty-one-year-old Salinger thought he had made it. But he couldn't sell another story for the following eight months. Frustrated, he reconsidered a career in acting or playwriting. Then he landed an agent—Dorothy Olding at Harold Associates, who represented Salinger's idol F. Scott Fitzgerald—and in 1941 his work was published in *Collier's*, *The Saturday Evening Post*, and *Esquire*. But all he got from *The New Yorker* were rejection letters. They passed on seven stories, and then finally accepted "Slight Rebellion off Madison Avenue," a story about a troubled teenager named Holden Caulfield. Before it could be published, Pearl Harbor was bombed and the magazine shelved the story.

Drafted in 1942, Salinger was stationed at Fort Dix in New Jersey and then in Georgia. His heart was broken when his sixteen-year-old celebrity girlfriend Oona O'Neill (Eugene O'Neill's daughter) dumped him for Charlie Chaplin. To cope with the breakup, Salinger threw himself into writing. He produced prolifically, even after being sent to Europe in 1944 as an agent for the Counter Intelligence Corps. Embedded in the army, he carried chapters of what would be *The Catcher in the Rye* during the D-Day invasion (his first day of active duty), considering the pages to be a sort of talisman. Normandy was carnage, the slow advance to Paris was a meat grinder, and he saw thousands of corpses upon his arrival at a subcamp of Dachau. Later he said, "You never get the smell of burning flesh out of your nostrils, no matter how long you live." After the war was over, Salinger had a nervous breakdown and checked himself into a hospital. Then he married a beautiful young Nazi named Sylvia. He claimed they could communicate telepathically. But soon after bringing his wife back to America, they divorced. He didn't write a word for the eight months they were together.

After five years of limbo, the postponed "Slight Rebellion off Madison Avenue" was taken off the shelf and published in December 1946, marking Salinger's *New Yorker* debut. But he had serious trouble writing after his return from Europe. In order to help him process the trauma he suffered during combat and his failed marriage, he turned to frequenting bars in Greenwich Village, dating as many women as possible, and studying Eastern religion. First came Zen Buddhism, which he discovered through the writings of D. T. Suzuki, the Japanese author most responsible for spreading Zen to the West. Salinger was rumored to give reading lists of Zen-related books to the women he was dating, apparently as a way of gauging their spirituality and compatibility. Zen was followed by Vedanta, which he learned through *The Gospels of Sri Ramakrishna* and the writings of Paramahansa Yoganada, after first encountering the Hindu philosophy at the Upper East Side's Ramakrishna-Vivekanada Center.

Salinger soon came to see writing fiction as a form of meditation, and understood his duty as an artist was to impart Eastern philosophy to our spiritually empty society—he just needed to find a way to do it without coming off as preachy, or so odd as to be alienating. Some critics say Salinger's turn toward spirituality killed his art. But around the time he started meditating is when something clicked, and in January 1948 *The New Yorker* published "A Perfect Day for Bananafish." For an entire year, Salinger worked closely with editors to revise the story, which introduced readers to the character Seymour Glass, a genius poet who commits suicide on a vacation in Florida, shooting himself while his wife sleeps in the next bed. We're not sure why. "Bananafish" was a huge success and *The New Yorker* offered Salinger their "first-reading agreement," which finally provided him with financial security. (The agreement gives the magazine rights of first refusal, and thus a monopoly on sought-after writers, whom they essentially keep on retainer; the magazine reportedly paid Salinger $30,000 a year for the right to review his work first.)

Over the following three years, the magazine published many more of his stories, several of which introduced other members of the Glass family; the second oldest sibling, Buddy Glass, is Salinger's alter ego and claims to be the "author" of these stories. In "Uncle Wiggily in Connecticut" (1948), a sauced-up woman describes her recently deceased boyfriend Walter, one of the Glass sons, who died during an accident in Japan after the war had ended. (Walt's twin Waker never gets his own story, but is frequently mentioned in later works; he's a Roman Catholic priest.) "Down at the Dinghy" (1949) features the middle Glass sister, Boo Boo, a Westchester mother of three. "For Esmé—with Love and Squalor" (1950) is narrated by Sergeant X, who many assume is Buddy, before and after a PTSD-induced nervous breakdown. Unlike his previously published work, Salinger was proud of these *New Yorker* stories, and in 1953 he published a collection of them, simply titled *Nine Stories*. By then, he had already published *The Catcher in the Rye* (1951), which made him The Most Famous Young Writer in America.

Uncomfortable in the spotlight, he retreated to Cornish, New Hampshire, where he devoted himself to writing stories about the Glass family. There was a couple of years of silence, and then in January 1955 he published a story about the youngest Glass child, Frances. A month later, Salinger gave the story as a wedding present to his new wife Claire, a college student half his age, with whom he would have two children.

"Franny" is about a young woman's existential crisis, which manifests in a nervous breakdown at an upscale restaurant. The mystery of her collapse caused a sensation. (*The New Yorker* received more mail about "Franny" than any other story in its history.) Two years later, Salinger sent in the sequel "Zooey," which was unanimously rejected by *The New Yorker*'s fiction editors. Ostensibly, the rejection was because of the story's length—at 41,130 words, it is the second-longest piece Salinger ever published, behind *The Catcher in the Rye*. They also claimed it was policy not to publish sequels. But the real reason was because the editors surely did not dig the overt religious nature of the story. It took the overruling of editor-in-chief William Shawn to get "Zooey" in the magazine. Never again would Salinger's work go through the editing gauntlet; it went straight to Shawn.

By then, Salinger was talking about the Glass family as if they were his relatives, giving them more attention than his real family (his wife Claire left him a few years later). In 1961, the two stories were published together as a book, and on the dust jacket he wrote, "I love working on these Glass stories, I've been waiting for them for most of my life." Despite critical derision, *Franny and Zooey* quickly went to number one on *The New York Times* best-seller list. The book was so popular, it put Salinger on the cover of *Time* magazine. I think that bears repeating: *Time* put J. D. Salinger on its cover because of *Franny and Zooey*, not *The Catcher in the Rye*.

Franny and Zooey would be his penultimate book to see print. The last was *Raise High the Roof Beam, Carpenters and Seymour: An Introduction* (1963), a couple of novellas fleshing out the life of Seymour—each initially appeared in *The New Yorker*, in 1955 and 1959, respectively. It, too, was a number one *New York Times* best seller, and also got horrendous reviews. By then, as Buddy writes in "Seymour," Salinger had lost interest in writing stories with what "that old Chekhov-baiting noise Somerset Maugham calls a Beginning, a Middle, and an End." This is most apparent in the final piece of writing Salinger would publish in his lifetime, "Hapworth 16, 1924," a very long letter written by an implausibly precocious seven-year-old Seymour away at summer camp. The piece took up most of the June 19, 1965 issue of *The New Yorker*, leaving little room for anything else but *Mad Men*–era advertisements for liquor and travel. It was met by an embarrassing silence. Later, it was widely panned for its indulgence, digressiveness, and exasperating tendency to go on and on.

Perhaps due to its negative reception, Salinger decided to quit publishing. With royalty checks paying the bills, he was happy to keep the fruits of his labor to himself. If writing was Salinger's religion, his religion was now pure. He kept it this way until he died at age ninety-one, in 2010.

Salinger's legacy may rest on *The Catcher in the Rye*, but it's through *Franny and Zooey* that he shares his spiritual wisdom with the world.

"Franny" begins at a train station. On the platform, a Burberry-clothed college student named Lane Coutell is waiting for his girlfriend to arrive. We're not sure which precise college Lane attends, but they plan to see "the Yale game," so we can assume it's in the Ivy League. Dressed in a sheared raccoon coat, Franny gets off the train and tells Lane she was on board with girls who "looked very Smith, except for two absol*ute*ly Vassar types and one absolutely Bennington or Sarah Lawrence type." It's also unclear which private college Franny attends, but my bet is on Radcliffe, where Salinger's second wife Claire was enrolled before he made her drop out—it's rumored that Claire served as a model for Franny. That's the world they're in: moneyed, privileged, elite. It should be a perfect world. And indeed, when they later sit down at a fashionable restaurant, Lane looks around the room "with an almost palpable sense of well-being at finding himself (he must have been sure no one could dispute) in the right place with an unimpeachably right-looking girl." But for Franny, something is definitely not right.

We get hints of her malaise, the first being a small, pea-green book Franny is clutching when she gets off the train. Lane asks her about it, but she suspiciously avoids the question, saying it's "just something." They get in a cab and after Franny tells Lane, "I've *missed* you," she realizes she doesn't. The lie causes her to feel guilty, and over the first few pages of the story her guilt is mentioned three times. Once they're seated in the restaurant, she attempts to make up for her guilt by intently listening to Lane's self-indulgent diatribe about an essay he recently wrote on Flaubert.

Lane embodies the arrogant yet ignorant college know-it-all—what we today would call a mansplainer. (Holden Caulfield would certainly call Lane "a phony.") After mentioning he's thinking to have his essay published, Lane says, "I mean to a certain extent I think I was perfectly justified to point out that none of the really good boys—Tolstoy, Dostoevsky, *Shakes*peare, for Chrissake—were such goddam word squeezers. They just *wrote*. Know what I mean?" It's clear Lane has no idea what he's talking about—try asking Sonia Tolstoy if her husband "just wrote." She'd show you the several messy drafts of *War and Peace* and *Anna Karenina* she had to painstakingly copy and recopy by hand, after Tolstoy's many revisions. Salinger himself was a notorious word-squeezer, writing and revising slowly and meticulously until he reached his idea of artistic perfection.

In response, Franny says she's "so sick of pedants and conceited tearer-downers" she could scream, and goes on to insult the famous poets teaching at her college. Just because someone has their poems published and "anthologized all over the place," she says, it doesn't make them a "real poet." Lane pushes back: "Do you have to be a goddamn bohemian type, or *dead*, for Chrissake, to be a *real poet*?" She asks him to drop it. He agrees to drop it, but only after she explains what a "real poet" is. She tells him to stop, and when he does, she gets going on another rant, growing even more pale and sweaty. And then she abruptly goes to the bathroom.

In the confines of a bathroom stall, Franny places the heels of her hands against her eyes. (This is actually a form of Tantric meditation, said to be calming and centering—perhaps Salinger picked it up somewhere along the way.) But after a moment, Franny breaks down. She cries for five minutes. Then she takes out the small, pea-green book. She places it on her lap, and then presses it to her chest—another hint this book is more than just a book. For her it's a transitional object, something Franny finds steadying. But we still don't know what the book is, or why it's so meaningful.

After the cathartic cry, Franny returns to the table with a smile. She tries to make herself normal again. But Lane is hungry and she's not. He orders snails, frog legs, and a salad. Franny orders a chicken sandwich, a barbaric choice that sets Lane off: "This is going to be a real doll of a weekend," he complains. "A chicken sandwich, for God's sake." Lane becomes further annoyed when Franny doesn't remember Wally, a friend of his they're seeing later. Franny says she doesn't remember Wally because she sees the same guy everywhere she goes. Of course he'll be charming and straddle a chair backwards. Of course he'll have spent the summer in Italy. (Lane corrects her: "He was in France last summer, for your information.") If Wally were a girl from Franny's dorm "he'd have been painting scenery in some stock company all summer. Or bicycled through Wales. Or taken an apartment in New York and worked for a magazine or advertising company." But it's not just Wally, she says, it's everybody: "Everything everybody does is so—I don't know—not *wrong*, or even mean, or even stupid necessarily. But just so tiny and meaningless and—sad-making." It's all so predictable, so conventional, their choices confined to what's already been done. "And the worst part is," she continues, "if you go bohemian or something crazy like that, you're conforming just as much as everybody else, only in a different way." It's lose-lose.

The "bohemians" Franny's referring to are Salinger's literary peers: those hipsters now known as the Beat Generation. Salinger was about the same age as Allen Ginsburg, Jack Kerouac, William Burroughs, Lucien Carr, and the rest. They had the same interest in Eastern mysticism, and were in the same location. (Salinger quit Columbia just a semester before Kerouac began attending.) But compared to the drug-fueled romp of these bohemians, Salinger remained straight and sober. He didn't hang out with hustlers and lowlifes in seedy Times Square. He didn't hitchhike back and forth across the country. He didn't partake in orgies. He hardly drank and didn't experiment with drugs. Despite his reclusive nature, Salinger remained within the establishment, rejecting the excesses of the burgeoning counterculture movement. He always kept a soldier's discipline. Yet his characters fight against social conformity and the mindless mass culture of postwar America. They simply do so in a refined, intellectual, and classy manner. A manner that reflects Salinger's own traditional disposition. And so Salinger falls between the camps. The intellectual New York literary establishment doesn't understand his indulgence in the spiritual. The beatniks and hipsters think him too square. He rejects both groups, and both reject him.

Franny, too, feels like she doesn't belong, and while she's venting to Lane, her anxiety increases along with her deepening pallor. She says she feels "so funny," and thinks she's "going crazy." To bring her back, Lane asks about her acting and the play she's in. The theater is Franny's passion. She's always wanted to be an actress. But she admits she not only quit the play, she quit the whole department. She quit acting altogether, explaining she "began to feel like such a nasty little egomaniac." Again, Lane interrupts, accusing her of talking as though she's "the only person in the world that's got any goddamn sense." (Though this is how he was talking a few moments earlier.) All Franny knows, she says, is that she's "sick of ego, ego, ego." Her own and everybody else's. She's "sick of everybody that wants to *get* somewhere, do something distinguished and all, be somebody interesting. It's disgusting—it is, *it is*." Using Freudian terminology, she's referring to the same natural narcissism Siddhartha saw in people, the self-importance for which he held them in disdain. People are in love with themselves, they have high hopes and ambitions, and both Siddhartha and Franny find it disgusting.

Getting psychological, Lane dismisses her points by suggesting she's simply afraid of competition. But she's not afraid to compete, she says. She's afraid she *will* compete. She's ashamed of her competitive self, of wanting to make a splash, of needing the applause and raves. She's "sick of not having the courage to be an absolute nobody." An absolute nobody? Who says they want to be an absolute nobody when they grow up? This is not how an elite young woman is supposed to sound. She's supposed to want to be successful. She's supposed to want to be somebody. By rejecting the values of her peers, Franny rejects who she is and what's she's supposed to be. Without a sense of self or a society, she leaps into an existential abyss. Her teeth begin to chatter. She's now perspiring so heavily that Lane offers her a handkerchief. Embarrassed at how she must look, Franny searches for her compact mirror, taking everything out of her purse. Then Lane again asks about the little green book, which is now on the table—literally and figuratively.

The book is *The Way of a Pilgrim*. It's a real book; its author is unknown, but thought to be a Russian peasant living in the mid-nineteenth century. (It takes place between the Crimean War of 1853 and the liberation of the serfs in 1861). First published in Kazan in 1884 as "Candid Narratives of a Pilgrim to His Spiritual Father" and translated into English by R. M. French in 1931, *The Way of a Pilgrim* is considered a classic of Eastern Orthodox spiritual literature. Its popularity is partly due to the endearing sincerity of the pilgrim himself, but also because the book presents the previously obscure *hesychast* tradition of unceasing prayer, a technique aimed at achieving union with God. (*Hesychasm* is Greek for "stillness," "rest," "quiet," or "silence.") It's a method that transforms prayer into a meditation, producing a form of Christianity that, in practice, has more in common with Eastern traditions of Buddhism and Hinduism than its Western Catholic and Protestant counterparts.

The narrator of *The Way of a Pilgrim* was born in Orel, about 220 miles southwest of Moscow. He was orphaned at age two, and his grandparents raised him along with his older brother, who is a total jerk. When the pilgrim was seven, his brother pushed him off the stove. His left arm was injured so badly it "withered up," leaving him unable to work the land or perform public duties. Using the Bible, his grandfather teaches him to read and write. At age twenty, he marries and inherits the grandparents' house and savings. But a year later, the brother gets drunk, lights the house on fire, and steals all the family's money, leaving the narrator ruined. After that, his wife dies of fever. Not knowing what else to do, the narrator decides to go venerate holy shrines in Kiev. And so he becomes a pilgrim, visiting churches and monasteries across the country, wandering through steppes, fields, and forests.

The book begins when the pilgrim is thirty-three years old and has been wandering for thirteen years. He's in church and hears a sermon that says Christians are supposed to "pray without ceasing." It's a line from Paul's first epistle to the Thessalonians. But what does this mean? "I heard a sermon on spiritual prayer," the pilgrim writes, "and unceasing prayer, but how it was to be done was not pointed out." This is what I've always found lacking in Christianity: the how. Unlike the Buddha, Jesus did not teach a technique. Yes, he taught the Lord's Prayer, but the pilgrim wants more than words—he wants to know *how* to pray unceasingly. And anyway, he wonders, what is prayer in itself? How is one supposed to actually pray? The pilgrim doesn't know, and he thinks church sermons leave "precise" answers to these questions behind "a veil of mystery." So he decides to stop attending public sermons.

He wanders from place to place, looking for a spiritual teacher who can tell him about ceaseless prayer. The first few he meets offer empty words. One abbot says: "Ceaseless interior prayer is a continual yearning of the human spirit toward God." Well, okay. But what does that mean? It's an abstract answer, not a practical one. The pilgrim is unsatisfied. Another abbot quotes a line from St. Dmitri's *The Spiritual Education of the Inner Man*, which says Paul's instructions to pray without ceasing should be "understood as referring to the creative prayer of the understanding. The understanding can always be reaching out toward God and praying to Him unceasingly." Again, the pilgrim is unsatisfied. He wants instruction. A method. A technique.

He walks on, carrying a Bible and a bag of dry bread, the only food he eats. Then he finds an old priest, a *starets*. In the Eastern Orthodox tradition, a *starets* is a monk distinguished by great learning and piety, someone who laypeople go to for spiritual council. Zooey later explains a *starets* is "a sort of Christian guru." (If you're familiar with *The Brothers Karamazov*, think of Father Zosima.) This *starets* tells the pilgrim that

> the continuous interior prayer of Jesus is a constant uninterrupted calling upon the divine name of Jesus with the lips, in the spirit, in the heart, while forming a mental picture of His constant presence, and imploring His grace, during every occupation, at all times, in all places, even during sleep. The appeal is couched in these terms, "Lord Jesus Christ, have mercy on me."

The pilgrim begins to understand what ceaseless prayer is: You constantly repeat "Lord Jesus Christ, have mercy on me," like a mantra. It's called the Jesus Prayer. He asks how to practice it, and the *starets* gives the pilgrim a copy of *The Philokalia*, which he says "contains the full and detailed science of constant interior prayer, set forth by twenty-five holy fathers." *The Philokalia* is a collection of ascetic and mystical writings by Eastern Orthodox saints, composed over a thousand years between the fourth and fifteenth centuries. The pilgrim later describes it as "a key to the mysteries of holy Scripture," and the *starets* later says it explains "in an understandable way the scientific knowledge of the truth and of the essence of prayer of the heart." The Greek word *philokalia* itself means "love of the beautiful," but also, according to the introduction of the edition I read, "the exalted, the excellent, understood as the transcendent source of life and the revelation of the truth." There are five volumes of *The Philokalia,* and aside from the Christian terminology, much of it sounds like guidance written by *ajahns* of the austere Buddhist Forest traditions—for instance, St. Mark the Ascetic's observation, "For he who entangles himself with the passions while trying to overcome them is like a man who tries to put out a fire with straw," or Ilias the Presbyter's advice that "if before indulging in pleasure you reflect on the pain inherent in it, you will escape the distress to which it gives birth." It's in *The Philokalia* where one can find specific instructions on the *heyschast* method of prayer, and the Jesus Prayer in particular, which was first mentioned in the fifth century by St. Neilos the Ascetic. The *starets* opens it to a passage by St. Simeon, who gives clear and specific instructions on how to pray without ceasing, as if from a meditation guru:

> Sit down alone and in silence. Lower your head, shut your eyes, breathe out gently, and imagine yourself looking into your own heart. Carry your mind, that is, your thoughts, from your head to your heart. As you breathe out, say "Lord Jesus Christ, have mercy on me." Say it moving your lips gently, or simply say it in your mind. Try to put all other thoughts aside. Be calm, be patient, and repeat the process very frequently.

After further illustration, the *starets* sends the pilgrim on his way to practice on his own. At first things seem to go well, but then he has difficulty. He becomes tired, feeling lazy and bored, sleepy and restless. This is a common experience during meditation. In Buddhism, lethargy and restlessness are two of the five hindrances (*nivaranas*), mental defilements that the purification process brings to the surface of the mind, and which block the road to spiritual progress. Frustrated, the pilgrim returns to his teacher. The *starets* explains the lethargy is "the attack of the world of darkness," which will try "by every means to hinder you and to turn you aside from learning the prayer." We're starting to see parallels.

The *starets* says the pilgrim needs further guidance. He opens *The Philokalia* and reads from the teaching of Nicephorous:

> If after a few attempts you do not succeed in reaching the realm of your heart in the way you have been taught, do what I am about to say and by God's help you will find what you seek. The

faculty of pronouncing words lies in the throat. Reject all other thoughts (you can do this as you will) and allow that faculty to repeat only the following words constantly: "Lord Jesus Christ, have mercy on me." Compel yourself to do it always.

Do it always. The Buddha also instructs his disciples to meditate continuously, saying we should meditate in all four bodily postures: standing, sitting, walking, and lying down. Similarly, the pilgrim's teacher clarifies: "Whether you are standing or sitting, walking or lying down, continually repeat 'Lord Jesus Christ, have mercy on me.' Say it quietly and without hurry, but without fail exactly three thousand times a day." To count the prayers, the teacher gives the pilgrim a rosary.

The pilgrim goes home and says the prayer three thousand times a day. A few days later, he's instructed to say it six thousand times a day. By then he becomes so used to saying the prayer that when he stops, he feels "as though something were missing," as though he had "lost something." The ceaseless praying initially causes physical weariness. It makes his tongue numb and jaws stiff. There is a slightly painful feeling in the roof of his mouth. His thumb hurts from counting the rosary beads, and his wrist becomes inflamed. But he moves on to saying the prayer twelve thousand times a day. At this point his tongue and lips pronounce the words "entirely of themselves." He feels as though "cut off from everything else," as if he "lived as though in another world." The prayer fills him with joy and relief.

His teacher soon dies and the pilgrim travels on. As he wanders, the ceaseless prayer protects him from cold and heat, from hunger and pain. After a while, the prayer passes from his lips to his heart: "My heart in its ordinary beating began to say the words of the prayer within each beat. Thus for example, *one*, 'Lord,' *two*, 'Jesus,' *three*, 'Christ,' and so on." He gives up saying the prayer with his mouth, and "simply listened to what [his] heart was saying." Finally, the pilgrim knows what it means to "pray without ceasing."

The bulk of the pilgrim's story is about the people he meets on his journey across Siberia to Irkutsk. He teaches them how to pray without ceasing, and he also continues to learn from others. One night an officer tells him: "What the Gospel is, that the prayer of Jesus is also, for the Divine Name of Jesus Christ holds in itself the whole gospel truth. The holy fathers say that the prayer of Jesus is a summary of the Gospels." The idea that a name can summarize a teaching is commonly found in the East, with some Hindus repeating "Rama, Rama" or "Hare Krishna, Hare Krishna" as their main spiritual practice. And as Franny will tell Lane, similarities also abound in Mahayana forms of Buddhism. In the Japanese Pure Land sect, you can supposedly become enlightened just by saying the name "Amithaba Buddha." There's a similar idea in the Nichiren tradition of Japanese Buddhism, and its offshoot the Soka Gakkai movement, in which it's believed one can achieve Buddhahood by repeating the mantra of the Lotus Sutra: *Namu Myoho Renge Kyo*. The core practice of the Tibetan Buddhist is to repeat the mantra *Om Mani Padme Hum* while counting the prayers on rosary beads or prayer wheels. It would be difficult to find practices more similar to the Orthodox Jesus Prayer than these Buddhist mantras. (It's also easy to understand why these Mahayana practices have become so popular over recent decades, not to mention centuries: it's much easier to repeat a few words than sit for thousands of hours of meditation!)

Later on his journey, the pilgrim meets a Polish Catholic who dismisses the ceaseless prayer as "odd sorts of schemes and tricks." The Pole says it is "like those fanatics in India and Bokhara who sit down and blow themselves out trying to get a sort of tickling in their hearts, and in their stupidity take this bodily feeling for prayer, and look upon it as the gift of God." The pilgrim objects, saying his teacher taught him "the monks of India and Bokhara took over the 'heart method' of interior prayer" from ancient Greek Christians, "only they spoiled and garbled it in doing so." More likely it's the other way around, with the Greeks learning from the Indians. (In fact, Buddhist missionaries spread west to Europe as early as the third century BCE; a beautiful work of Buddhist scripture is the first-century *Milinda Panha*, or the Questions of Milinda, a dialogue in which the Greek king of Bactria poses questions to an Indian Buddhist monk.) But the significance of this section is in its symbolism: the Roman Catholic Church, represented by the Pole, never explicitly condemned *hesychasm* as heresy, but many Catholic theologians rejected ceaseless prayer as heretical, which led to it having little influence in the West.

At one point, the pilgrim's deceased teacher appears in a dream and gives a specific order in which to read *The Philokalia*. In the pilgrim's book, he even marks specific instructions by Callistus, patriarch of Constantinople—marks that are still there when the pilgrim awakes. After reading this section, the pilgrim shuts his eyes and, using his imagination, gazes upon his heart: "I tried to picture it there in the left side of my breast and to listen carefully to its beating." After several days of practicing he says, "I was able to picture my heart and to note its movement, and further with the help of my breathing I could put into it and draw from it the prayer of Jesus in the manner taught by the saints." Then he begins "to fit the words of the prayer to the beats of the heart."

As he develops in the practice, he explains how to pray ceaselessly with more refined instructions: "Thus with the first beat, say or think 'Lord,' with the second, 'Jesus,' with the third, 'Christ,' with the fourth, 'have mercy,' and with the fifth, 'on me.' And do it over and over again." Once this comes easily, then "you must begin bringing the whole prayer of Jesus into and out of your heart in time with your breathing." When breathing in, he looks into his heart and says "Lord Jesus Christ." When breathing out he says, "Have mercy on me."

This method of linking breath, heart, and mantra is what transforms prayer into meditation. When praying in this methodical manner, the pilgrim feels a "joyous 'bubbling' in the heart." The prayer now goes on of its own accord. It never stops, not for a single moment, no matter what the pilgrim is doing. He can listen or read carefully while the prayer continues as if he "were made into two people, or as if there were two souls in [his] one body."

At the end, the pilgrim begins a journey back across Russia to Odessa, where he's to board a ship for Jerusalem. And as he travels, the ceaseless repetition of the Jesus Prayer makes him feel as joyful as if he "had been made a czar." He's now enjoying the fruits of ceaseless prayer.

Perhaps this spiritual joy is what so attracts Franny. But she's also attracted by the simplicity of the pilgrim himself. He's the opposite of everything she hates. The antithesis of all those Smith and Vassar and Bennington types, those Joe Yales. The pilgrim is constantly diminishing his ego. He doesn't compete. He doesn't want to get anywhere, or do something distinguished, or be somebody interesting. He has "the courage to be an absolute nobody."

Back at the table, Franny avoids Lane's question about her book. Then she says, "It's just something I brought to look at on the train." Skeptical, he presses, asking if the book "is a goddam secret or something." Franny claims she got the book out of the library, after the professor of her religion survey course mentioned it, and that she simply keeps forgetting to return it. But Lane doesn't let her off, and Franny reluctantly reveals her obsession with *The Way of a Pilgrim*.

While Lane eats frog legs, she tells him about the Jesus Prayer and *The Philokalia*. For the first time since we've met her, she's positively interested in something. Oblivious to her excitement, Lane comments, "I hate to mention it, but I'm going to reek of garlic." He couldn't care less. But Franny gets on a roll, talking about the people the pilgrim meets along his way, and how he teaches them "the method of praying without ceasing." Uninterested, Lane again brings up his essay, asking if Franny will read it.

She quickly agrees and moves back to the Jesus Prayer, explaining how after first saying it with your lips, it later becomes "self-active." That is, she says, "Something *happens* after a while," and the "words get synchronized with the person's heartbeats, and then you're actually praying without ceasing." She says the result of ceaseless prayer will "purify your whole outlook and get an absolutely new conception about what everything's about." (Zooey later refers to this new conception as "Christ-Consciousness," a phrase that means different things to different people, but which Salinger got from his readings of Paramahansa Yogananda, who used Christ-Consciousness as a term for spiritual perfection.)

Showing Salinger's familiarity with world religions, Franny relates the Jesus Prayer to the "Nembutsu sects of Buddhism," in which "people keep saying 'Namu Amida Butsu' over and over again," and "the *same thing* happens." She says the same thing also "happens in 'The Cloud of Unknowing,' just with the word 'God.' I mean you just keep saying the word God." *The Cloud of Unknowing* is an anonymous work of Christian mysticism from fourteenth-century England, which served as a prayer guide during the later Middle Ages, as well as to contemplative Christians today. Franny is referring to an instructive line from the book: "When we intend to pray for goodness, let all our thought and desire be contained in the one small word 'God.' Nothing else and no other words are needed." She then says the "same advice" is found "even in India," where "they tell you to meditate on the 'Om,' which means the same thing really, and the exact same result is supposed to happen." After explaining these cross-cultural similarities, she looks directly at Lane and asks, "Did you ever hear anything so fascinating in your *life*?" Cautioning her to "take it easy," Lane wonders if she can actually "believe that stuff." Franny says it's not a matter of belief; she simply finds the similarities fascinating. Being a practical American (like Isabel Maturin), Lane asks what's the point of "all this synchronization business and mumbo-jumbo." Franny answers: "You get to see God."

This idea of getting "to see God" isn't actually found in *The Way of a Pilgrim*; it's Salinger's own mixture of Christian mysticism and Hindu Vedanta, and he has Franny explain it using themes found in *The Razor's Edge* and *Siddhartha*: "Something happens," she says, "in some absolutely nonphysical part of the heart—where Hindus say that Atman resides, if you ever took any Religion—and you see God, that's all." She's not sure who or what God is, or even if he exists, but before she can go on, the waiter comes to their table and Lane realizes they're late for the football game. He admits what she's talking about is "interesting," but dismisses it by saying "all these religious experiences have a very obvious psychological background." Then he smiles and tells her, "I love you."

By then it's too late. As if she didn't hear his declaration of love, Franny abruptly excuses herself and again heads to the bathroom. But she only makes it to the bar. She steadies herself, dramatically raises her left hand to her forehead, "weaved a trifle," and then faints, collapsing to the floor. She revives five minutes later, terribly embarrassed. She can't believe she actually fainted, and that she had to be carried to a back room, where Lane is with her. Once he sees she's feeling better, he alludes to the sex he hopes to have later, since it's been "too goddam long between drinks. To put it crassly." He then leaves to find them a taxi. Alone, Franny's "lips began to move, forming soundless words."

As "Franny" comes to a close, her lips continue to move. She's repeating the Jesus Prayer.

Like Somerset Maugham, J. D. Salinger knows very well that he shouldn't be writing so explicitly about religion in his fiction. And in the very beginning of "Zooey," he acknowledges the taboo through his alter ego, Buddy Glass, the "author" and narrator of these stories about his youngest siblings. (We can assume that Buddy has published with some success; despite not even having a BA, he is a writer-in-residence at an all-girls college in upstate New York, teaching advanced writing and giving informal lectures on Zen and Mahayana Buddhism. After dropping out of NYU, Ursinus College, and then Columbia, Salinger also never earned a degree.)

Buddy claims that after reading his story about their sister, Zooey "feels the plot hinges on mysticism, or religious mystification—in any case, he makes it very clear, a too vividly apparent transcendent element of sorts," which will only expedite the author's "professional undoing." Buddy further says, "People are already shaking their heads over me, and any immediate further professional use on my part of the word 'God,' except as a familiar, healthy American expletive, will be taken—or, rather, confirmed—as the very worst kind of name-dropping and a sure sign that I'm going straight to the dogs." In other words, Salinger knows he could ruin his reputation by writing about religion.

Sure enough, the saturation of religiosity is a reason why these stories were not and are still not necessarily well received by the literary establishment. It's not surprising that *The New Yorker*'s fiction editors initially rejected "Zooey"—what's surprising is that it was published in the magazine in the first place. By standards of both its length and content, it's something the likes of which I could never imagine seeing in the magazine's pages today. But in Buddy's opinion, what he's offering "isn't a mystical story, or a religiously mystifying story," but rather a "love story, pure and complicated." And it is indeed a love story. A story of familial love, as well as a religious love.

Salinger's acknowledgment of the taboo can also be understood as a response to the criticism he'd been getting for several years; neither "Franny" nor "Zooey" was Salinger's first foray into writing explicitly about Eastern religion and matters of the spirit. The first piece of spiritual fiction he wrote was the story "Teddy," which was first published in *The New Yorker* in 1953, and then collected in *Nine Stories*. The story is named after its protagonist, a ten-year-old genius. It takes place on a cruise ship, and within the time frame of an hour, mostly while Teddy is waiting for a swim lesson and answering questions from a professor. Relatively famous in academic circles, Teddy is returning from a European tour of being interviewed by professors of religion and philosophy, who record their sessions with him and then spread the tapes amongst their colleagues.

It doesn't take long to see that Teddy isn't your typical ten-year-old. For starters, he writes in a diary. One of his entries reads: "Try the sports deck for meditation tomorrow morning before breakfast but do not lose consciousness." Yes, a ten-year-old meditator, and an apparently skilled one at that. But he's been at it for lifetimes. Not long into their conversation, the professor says Teddy holds "pretty firmly to the Vedantic theory of reincarnation." Here's the first mention of Vedanta in Salinger's writings, the philosophy that would hold the author under its sway for most of his life, and which Larry Durrell explained to Somerset over that long night in Paris.

By 1953, Salinger was seriously interested in Vedanta. He was heavily under the influence of *The Gospel of Sri Ramakrishna*, which was published a few years earlier, and the writings of Ramana Maharshi, whom Maugham used as a model for Larry's guru Sri Ganesha. In 1955, after reading Paramahansa Yogananda's *Autobiography of a Yogi* and *The Second Coming of Christ*, Salinger and his wife Claire were initiated into Yogananda's path of Kriya Yoga. They were taught a mantra and breathing exercises to practice for ten minutes twice a day. (I should also note that Claire let Salinger borrow her copy of *The Way of a Pilgrim*, which she was reading at Radcliffe when they became engaged.) All this is to say that we can assume Salinger himself held pretty firmly to the Vedantic theory of reincarnation. But Teddy interrupts the professor, protesting that reincarnation "isn't a theory, it's as much a part—." He's counter-interrupted by the professor, who questions the claim that Teddy has "acquired certain information, through meditation," which has given the child the "conviction" that in his "last incarnation" he was "a holy man in India," but "more or less fell from Grace before final Illumination."

Incarnation. Holy man. Vedantic. Illumination. Other than readers of *The Razor's Edge*, how many Americans in 1953 would've heard these terms before? Not many.

Teddy clarifies he wasn't necessarily a holy man, but simply "a person making very nice spiritual advancement." He elaborates that in this past life he "met a lady," which caused him to stop meditating. He wasn't so spiritually advanced that he could have "gone straight to Brahma and never have to come back to earth." But if he hadn't met the lady, he "wouldn't have to get incarnated in an American body." Being an American, it seems, is a spiritual disadvantage. "It's very hard to meditate and live a spiritual life in America," Teddy says. "People think you're a freak if you try to." Teddy's father thinks he's a freak, and his mother doesn't think it's good for her son to "think about God all the time."

So now we have "Brahma," the highest being in the Indian order of beings, and the more familiar "God." Like Maugham, Salinger has a different definition of the word. He's not referring to Yahweh, or any sort of omniscient father figure in the sky. He has Teddy make this clear when the boy says, "I was six when I saw that everything was God, and my hair stood up, and all that." This, as the professor confirms, was Teddy's "first mystical experience." For once it's an accurate use of the word mystical, as we see when Teddy further explains his version of God: "My sister was only a very tiny child then, and she was drinking her milk, and all of a sudden I saw that she was God and the milk was God. I mean, all she was doing was pouring God into God, if you know what I mean." For Salinger, God is everything. Like Hesse, he believes God is the Unity of All Things.

Perhaps not understanding what Teddy means, the professor doesn't respond. Teddy continues, saying that by age four he was able "to get out of the finite dimensions fairly often," but the professor can't follow logically. Teddy scolds him for his insistence on logic, saying, "logic's the first thing you have to get rid of" if you want to "get out of the finite dimensions." To Teddy, logic is the apple Adam and Eve ate in the garden of Eden. The apple is "logic and intellectual stuff." And "if you want to see things as they really are" then all you have to do is "vomit up" the apple. The problem, he thinks, is "that most people don't want to see things the way they are. They don't even want to stop getting born and dying all the time. They just want new bodies all the time, instead of stopping and staying with God, where it's really nice." Using familiar terms from the Genesis story, Salinger is actually explaining the Vedantic conception of illumination, the goal of *moksha*, where one can "stop and stay with God."

But the professor isn't concerned with these mystical ideas. He's rather fixated on Teddy's notorious predictions. Specifically, predictions Teddy made concerning "where and when and how" fellow professors would die. Like Larry Darrell and Hesse's Siddhartha, Teddy, too, has apparently acquired spiritual powers. He even predicts his own death, which implicitly happens at the end of the story, an ambiguous end that has made it one of the most controversial endings in the history of the short story.

For its twenty-odd pages, "Teddy" is packed with references to Eastern religious concepts, containing more spiritual ideas than all contemporary *New Yorker* stories I've ever read put together. But here they remain ideas, allusions, name-droppings. Salinger mentions meditation, but we don't see Teddy meditate, or know how he does it—that is, which technique he uses. It all comes off rather abruptly and unnatural. A few years later, Salinger (as Buddy writing in "Seymour") admits his story "Teddy" was "thoroughly unsuccessful." It's not until *Franny and Zooey* that Salinger ventures further into spiritual fiction, not only getting more specific but getting it right.

Some see "Franny" as a prologue to "Zooey," which is three times as long. But to me, it's "Franny" that can stand alone, with "Zooey" being an epilogue, a coda providing context for understanding Franny's breakdown. In the beginning of the story, Zachary Glass, known by his family as Zooey, is in the bath. At age twenty-five, he's a successful television actor. Smoking a cigarette, he's reading a four-year-old letter from his older brother Buddy. The letter was written three years after Seymour's suicide, an event from which no members of the Glass family seem to have been able to recover. Before revealing the contents of the letter, Buddy (as the narrator) sketches a crucial background of the Glass family—crucial because without it, we might simply dismiss Franny as another naïve and privileged college-age fool who, after taking her first religious studies course, disdains the phonies of society and declares the world to be meaningless. No, Salinger wants to make sure his readers know there's much more to her breakdown than a cliché.

The parents Les and Bessie Glass made a career in vaudeville. Bessie is Irish-Catholic, and Les is Jewish—ethnicities identical to Salinger's own parents. The Glasses have seven children, all of whom appeared regularly on a network radio program, a children's quiz show called *It's a Wise Child*. Due to the age difference of eighteen years between the eldest, Seymour, and the youngest, Franny, the Glass children held a "dynastic seating arrangement" on the show from 1927 through 1943. On *It's a Wise Child*, the children answered "deadly bookish and deadly cute questions—sent in by listeners—with a freshness, an aplomb, that was considered unique in commercial radio." Buddy tells us that Seymour and Zooey were considered the most appealing, with the latter having a "somewhat preposterous ability to quote, instantaneously and, usually verbatim, almost anything he had ever read, or even listened to." Listeners of the show either thought the "Glasses were a bunch of insufferably 'superior' little bastards that should have been drowned or gassed at birth" or that "they were bona-fide underage wits and savants, of an uncommon, if unenviable, order." They are, in other words, a family of geniuses. (The influence of such a family still trickles down through pop culture, seen most clearly in Wes Anderson's film *The Royal Tenenbaums*, also about a family of former childhood geniuses who fall on hard times as adults. Anderson even goes so far as to have an early scene showing one of his characters, Margot Tenenbaum, played by Gwyneth Paltrow, soaking in the bath, and in a near verbatim cribbing, has the mother say staying in a bath so long "isn't even healthy," just as Bessie tells Zooey. Also, Tannenbaum is the married last name of the middle Glass sister, Boo Boo, so there's the nod.) As they were public radio stars, Buddy says "all seven of the children had been fair game for the kind of child psychologist or professional educator who takes a special interest in extra-precocious children." Zooey made his debut as a public performer at age seven. Being a famous child genius is enough to give someone complexes for the rest of their life. But on top of having "wise child syndrome," there's the "education" that Seymour and Buddy gave their younger siblings.

In his letter, Buddy explains why he and Seymour "took over" their younger siblings' education, throwing "in the Upanishads and the Diamond Sutra and Eckhart and all our other old loves with the rest of your recommended reading when you were small." He thinks Zooey would have "made a damn site better-adjusted actor" otherwise, and the essence of the letter is worry. After Seymour's suicide, Buddy is worried about Zooey, who at eighteen had a "reputation" in his college dorm "for going off and sitting in meditation for ten hours at a time." Ten hours! Clearly, Zooey is a not a normal young man—Buddy gives us the gossip that Zooey once "got over an unhappy love affair by trying to translate the Mundaka Upanishad into classical Greek." And Buddy's letter is an apology for making his brother and sister abnormal. Looking back on what he's done, he's always been afraid his youngest siblings would "take up a position across the room and fire Max Mueller's Sacred Books of the East" at him, which he says would have probably been "masochistic ecstasy."

So maybe it was too much. But their intentions were pure. Education, Buddy and Seymour thought, would be all the better "if it didn't begin with a quest for knowledge at all but with a quest, as Zen would put it, for no-knowledge." Buddy references D. T. Suzuki's statement that "to be in a state of pure consciousness—*satori*—is to be with God before he said, Let there be light." Buddy and Seymour thought it was a good idea to "hold back this light" from Franny and Zooey. They wouldn't be taught the arts, sciences, classics, and languages until they were both "able to conceive of a state of being where the mind knows the source of all light." That's why Seymour and Buddy wanted to teach their youngest siblings about all "the men—the saints, the arhats, the bodhisattvas, the jivanmuktas—who knew something or everything about this state of being." And so before puberty, Franny and Zooey learned "who and what Jesus and Gautama and Lao-tse and Shankaracharya and Huineng and Sri Ramakrishna, etc., were before" they learned "too much or anything about Homer or Shakespeare or even Blake or Whitman, let alone George Washington and his cherry tree or the definition of a peninsula or how to parse a sentence." Well before puberty, in fact: When Franny was all of ten months old she had to sleep in her older brothers' room for a few nights; Seymour soothed her crying and put her to bed by reading her Taoist tales.

Salinger expressed a similar idea about education in "Teddy." At one point, the professor asks the ten-year-old how he would change the education system. "I think I'd first just assemble all the children together and show them how to meditate," Teddy answers. "I'd try to show them how to find out who they *are*, not just what their names are and things like that. . . . I guess, even before that I'd get them to empty out everything their parents and everybody ever told them." He'd "make them vomit up every bit of apple their parents and everybody made them take a bite out of." Teddy says it's fine for students to learn "all that other stuff—names and colors and things," but he'd want "them to *begin* with all the real ways of looking at things." That is to say, he'd begin like Seymour and Buddy did, by holding back the light.

According to Salinger, our education system has its priorities all wrong. It ignores the most fundamental and focuses on the most trivial. It doesn't teach about anything spiritual, which has always been left to organized religion. Yet as our essence is spiritual, we miss learning the essential. With this oversight, education focuses on the quantitative. Consequently, we never learn about the qualitative—about well-being, happiness, and peace. We're forced to take physical education, but we're not taught how to exercise our minds through meditation, or take care of our bodies through yoga. We're taught to memorize and repeat, but not how to understand and to think. Education, implies Salinger, should begin from the beginning, with the essential, and move on from there. If it were this way, seekers wouldn't have to spend years unlearning what they were taught. As Salinger has Seymour say, "all legitimate religious study *must* lead to unlearning the differences, the illusionary differences, between boys and girls, animals and stones, day and night, heat and cold." In other words, religious study leads to the "unity of all things" that Siddhartha realizes in the Om and the river. If this is the goal, the fruits of such an education should be nothing but beneficial. It should produce wise, peaceful, and happy individuals. Franny and Zooey should have an advantage over everyone else. But the results say otherwise. Franny is having a nervous breakdown, and Zooey is a jerk. "We're *freaks*, the two of us, Franny and I," Zooey tells his mother Bessie. "I'm a twenty-five-year-old freak and she's a twenty-year-old-freak, and both those bastards are responsible."

Yes, despite professional success, Zooey has issues. For starters, he has an ulcer. But he dismisses it as just part of the dark eon we're living in: "This is the Kaliyuga, buddy, the Iron Age. Anybody over sixteen without an ulcer's a goddamn spy." Moreover, he has social issues. He can't talk to people. Bessie says he makes people nervous. If he likes somebody, he does all of the talking "and nobody can get a word in edgewise." And if he doesn't like someone, he'll just "sit around like death it*self* and let the person talk themselves into a hole." Despite whatever spiritual wisdom he has, Zooey comes off as arrogant and smug. In fact, he's downright insufferable. "You're not kind," Bessie tells her son.

Out of all the Glass children, Zooey has been the most analyzed, "the most voraciously examined, interviewed, and poked at." With the consequential self-awareness, he's the first to admit his social shortcomings: "I can't even sit down to lunch with a man any more and hold my end of a decent conversation. I either get so bored or so goddamn preachy that if the son of a bitch had any sense, he'd break his chair over my head." He thinks Franny has the same complex, just that her symptoms are more delayed. Zooey blames these social problems on their religious education. He—and, he assumes, Franny—can't even eat a meal without first saying the Four Great Bodhisattva Vows: "However in*num*erable beings are, I vow to save them; however inexh*aust*ible the passions are, I vow to extinguish them; however immeasurable the Dharmas are, I vow to master them; however incomparable the Buddha-truth is, I vow to at*tain* it." He's been mumbling these vows under his breath since he was ten. It's become a neurosis, as if he's got spiritual OCD. Understandably, he resents his eldest brothers. "I swear to you," he tells Bessie, "I could murder them both without even batting an eyelash"—and this despite Seymour being dead for seven years.

Now, this is a lot to dump on a reader. A lot a lot. The saints, the arhats, the bodhisattvas, the jivanmuktas. Buddha-truth and the Four Great Vows. When I first read *Franny and Zooey*, I didn't know what any of this stuff was about. I think I can safely assume that most readers in postwar America didn't either. But each reference, each allusion is like a little seed

Salinger scattered in the wind. Some seeds would land on stone, but others would find fertile soil and grow. For some readers, it might have been the mentions of Sri Ramakrishna that led to a lifetime of studying Vedanta, and others might have become Taoists following the mention of Lao-tse. And many might have taken up the Jesus Prayer and turned Eastern Orthodox. For me, it was Zen. Though most of Salinger's religious references didn't initially resonate, his mentions of Buddhism and Zen are what motivated me to walk across campus to the UCLA bookstore and excavate the contents of the religion section, so I could find out what this Zen stuff was all about. I came home with *Buddhism Explained* by Laurence-Kantipalo Mills, *Zen Mind, Beginner's Mind* by Shunryu Suzuki, and *The Way of Zen* by Alan Watts. Next stop was the Los Angeles Zen Center, and two years later I was sitting my first Vipassana course.

From one perspective, the story "Zooey" is an introduction to Eastern religion; it's practically an index. And many of us are grateful for that. But if someone actually had to survive Seymour and Buddy's education curriculum, it would be enough to make them not only resentful but neurotic. It might even cause a nervous breakdown.

After her collapse in the restaurant, Franny came home to the Glass apartment in Manhattan's Upper East Side. When the story "Zooey" begins, she's been "lying in a room crying and mumbling to herself for forty-eight hours." She refuses her mother's offer of chicken broth, not once but a dozen times, and has thrown up nearly everything she's eaten. Understandably, Bessie is very worried about her daughter. The woman is all fret, saying "the child's laying there by the hour crying her eyes out if you say boo to her, and *mumbling* heaven knows what to herself." Bessie wants Zooey to do something about it. If Zooey can't help, Bessie will send for a psychoanalyst.

The repeated mentions of mumbling let us know Franny is still practicing her mantra, the Jesus Prayer. Bessie doesn't know about her daughter's experiment with the prayer, but she does know Franny's "been reading too many religious books." Lane has called several times and from him Bessie learned that "the *root* of this whole business" is that "little book she carried all around the whole house." But she doesn't know what the book is. After teasing and joking and calling her stupid, not to mention an "old fat Druid," Zooey informs his mother that the book is *The Pilgrim Continues His Way*, which is the sequel to *The Way of a Pilgrim*. He says Franny got them both from Seymour and Buddy's old room, where they've been sitting on the desk for as long as Zooey can remember. Franny lied to Lane about getting the book from the library.

The Pilgrim Continues His Way is drier and less plausibly a memoir than *The Way of a Pilgrim*—Zooey says it's "mostly a dissertation in dialogue form on the whys and wherefors of the Jesus Prayer." He's right, but the sequel also offers more nuanced instructions on how to pray unceasingly. As it turns out, the pilgrim was unable to go to Jerusalem as planned. From Odessa he returns to Kiev, and then wanders back across Russia to Irkutsk. On the way, he meets a fellow pilgrim, a former professor who joins him on his journey. As they walk, the professor reveals a kind of Orthodox Christian Kabbalah. That is, *The Pilgrim Continues His Way* reveals an esoteric way of reading the Gospels to find "the hidden meaning of the Word of God," just like the mystical Jewish Kabbalists interpret secret instructions of how to pray from a close reading of the Torah. (It's intriguing, but too far into the weeds to present here.)

Anyway, after Zooey reveals that Franny has been reading *The Way of a Pilgrim* and *The Pilgrim Continues His Way*, he explains the books to Bessie. The line in Thessalonians, the pilgrim's desire to learn how to pray without ceasing, and his journey all over Russia. Zooey says the full Jesus Prayer is actually "Lord Jesus Christ, have mercy on me, a miserable sinner," and he's grateful the books left out the miserable sinner part. Now having his mother's full attention, he explains that "once the prayer moves from the head down to the center in the heart and becomes an automatic function, right along with the heartbeat," the person is "supposed to enter into the so-called reality of things." Explaining what "doesn't come up in either of the books," Zooey goes on to put the prayer in a wider religious context: "It didn't just start with the little pilgrim's crowd," he says. In India, "for God knows how many centuries, it's been known as *japam*," which is the repetition of any of the human names of God, or the names of his incarnations. Ram or Krishna. Further linking the Jesus Prayer with Indian religion, Zooey tells Bessie about

> the seven subtle centers in the body, called *chakras*, and the one most closely connected with the heart is call *anahata*, which is supposed to be sensitive and powerful as hell, and when it's activated it, in turn, activates another of these centers, between the eyebrows, called *ajna*—it's the pineal gland, really, or, rather, an aura around the pineal gland—and then, bingo, there's an opening of what mystics call the "third eye." It's nothing new, for God's sake.

Wait, is this a work of fiction or a lecture? It's not surprising that when *Franny and Zooey* came out, critic Maxwell Geismar called it an "appalling bad story," and George Steiner said it was "a piece of shapeless self-indulgence." Joan Didion dismissed the book as "spurious, and what makes it spurious is Salinger's tendency to flatter the essential triviality within each of his readers, his predilection for giving instructions for living." In a respectful yet ultimately deriding critique for *The New York Times Book Review*, John Updike wrote that "'Zooey' is just too long; there are too many cigarettes, too many goddams, too much verbal ado about not quite enough." It's true there are pages and pages of detailed descriptions of furniture, decorations, and step-by-step gestures that are all bound to irritate a certain kind of reader. But that's not why a writing professor of mine once dismissively referred to the book as "Franny and *Hooey*." The hooey was the spiritual. The hooey was because the story is saturated with religion. So it's not hard to see why critics would hate it.

And yet, despite the ire of critics, the book was a number one best seller. To account for its popularity with the general reading public, Didion wrote, "What gives the book its extremely potent appeal is precisely that it is self-help copy: it emerges finally as *Positive Thinking* for the upper middle classes, as *Double Your Energy and Live Without Fatigue* for Sarah Lawrence girls." To equate the spiritual with self-help is to woefully miss the point, as so many do. Though Didion's insight is misconceived, she's correct that the popularity of *Franny and Zooey* is not necessarily due to the artistic perfection, flamboyance, and originality of Salinger's writing style, but rather his serious treatment of Eastern religion, which many readers of the time must have experienced as a kind of opening to a world hitherto unknown, as it was for me. If you're not interested in matters of the spirit—and in my experience, most New York intellectuals are not—then such religious fiction will be dismissed, and in this case loathed. It is interpreted as anachronistic, having no place in modernity. But as Janet Malcolm wrote, in a redemptive piece on Salinger in a 2001 issue of *The New York Review of Books*, "it is the contemporary criticism that has dated" and now seems "magnificently misguided." She says it's similar to how contemporary critics of Tolstoy's *War and Peace* raged at the novel's "shapelessness." Negative contemporary criticism, Malcolm writes, "is helpful to later critics, acting as a kind of radar that picks up the ping of the work's originality. The 'mistakes' and 'excesses' that early critics complain of are often precisely the innovations that have given the work its power." To her, *Franny and Zooey* "remains brilliant" and is "arguably Salinger's masterpiece."

I'm not sure I agree, though I do wonder how things would be different if certain trigger-pulling nutjobs were obsessed with *Franny and Zooey* instead of *The Catcher in the Rye*. We'd likely have more wannabe bodhisattvas than we do phony-haters. And John Lennon might have lived a lot longer.

Such praise would be small consolation to poor Franny, who's still sleeping on the living room couch. Asleep, she is in the underworld. The nadir of her spiritual crisis. She's on the couch because the Glass apartment is being painted, and the painters are in her bedroom. Reflecting Franny's mental state, even the physical setting is unsettled, in a period of transition.

When Bessie finds out her daughter is saying the Jesus Prayer, she asks Zooey how long one has to do it. "How long?" Zooey answers. "Oh, not long. Till the painters want to get in your room. Then a procession of saints and bodhisattvas march in, carrying bowls of chicken broth." After he's done teasing his mother, he goes into the living room to wake Franny up, literally and figuratively. It will be his job to bring his sister back from the underworld. If he fails, she'll remain in Hades among the shades—early in their conversation, Zooey asks if Franny wants to talk to Buddy, but she replies, in a barely audible voice, "I want to talk to Seymour." Their house is filled with ghosts.

We can hear echoes of *The Catcher in the Rye*. Holden Caulfield, too, has never gotten over the death of his younger brother Allie, whom he idealizes, as the Glass family idealizes Seymour. Wanting to be "the catcher in the rye," saving kids from falling over an imagined cliff, Holden's mission is to preserve the innocence of children. At the end, it's his love for his sister Phoebe that saves him. We have another sibling-saving-sibling situation going on, but where Holden sees his mission as preserving his sister's innocence, Zooey's is to preserve Franny's sanity. So far, he's not doing so well. He had a failed attempt the previous night, a long talk that apparently ended with Franny in tears.

Zooey wakes her up and then plays Freud—cigar and all—while Franny describes a dream, which featured the teacher of her religion seminar, Professor Tupper. Franny says Tupper "keeps dropping idiotic hints that he's a *Realized Man* himself," but the only thing he does "with any *zing*, when he isn't bragging, is correct somebody when they say something's Sanskrit when it's really Pali." To Franny, Professor Tupper represents everything wrong with the higher education system. She says "college was just one more *dopey, inane* place in the world dedicated to piling up treasure on earth." After all, "what's the difference whether the treasure is money, or property, or even *cul*ture, or even just plain knowledge?" To her "knowledge for knowledge's sake" is "the worst of all." She's disgusted because she's never heard even "some polite per*func*tory implication that knowledge *should* lead to *wisdom*, and that if it *doesn't*, it's just a disgusting waste of time!" She's partly so upset because in nearly four years of college she's "hardly even heard the word 'wisdom' mentioned." And she has a point, because if our higher education system did aim to produce wise citizens, rather than simply knowledgeable ones, we'd have a lot fewer educated idiots squawking on social media, and the halls of congress might be filled with wise men instead of embarrassing clowns.

Zooey patiently listens to Franny, and then he tells her, "You look like hell. You know that?" Wonderful. Exactly what every woman wants to hear. Especially a twenty-year-old woman going through a spiritual crisis. Franny begs Zooey to "not start in on" her like he did the night before. He sees her lips are moving quietly throughout their conversation, and so he mocks, "The Prayer is rising." He's been chipping away at her new obsession, but his main point of disapproval is not that his sister is saying the Jesus Prayer. He likes the prayer. In fact, after reading the same books several years earlier, he "went to every Army & Navy store looking for a nice, pilgrim-type rucksack." He planned to "fill it with bread crumbs and start walking all over the goddam country. Saying the prayer. Spreading the word. The whole business." No, Zooey has nothing against the prayer itself.

His problem is with Franny's mistaken motivation for saying it, and how she's handling the whole thing. There's something about the way she's "going about this prayer" that gives him "the *willies*." What he perceives to be her holier-than-thou woe-is-me attitude. It's her thinking that he has issue with. "There's nothing tenth-rate about you," he tells her, "and yet you're up to your neck at this minute in tenth-rate thinking." By spending dozens of pages to fine-tune such spiritual thinking, Salinger not only provides a guide for fellow seekers, he hashes out an argument he's having with himself. How to be spiritual without becoming pious? How to follow a religious path without having disdain for those who don't? In *The Dhammapada*, the Buddha says: "Whoever stills negativity, coarse or subtle, in every way, because of the stilling of that negativity, that person is called a seeker." It is the stilling of all negativity that shows a seeker is properly walking the spiritual path. As long as negativity remains, the seeker is missing something. And because she's so negative, so judgmental, Zooey feels Franny is missing something.

As a recluse himself, Salinger most likely agrees with Franny on many points, particularly the disgust at everybody's "ego, ego, ego." But ego isn't all bad. "What about your beloved Epictetus?" Zooey asks. Or "your beloved Emily *Dick*inson?" What if every time Dickinson had an urge to write a poem she said "a prayer till her nasty, egotistical urge goes away?" No, when it serves artistic purpose, ego is all fine and good. Zooey doesn't want Franny "to go screaming about egos in general." That would be mistaken. It's not about others, he says, "it's *us*." Trying to gain some solidarity, he tells her, "We're freaks, that's all. Those two bastards got us nice and early and made us into freaks with freakish standards, that's all. We're the Tattooed Lady, and we're never going to have a minute's peace, the rest of our lives, till everybody else is tattooed, too." He further analyzes that they have "wise child complexes," and have "never really got off the goddam air." They don't talk, they hold forth. They don't converse, they expound. By calling Franny a freak with a complex, he's perversely trying to make her feel better. He's like her, after all, and they should bond because they're "bothered by the same kind of things" and "for the same reasons." He's disappointed in his sister because she should know to not go looking for the speck in the eyes of others, before taking out the beam in her own. She's being a hypocrite, is the implication. And so she's committing a serious spiritual sin. The one that really got Jesus's feathers ruffled.

Pressing the point of hypocrisy further, Zooey says there's no difference "between the man who's greedy for material treasure—or even intellectual treasure—and the man who's greedy for spiritual treasure." By now, Franny can hardly keep herself from exploding, furious to a degree only loved ones are capable of infuriating us. She knows what Zooey is implying. If she wants something from the Jesus Prayer then she's just as acquisitive as "somebody who wants a sable *coat*, or to be *fam*ous, or to be dripping with some kind of crazy pres*tige*." She knows all that. "My gosh," she rallies, "what kind of imbecile do you think I am?" She has her own motives in check, thank you very much. Just because she's choosey about what she wants, "in this case, en*light*enment, or *peace*, instead of money or pres*tige* or *fame* or any of those things," doesn't mean she's "not as egotistical and self-seeking as everybody else." By establishing she's well aware of what Zooey's saying, Franny successfully parries her brother's thrust of hypocrisy.

Okay then, Zooey tries a different approach. If she's not being hypocritical about her motivation, she's still mistaken in the overly dramatic way she's handling everything. After all, he reminds her, she had previously gone through "a little apostasy from the New Testament." As a child, it seems Franny "didn't like Jesus any more" after reading Matthew chapter six, which made her terribly upset. She "didn't approve of his going into the synagogue and throwing all the tables and idols all over the place." "I was all of ten years old!" Franny protests. But Zooey doesn't care how old she was. His point is that she doesn't understand who Jesus is. Like "ninety-eight percent of the Christian world," she has Jesus confused with "about five or ten other religious personages," specifically Saint Francis of Assisi. But Jesus is not as lovable as Saint Francis. And Zooey doesn't think she should go ahead with the Jesus Prayer until she knows "who's who and what's what." He doesn't see how someone can pray to a Jesus they can't understand. If Franny were a simple person, or a desperate person, he'd forgive her for not praying to the right Jesus. But she's not desperate, and she's not simple, and so it irritates him that she's not saying the Jesus Prayer to the actual Jesus.

To him, this misunderstanding is the reason she chose to have her breakdown at home, which is Zooey's other concern. Only at home can she say her prayer "and roll Jesus and St. Francis and Seymour and Heidi's grandfather all in one." In addition to her misconception of Jesus, he disapproves of her breakdown for aesthetic reasons. "All this hysteria business," he says, "is unattractive as *hell*." The way she lays around mumbling to herself, crying, and vomiting gives off "a little stink of piousness." To Zooey, there "isn't any prayer in any religion in the world that justifies piousness." He doesn't like "this little hair-shirty private life of a martyr" she's living back at college, this "snotty crusade" she thinks she's "leading against everybody." But what really bothers him is that she's taken her crusade home, where she's being waited on by their parents, and worrying them half to death while she's at it. If Franny is "going to go on with this breakdown business," Zooey wishes she'd go back to college to have it, where she's "not the baby of the family." Because of her choice of where she's having her breakdown, and the way she's going about it, Zooey's tirade culminates with the accusation that Franny is "missing the whole point of the Jesus Prayer."

At this point, after periodic shrieks and sobs, Franny starts bawling in a "wretched, prostate, face-down position" on the couch. Zooey finally shuts up. Distraught by his sister's utter anguish, he turns pale. To create a palpable sense of what has happened, Salinger writes, "Failure had suddenly filled the room with its invariably sickening smell." Smelling his own failure, Zooey apologizes, formally and sincerely. And then he leaves the room.

Temporarily defeated, Zooey can't completely give up. He retreats to the former bedroom of Buddy and Seymour, where he hasn't set foot in seven years. Like Franny, the reader is offered a respite from Zooey's preaching, and Salinger uses the opportunity to inject even more spiritual wisdom into his story.

On a beaverboard nailed to the back of the bedroom door, Buddy and Seymour have written four floor-to-ceiling columns of quotations from a variety of the world's sages, philosophers, and authors. There follows two and a half pages of quotes that cover most bases, starting with one of the most influential sections of the *Bhagavad-Gita*:

> You have the right to work, but for the work's sake only. You have no right to the fruits of work. Desire for the fruits of work must never be your motive in working. Never give way to laziness, either.
>
> Perform every action with your heart fixed on the Supreme Lord. Renounce attachment to the fruits. Be even-tempered in success and failure; for it is this evenness of temper that is meant by yoga.
>
> Work done with anxiety about results is far inferior to work done without such anxiety, in the calm of self-surrender. Seek

refuge in the knowledge of Brahman. They who work selfishly for results are miserable.

The passage not only indicts the American way of life and the consumerism it imposes—in which we work in order to gain material and social success, and are perpetually dissatisfied as a result—but it encapsulates the deeper meaning, if not the solution of the story, which is revealed at the end: the essence of any spiritual practice is to act without ego or expectation. The quotes continue through the Stoics Marcus Aurelius and Epictetus, the Zen Buddhists Kobayashi Issa and Mumon Ekai, the French Jesuit priest Jean Pierre de Caussade, and Salinger's beloved Sri Ramakrishna. There are also quotes from Ring Larder, Tolstoy, and two from Kafka. Those are all we get, but we're told Zooey could have kept reading the same column for five minutes without having to bend his knees.

Being in his brothers' room among these sages gives Zooey an idea. Using the room's telephone, a separate line, he calls the Glass home's main line and pretends he's Buddy. Covering the phone with a handkerchief to muffle his voice, he fools Bessie, who hurriedly gets Franny on the line. For a while, he fools his sister, too. (For plausibility's sake, let's keep in mind he's an actor.) She tells "Buddy" about the abuse she's been taking from Zooey: "It's like being in a *lun*atic asylum and having another patient all dressed up as a *doc*tor come over to you and start taking your pulse or something . . . it's just awful." But then Zooey lets slip a little too flamboyant "verbal stunt" for Buddy to pull off, and Franny realizes who she's really talking to.

But she doesn't hang up. She tells Zooey she's exhausted, but if he called with something special to say, she's not going to hang up on him. He hesitates. Then he meekly says he called to tell her to go on with her Jesus Prayer. He never wanted to stop her from saying it, and admits he had no business talking like he'd been—like an authority, or a seer. This gets Franny's attention; she straightens her posture. But, he reminds her, when she felt the urge to say the prayer, "the *call*," she didn't "search the four corners of the world for a master." She came home. And because she came home, she's "entitled to the low-grade spiritual counsel" she's gotten there, because that's all her family is able to give. He's admitting he *is* a patient in a lunatic asylum playing doctor to another patient. He is the blind leading the blind. But he's doing his best.

He still has a point to make, however. If it's the religious life Franny wants, then she should open her eyes, because she's "missing out on every single goddam religious action that's going on around the house." Bessie's been bringing her chicken soup, right? Well, how is Franny going "to recognize a legitimate holy man" when she "doesn't even know a cup of consecrated chicken soup" when it's under her nose? Zooey is basically asking, *What's holier than a mother's love, you dummy?* Let's not separate the spiritual from the mundane. It's this duality that's the problem with her approach, the mistake with her thinking. She doesn't like college because of the egos of her professor and classmates, because they're looking for knowledge and not wisdom. She doesn't want to act because of "the stupidity of audiences," because of "the unskilled laughter coming from the fifth row." Well, Zooey says, that's none of her business. "An artist's only concern is to shoot for some kind of perfection, and on his own terms, not anyone else's." That is, *work without the desire for the fruits of your work.* If they had a "freakish education," then at least they need to use it. Franny can say the Jesus Prayer "from now till doomsday," but if she doesn't understand that "the only thing that counts in the religious life is detachment," she'll "never move an inch." This is the key to the spiritual path: "Detachment, buddy, and only detachment. Desirelessness. 'Cessation from all hankerings.'" In other words, don't get yourself so worked up.

In one incarnation or another, he says, she must have had a hankering to be an actress, and be a good one at that. She can't just walk out on the results of her own hankerings. "Cause and effect, buddy, cause and effect." At this point, "the only re*li*gious thing" Franny can do is act. Zooey tells her, "Act for God, if you want to—be God's actress." (Acting for God seems to be another idea Salinger got from Paramahansa Yogananda, who taught that the entire universe is God's cosmic motion picture, a divine play, and that human beings are actors who change roles with each incarnation—we suffer only when we cling too closely to a specific role.)

He then brings up something Seymour once said to him, when Zooey didn't want to shine his shoes before going on *It's a Wise Child.* Seymour told him to shine his shoes "for the Fat Lady." This gets Franny really excited—she's standing now—because Seymour once told her "to be funny for the Fat Lady." Franny and Zooey each pictured a different Fat Lady in their minds, but the motivation worked. And now Zooey brings it all back around. "Don't you know who the Fat Lady is?" he asks. There isn't anyone out there who isn't Seymour's Fat Lady. This includes her professors and classmates and Lane and the predictable Ivy League guys and Vassar types. The Fat Lady, Zooey says, "is Christ Himself." Jesus is everyone, and everyone is Jesus. The presence of God is in us all. And so treat everyone as you would treat God.

Overwhelmed with joy, Franny holds the phone with both hands. Then Zooey abruptly says he can't talk anymore and hangs up. But now his mission has been successful. He's saved his sister. For several minutes, Franny listens to the "extraordinarily beautiful" sound of the dial tone, smiles for several minutes more, and then falls into a "deep, dreamless sleep."

A deep, dreamless sleep is Salinger's way of saying Franny, too, has achieved some sort of illumination, albeit in a more relatable way than Larry Durrell and Siddhartha. Because for an American in the twentieth century—or twenty-first, for that matter—there's no getting away with separating the religious from the everyday. That's only for the naïve. This isn't nineteenth-century Russia. We can't just go off and be a pilgrim. And we're not in Asia. We can't become a begging monk. Our culture has no place for the samana. There are no wandering seekers here. And if there are, we see them as just another bum. So get real. Take a yoga class, but don't try to *be* a yogi. Meditate every day, but not *all* day. Say your prayers, but don't try to pray without ceasing. That'll just make you crazy.

In the Protestant West, the wholly spiritual life is not readily available—unless one wants to hide themselves away in a monastery, and then one's dismissed as a fanatic. So the only way to follow a spiritual path and not be a fanatic—or a hypocrite, or pious, or righteous, or negative, or judgmental—is to find the middle path. Practice seriously, but practice playfully. See the spiritual in the mundane. Make every act a holy act. Accept that people are on different levels of spiritual progression, and that most people are unaware they should be progressing spiritually at all. So have compassion instead of judgment. Have sympathy instead of negativity. Forgive instead of taking offense, and never hold a grudge. Be sure your ego is steadily deflating, not inflating. Be kind instead of being right. Know that though enlightenment is well out of reach, it's quite possible to be a wise person. And most importantly, be even-tempered through life's ups and downs, for this evenness of temper, this cultivation of equanimity, is itself the core of the spiritual path.

4

The Dharma Bums

IN ANTHONY CURTIS'S INTRODUCTION to Somerset Maugham's *The Razor's Edge*, Larry Darrell is described as "the forerunner of a kind of hero that proliferated in postwar fiction: the dharma bum." And in the beginning of "Seymour: An Introduction," J. D. Salinger (as Buddy) directly addresses the reader, offering a bouquet of parentheses in advance warning of his digressions, before he and his reader "join the others." Who are these others? Along with "the middle-aged hot-rodders who insist on zooming us to the moon" and "all the lofty experts who know so well what we should or shouldn't do with our poor little sex organs," these others include "all the bearded, proud, unlettered young men and unskilled guitarists and Zen-killers." Zen-killers? Who are Zen-killers? They are "the Beat and the Sloppy and the Petulant." The Zen-killers, Buddy declares, are "the Dharma Bums."

Salinger wrote "Seymour" in 1959, a year after Jack Kerouac published *The Dharma Bums*. It was a clear reference, and a disdainful one at that. Salinger didn't approve of Kerouac's vision of Buddhism and the spiritual life, much less his philosophy of "spontaneous writing"—that is, writing without revision, which is as far from Salinger's word-squeezing as you can get. And though the quality of Kerouac's writing is inferior to Salinger's, Kerouac's influence has been much greater. Salinger's work never started a movement, and he was mostly ignored by the time the hippie generation came around. On the other hand, there might not have been a hippie generation if it weren't for Kerouac.

His two most popular books—*On the Road* and *The Dharma Bums*—showed people they could live a completely different way of life: a bohemian existence at odds with postwar American consumerism. Both books are about freedom. Both depict a life free from thirty-year mortgages, nine-to-five jobs, conventional relationships, and family responsibilities. They present the liberating idea that you could do whatever you want with your life—what you want to do, not just what you were supposed to do. For many readers, this idea was profound.

Yet despite their similarities, the books are quite different. Stylistically, *On the Road* is far superior. When reading it out loud, the prose sounds like poetry. It has the spontaneous shifting rhythms of jazz, with the words tumbling forth like a roller coaster, rising and falling in a mesmerizing flow. Some passages are truly ecstatic, in the transcendent sense. But for the most part, the language of *The Dharma Bums* is flat, perhaps too spontaneous, perhaps even too contrived. Either way, it doesn't have that magic.

Yet for the purpose of influence, this doesn't matter. Just as *On the Road* set countless young people off to a freewheeling life of hitchhiking, train hopping, and overall dropping out, *The Dharma Bums* inspired many to become the sort of wandering religious pilgrims unaccepted in the West. More importantly, it brought Buddhism to the mainstream, whereas it was previously the obscure interest of scholars and beatniks. (For instance, around a year after the book was published, a group of young men wearing matching jackets with the words "DHARMA BUMS" written across the back showed up at Kerouac's house in Northport, Long Island.) Essentially a book of Buddhist propaganda, *The Dharma Bums* arguably turned more people on to the religion than any other work of American fiction.

But Kerouac is all energy and attitude, not depth, and many of the misconceptions we have about Buddhism today are due to his flawed presentation. His friend Locke McCorkle, who studied with the philosopher Alan Watts at the American Academy of Asian Studies and served as the model for *Dharma Bums* character Sean Monahan, later said that though Kerouac's "intuitions were right," he "made up his Buddhism" and "didn't know a lot about it, didn't have a lot of training in it." Watts himself said Kerouac had "Zen flesh but no Zen bones." Poet, essayist, and translator Kenneth Rexroth said "Kerouac's Buddha is a dime-store incense burner." (Both Watts and Rexroth have characters based on them in *The Dharma Bums*.) During a meeting with D. T. Suzuki, Kerouac felt the famous Zen teacher and translator was looking at him as if he were "a monstrous imposter."

Perhaps this harsh dismissal of his work by leading Buddhist scholars is why Kerouac eventually gave up on Buddhism, turning back to Catholicism, and alcoholism, before dying of a cirrhosis-caused hemorrhage at age forty-seven, in 1969. We see the seeds of this fate beginning to sprout in *The Dharma Bums*. About a third of the way through the book, Kerouac's alter ego mentions his "recent years of drinking and disappointment." What he's referring to is his stalled literary career.

After getting accepted to Columbia on a football scholarship, Kerouac dropped out in 1942. He worked for the Merchant Marines during the Second World War, never seeing combat. (Another bit that would arouse Salinger's disdain.) All the while and afterward, Kerouac lived the bohemian life, tracing and retracing a big triangle between New York, San Francisco, and Mexico City. He was writing constantly, and in 1950 "John Kerouac" published his first book, *The Town and the City*. It's a traditional type of novel, longer than anything else he wrote, and based on his experiences growing up in Lowell, Massachusetts, and his transition to New York City, where he met a circle of eccentric friends he'd later call the Beat Generation. At twenty-eight, Kerouac thought he'd made it.

Then came the disappointment. The novel didn't sell. Worse, no house would publish his second novel. Halfway to the jazz-inspired epiphany of "writing spontaneously," Kerouac typed this book on one 120-foot-long scroll over the course of twenty days, high on Benzedrine. A single 120,000 word paragraph, the novel was about his experiences during 1947–50, taking road trips with Denver-raised delinquent Neal Cassady, the model for the book's antihero, Dean Moriarty. Kerouac called it *On the Road*. He took the scroll to Roger Giroux, his editor at Harcourt Brace who had bought *The Town and the City*. Giroux rejected it immediately.

For six years, Kerouac continued to receive rejections. No one would touch it, particularly because of the book's depictions of drug use and sexual promiscuity. He became disappointed. But he continued to write. After finishing *On the Road* in 1951, Kerouac wrote *The Subterraneans, Doctor Sax, Maggie Cassidy, Visions of Cody, Visions of Gerard*, and *Tristessa*, all of which would remain unpublished for years. He also married and divorced, twice. In the second marriage, he fathered a daughter he refused to recognize as his own, mainly for fear of having to make child support payments. So there was failure in literature, failure in love, and moral failure. During these years, he developed his drinking habit—a habit that often accompanies disappointment—but he also became interested in Buddhism.

In 1954, while staying with Neal and Carolyn Cassady at their home in Los Gatos, California, Kerouac found Dwight Goddard's *A Buddhist Bible* in the San Jose Public Library. Originally published in 1932, this nearly seven-hundred-page book gave Kerouac a foundational knowledge of Buddhist concepts—from *dharma* to *karma* to *maya* to the cyclical idea of the universe. He dove into it. Friends recall him carrying the book around wherever he went. He didn't have a guide or teacher, but he felt he could intuitively digest the ideas of Buddhism on his own. Over the following two years, he wrote a sprawling book of Buddhist notes called *Some of the Dharma*, which began as letters aiming to teach Allen Ginsburg about Buddhism. Kerouac also wrote a biography of the historical Gotama Buddha, titled *Wake Up: A Life of the Buddha*. (Both books were published posthumously.) These works show his serious interest in Buddhism, an interest that quickly overwhelmed everything else in his life.

For instance, in January 1955 Kerouac wrote his new agent, Stanley Colbert at Sterling Lord, saying, "I think the time has come for me to pull my manuscripts back and forget publishing." He wanted all his projects returned, including *On the Road*, which he was then pitching as "The Beat Generation." He claimed that being unable to publish "worked out fine," because from then on, all his writing was "going to have a basis of Buddhist Teaching free of all worldly and literary motives." He said he could only have published "Beat G." as a "Pre-enlightenment work." *Some of the Dharma* grew to over two hundred pages, and spreading the Buddhist Word became Kerouac's main focus. In a letter to his sister, he wrote: "I intend to be the greatest writer in the world and then in the name of Buddha I shall convert thousands, maybe millions." Among editors, there was little interest in his Buddhist writings. But his passion only deepened after becoming friends with Gary Snyder, the poet, scholar, and translator studying Asian culture and languages as a grad student at Berkeley, where Kerouac lived with Ginsberg in late 1955. Snyder was able to read Chinese and Japanese Buddhist texts in their original languages, and Kerouac loved learning from him, especially about Buddhist lore. Snyder quickly replaced Neal Cassady as Kerouac's new hero. Following Snyder's advice, Kerouac became a fire lookout on Desolation Peak in the Cascades—the only book he brought with him was the *Diamond Sutra*, one of the most influential Mahayana Buddhist texts.

Everything changed in late 1956, after he came down from the mountains. With the help of editor and critic Malcolm Cowley, Kerouac was able to publish excerpts of "The Beat Generation" in the literary magazines *New World Writing* and *The Paris Review*. With this push—and the publicity that followed Ginsburg's success with his poem "Howl," which was dedicated to "Jack Kerouac, new Buddha of American prose"—the time for Kerouac became ripe. Finally, after many revisions to the original manuscript, Viking accepted *On the Road*, publishing it in the fall of 1957. Within a few weeks, *The New York Times* hailed Kerouac as the voice of a new generation. He became famous overnight. He was on the radio. He was on television. He was in the newspaper. He made appearances at campuses. And he quickly became uncomfortable with fame.

By then, he was thirty-five. His twenty-one-year-old girlfriend at the time, Joyce Glassman, recalls this tumultuous period of Kerouac's sudden celebrity status, saying, "I felt this kind of anger in people. They were fascinated by him. They also thought he was very threatening. They hated him. All the men wanted to fight him. All the women wanted to fuck him, not in a nice way, but in an aggressive way." Interviewers were hostile, as if Kerouac were the despicable Dean Moriarty himself. When Kerouac went out at night in Greenwich Village, he'd get drunk and obnoxious. Men would recognize him and try to beat him up. Once, he was beaten quite badly, his head smashed against a curb. He needed to get away. And despite his fame, Viking didn't want any of his unpublished novels. They wanted him to write another book like *On the Road*. So Kerouac retreated from the public eye to his sister's house in Orlando, Florida, where he wrote *The Dharma Bums* in less than two weeks.

In this time of turmoil—before his drinking habit turned to outright alcoholism, and after his years of wandering and creative fury—he wrote about what was perhaps the happiest time in his life. *The Dharma Bums* chronicles his adventures with Gary Snyder, Ginsburg, and other Bay Area poets on the West Coast during 1955 and 1956—the time immediately before *On the Road* was published. As his friend John Clellon Holmes said, Kerouac's fame "so discombobulated him that for the rest of his life he never, never got his needle back on true north."

Indeed, by the time *The Dharma Bums* was published, in 1958, Snyder was living in Japan with fellow Beat and soon-to-be-Zen monk Philip Whalen, who invited Kerouac to join them. Kerouac wrote back that he'd be too embarrassed for them to see him, admitting, "I've become so decadent and drunk and don't give a shit. I'm not a Buddhist anymore." But by then it was too late. *The Dharma Bums* was already on the way to converting thousands, maybe millions of readers—or at least leading them to the Buddha's path, as it did to me.

The Dharma Bums begins in Los Angeles, California. It's late September 1955, three days after narrator Ray Smith came up from Mexico City. Like all of Kerouac's novels, the book is a *roman á clef*, or a "true story novel," as he called them, with Ray Smith being Kerouac's alter ego.

In real life, Kerouac spent late summer of 1955 in Mexico City, staying in William Burroughs's apartment—Burroughs was then in Tangier, Morocco, writing what would become *Naked Lunch*. Kerouac had just received an advance from Viking after they accepted *On the Road*, and a $200 grant from the Academy of Arts and Letters to tide him over until royalties would come in. (This wouldn't be for another two years, as the revision process was slow.) In Mexico, he wrote his most celebrated poetry collection, *Mexico City Blues,* which features Kerouac's first foray into blending Buddhist ideas into his writing. And in the opening pages of *The Dharma Bums,* it immediately becomes clear that Kerouac has developed a new obsession since the days of *On the Road.*

In Los Angeles, Ray Smith hops a northbound freight train and is soon joined by a hobo. Ray shares some wine, bread, and cheese with the hobo, and then—not two pages in—mentions "a line in the Diamond Sutra that says, 'Practice charity without holding in mind any conceptions about charity, for charity after all is just a word.'" In the next sentence, Ray explains to the reader: "I was very devout in those days and was practicing my religious devotions almost to perfection." But in a culture without a system of Buddhist monasteries, what can he mean by devout? How can he have been perfectly practicing religious devotion? Has he been ordained as a monk? Has he taken vows to observe Buddhist precepts? If not, what would being devout mean? He doesn't say. Because there was no path for devout Buddhists in postwar America. If he were in Asia, he could simply join a monastery, observe the precepts, fulfill the duties of a monastic life, and meditate diligently. There would be guidance from experienced teachers, support from fellow members of the *sangha,* and a disciplined daily schedule. But at the time, there were no such pathways in the West, no structure that supported a devout practice. So even if he wanted to be devout and practice perfectly, it was basically impossible to do so. He'd essentially be on his own, and could easily go astray. And once astray, he'd get lost. This is exactly what happened.

Ray admits, "I've become a little hypocritical about my lip-service and a little tired and cynical." But for a while, he really "believed in the reality of charity and kindness and humanity and zeal and neutral tranquility and wisdom and ecstasy." In so many words, this was his Buddhism. He also believed he was "an oldtime bhikku in modern clothes wandering the world." The Pali word *bhikkhu* literally means "beggar," as in a mendicant, but has traditionally been translated as "monk." Today, *bhikkhu* is often translated more secularly as "meditator" or "practitioner." The use of the (misspelled) word bhikkhu and the mention of the *Diamond Sutra* announce that *The Dharma Bums* is different than *On the Road.* It alerts the reader that Ray Smith is not merely another bohemian beatnik. Like the narrator of *The Way of a Pilgrim,* or the *samanas* in *Siddhartha,* Ray considers himself to be "a religious wanderer." To clarify, Ray explains he was wandering with the purpose of turning "the wheel of the True Meaning, or Dharma, [to] gain merit" for himself "as a future Buddha (Awakener)." At this point, he hadn't yet met Japhy Ryder—the book's hero, based on Gary Snyder—nor heard anything about "Dharma Bums." In hindsight, however, he sees himself as "a perfect Dharma Bum."

Bhikkhu. Sutra. Dharma. Few of Kerouac's readers would be familiar with these terms in 1958, and with the barrage of them being thrown, the meaning seems to matter less than the impression. Something different, something new is happening here—that's what is important. Kerouac is on to something. And he wants to share it. He provides his own definitions of the words Buddha (Awakener) and Dharma (True Meaning) so that the uninitiated can understand.

In the second chapter, Ray Smith arrives in San Francisco and immediately meets Japhy Ryder. Ray relates that Japhy was "brought up in a log cabin deep in the woods" of eastern Oregon, and in addition to being "a woods boy, an axman, farmer, interested in animals and Indian lore," he also "got interested in oldfashioned I.W.W. anarchism." After studying anthropology at Reed College, Ryder "learned Chinese and Japanese and became an Oriental scholar and discovered the greatest Dharma Bums of them all, the Zen Lunatics of China and Japan."

These "Zen Lunatics" are Kerouac's ideal religious figures. Foremost is the Chinese poet Han Shan, to whom *The Dharma Bums* is dedicated. When he first meets Ray, Japhy is translating Han Shan's series of poems "Cold Mountain." Japhy describes Han Shan as "a Chinese scholar who got sick of the big city and the world and took off to hide in the mountains." Han Shan, whose name literally means "cold mountain," lived in the eighth century during the Tang dynasty and inscribed his poems on rocks in the mountains. A popular subject of Japanese painting, he's known as a central figure within Zen history and legend. Living in caves near a Buddhist monastery, Japhy tells Ray, "Han Shan would come down from Cold Mountain in his bark clothing and come into the warm kitchen and wait for food, but none of the monks would ever feed him because he didn't want to join the order and answer the meditation bell three times a day." Han Shan is Japhy's hero because he "was a man of solitude who could take off by himself and live purely and true to himself." This choice of hero is crucial to understand Kerouac's misunderstanding of the religion he's espousing; Han Shan was a poet influenced by Buddhism, not necessarily a Buddhist practitioner, nor a disciplined meditator.

Ray described Japhy as "strangely Oriental-looking." With his little goatee and slanted green eyes, Japhy "did not look Bohemian at all." Ray defines a bohemian as "a hanger-onner around the arts," but they're all bohemian beatniks; on the night they meet, they go to a poetry reading at Gallery Six in North Beach, the reading that in real life launched the San

Francisco Poetry Renaissance. First they watch Alvah Goldbrook (that is, Allen Ginsberg) read the revolutionary poem "Wail" (that is, "Howl"), with everyone yelling "Go! Go! Go! (like a jam session)." Following Alvah, Japhy reads a few poems, and Ray liked "something earnest and strong and humanely hopeful" about him. Unlike Japhy, other poets "were either too dainty in their aestheticism, or too hysterically cynical to hope for anything, or too abstract and indoorsy, or too political." After the reading, Ray wants to become closer with Japhy.

In Berkeley, Ray lives in a cottage with Alvah Goldbrook. Japhy lives nearby in a shack without furniture. The only items in the shack are straw mats and orange crates filled with "beautiful scholarly books, some of them in Oriental languages, all the great sutras, comments on sutras, the complete works of D. T. Suzuki and a fine quadruple-volume edition of Japanese haikus." When Ray first visits the shack, Japhy makes them a pot of green tea and asks, "Did you ever read the Book of Tea?" Japhy calls the book "a scholarly treatise on how to make tea utilizing all the knowledge of two thousand years of tea-brewing."

The Book of Tea is another book I received as a birthday present around the time I first read *Siddhartha, Franny and Zooey*, and *The Dharma Bums*. It was written in English by the Japanese scholar Okakura Kakuzo and first published in 1906, when Kakuzo was curator of Oriental art at the Boston Museum. (The book was reissued in 1956, the very year that *The Dharma Bums* takes place, so it makes sense that Gary Snyder would have it.) In *The Book of Tea*, Kakuzo presents Japanese "Teaism" as an aesthetic concept unifying art and life. But Kakuzo also wrote his delightful book as a protest against the mutual misunderstandings that separated East and West, the prejudices that went both ways. Kakuzo playfully writes that it's okay if Westerners pictured Asians "as living on the perfume of the lotus, if not on mice and cockroaches," because "our writers in the past—the wise men who knew—informed us that you had bushy tails somewhere hidden in your garments, and often dined off the fricassée of new born babes." Even worse, Kakuzo says, "we used to think you were the most impracticable people on earth, for you were said to preach what you never practiced." Chapters explain the history of tea drinking, and tea's relation to Taoism and what Kakuzo refers to as "Zennism," which is appropriate because Zen is really its own thing. But overall, Kakuzo attempts to dispel the false values shared by both cultures. For instance, the Westerner "was wont to regard Japan as barbarous while she indulged in the gentle arts of peace: he calls her civilized since she began to commit wholesale slaughter on Manchurian battlefields." Rather than focus on the Code of the Samurai and its Art of Death, Kakuzo says it would do better for us to pay attention to Japan's Tea Cult. After all, in the worship of Bacchus, we have sacrificed too freely; and we have even transfigured the gory image of Mars. Why not consecrate ourselves to the queen of Camelias, and revel in the warm stream of sympathy that flows from her altar? In the liquid amber within the ivory-porcelain, the initiated may touch the sweet reticence of Confucius, the piquancy of Laotse, and ethereal aroma of Sakyamuni himself.

For Kakuzo, Teaism is as veritable an Eastern religion as Confucianism, Taoism, and Buddhism.

After mentioning *The Book of Tea*, Japhy tells Ray about Han Shan. Even though Han Shan was a vegetarian, Japhy "hasn't got on that kick from figuring maybe in this modern world to be a vegetarian is to split hairs a little since all sentient beings eat what they can." Japhy's reasoning actually isn't far off from the Buddha's, and the Buddha was certainly the most assiduous of hairsplitters. Most people assume that Buddhists are necessarily vegetarians, but that's not actually the case. The first moral precept of Buddhism is to abstain from taking life. This is because the act of taking life requires an unwholesome mental volition that creates unwholesome karma. In the Jivaka Sutta, the Buddha clarifies the rule about eating meat: As long as it is not seen, heard, or suspected that a living being has been slaughtered for oneself, it does not create unwholesome karma to eat it. In other words, a Buddhist cannot do the actual killing, and cannot request someone else do the killing on their behalf. This means that if a monk is offered meat during his begging rounds, and the animal was not killed specifically for the monk, he should humbly accept what was given, and eat what was offered. He is a beggar, after all. And as for Japhy's point about "this modern world," the Buddha's specification means that buying meat in a grocery store or ordering meat in a restaurant is actually not breaking the first precept—as long as one doesn't order a live lobster.

Despite the age difference of ten years, Ray and Japhy get along swimmingly. Already familiar with Buddhist terminology, Japhy claims Ray is "a great Bodhisattva, meaning 'great wise being' or 'great wise angel.'" Ray says he and Japhy have "the same favorite Buddhist saint, too: Avalokitesvara." Avalokitesvara is first mentioned in the Mahayana text the *Lotus Sutra*, and is the quintessential bodhisattva who vowed never to rest until he freed all sentient beings from *samsara*. This is kind of like saying Francis of Assisi is my favorite saint. A bit obvious.

In a section revealing deep confusion, Ray then says Japhy knows "all the details of Tibetan, Chinese, Mahayana, Hinayana, Japanese and even Burmese Buddhism." Ray himself "doesn't give a goddamn about the mythology and all the names and national flavors of Buddhism." He's "just interested in the first of Sakyamuni's four noble truths, *All life is suffering*." Nonsensically, Ray tells Japhy, "I'm not a Zen Buddhist, I'm a serious Buddhist, I'm an oldfashioned dreamy Hinayana coward of later Mahayanism." His qualm with Zen, he says, is that "Zen Buddhism didn't concentrate on kindness so much as on confusing the intellect to make it perceive the illusion of all sources of things." That is to say, "it's *mean*." Ray doesn't appreciate "all those Zen Masters throwing young kids in the mud because they can't answer their silly word questions." But he's undoubtedly influenced by Buddhist mythology. For instance, he accepts the third noble truth, *The suppression of suffering can be achieved*, only after he "digested the Lankavatara Scripture." This is a Mahayana sutra that takes place on the mythical island-kingdom of the legendary Hindu demon king Ravana, to whom the Buddha taught that all objects in the world are simply manifestations of the mind. It's very important to the Chan and Zen traditions, in that it further develops the concept of "Buddha-nature" that was introduced in the *Lotus Sutra*.

Avalokitesvara. Sakyamuni. Mahayanism. Lankavatara. Like Zooey's rants, this is a lot. But here it's merely a bunch of name-dropping, and nothing is explained. Kerouac moves too quickly for explanation, or even discussion. In *Franny and Zooey*, Franny explains the Jesus Prayer to Lane, Zooey explains the prayer to Bessie, and Zooey explains the proper way of approaching the spiritual life to Franny. In having his characters do all that explaining to each other, Salinger explains a lot to his readers. But unlike Salinger, Kerouac isn't interested in the fine-tuning of religious thinking, or the proper approach to a spiritual practice. He just wants to *go go go*.

But what's this word *bodhisattva*? And what are these "sutras" he keeps mentioning? I think now's the time to clarify Kerouac's confusion, and explain the difference between Theravada and Mahayana Buddhism.

The arising of the Mahayana is the fundamental unanswerable question that plagues the field of Buddhist studies—no one knows exactly how, where, and when the Mahayana arose. But according to Buddhist scholar Paul Williams, the separation between Theravada and Mahayana Buddhism is not due to a schism. That is, it cannot be compared to the separation between the Eastern Orthodox Church and the Roman Catholic Church during the Byzantine era, or the separation of Catholicism and Protestantism during the Reformation. In both of those cases, there was a doctrinal dispute that resulted in a schism. Nothing of the sort happened within Buddhism. That is, Theravada and Mahayana are not sects, and they are not separate schools, like the distinct Rinzai and Soto schools within Zen Buddhism. So what happened? What's the difference?

As Williams presents it, there are two main differences. The first is not in doctrine but in motivation. In vision. In goal. Since the time of Gotama the Buddha, the goal of a Buddhist was to become an *arahant*, a fully liberated being. However, centuries after the Buddha's death, some people thought there should be a different goal. Their goal was not to simply become an *arahant*, but to attain full Buddhahood, and become a *samasambuddha*. That is, to become one of the future buddhas. As a full buddha, they could alleviate the suffering of all sentient beings. From a certain logic, this goal seemed nobler, higher, and greater than the liberation from one's own personal suffering. Accordingly, as *maha* means "great," the goal of achieving full Buddhahood was called *Mahayana*, the Great Vehicle. The Greater Path. In sutras that promoted this idea, the goal of merely becoming an *arahant* was denigrated with the term "Hinayana," or the Lesser Vehicle. The Inferior Path. Otherwise, the term Hinayana did not exist, and really has no substance other than a polemic, a pejorative.

The term Mahayana was used to indicate the new motivation. Not to become an *arahant*, but a buddha. And so rather than work for one's own liberation, a Mahayana Buddhist works to become a *bodhisattva*. During his life, the Buddha used the term "bodhisatta" to refer to himself before he became liberated, not only as a young man but also his previous incarnations. By "bodhisatta," he meant someone who is bound to become a buddha. In the words of monk and scholar Bhikkhu Bodhi,

> According to common Buddhist tradition, a bodhisatta is one who undertakes a long course of spiritual development consciously motivated by the aspiration to attain future Buddhahood. Inspired and sustained by great compassion for living beings mired in suffering of birth and death, a bodhisatta fulfills, over many eons of cosmic time, the difficult course needed to fully master the requisites for supreme enlightenment. When all these requisites are complete, he attains Buddhahood in order to establish the Dhamma in the world. A Buddha discovers the long-lost path to liberation, the "ancient path" traveled by the Buddhas of the past that culminates in the boundless freedom of nibbana. Having found the path and traveled it to its end, he then teaches it in all its fullness to humanity so that many others can enter the way to final liberation.

Gotama the Buddha, however, did not teach "the bodhisattva path." This is the idea that out of compassion, a practitioner purposely delays their own enlightenment, in order to remain in samsara and help others progress toward liberation. In fact, the Buddha taught quite the opposite; as he says in the *Dhammapada*:

> One should not neglect one's goal
> for the goal of another, even if great.
> Knowing well his goal,
> Let him be a person who pursues
> The true goal.

The Mahayana sutras that promote the bodhisattva path suggest something quite different. And it is the existence of these sutras themselves that differentiate Theravada and Mahayana Buddhism. Because you can't have the Mahayana without writing. That is, Mahayana could only have come into existence after the Pali Canon was written down. In other words, the difference between the two forms of Buddhism is canonical, not necessarily doctrinal.

The difference is also not necessarily due to time period, because the Pali Canon includes texts written long after the Buddha died, and even after the time the Mahayana arose, such as the *Milindapanha*, or Questions of King Milinda, which was believed to have been written between 100 200 CE. Many people think the separation is due to a different monastic code of discipline, but even that's not true: interestingly, in the centuries after Mahayana arose, there were monasteries where Theravada and Mahayana monks lived and practiced side by side, often keeping the same code of discipline. They differentiated themselves only by the texts they considered scripture. Like the New Testament looks at the Hebrew Bible, the Mahayana sutras look at the Pali Canon—the latter is integral to the former, but was missing a few things and needed to be updated. (My teacher Charles Hallisey likes to say that the Theravada Buddhists "left class early.") Similarly, as Jewish people have no use for the New Testament, Theravadins could not care less about Mahayana texts. Mainly this is because of the revelatory nature of these texts, and this revelatory nature highlights the second difference between Theravada and Mahayana, which is, according to Paul Williams, the idea that the Buddha did not really die.

Three months after the Buddha's death at age eighty, there was the First Buddhist Council, where Ananda recited all of the Buddha's discourses, or *suttas*. After getting approval by the five hundred fully enlightened monks, these *suttas* were orally transmitted until committed to writing in Pali during the Fourth Buddhist Council, which was held in Sri Lanka during the first century BCE. Along with the *suttas*, there is the *Vinaya*, the code of discipline, and the *Abhidhamma*, or "higher teachings," which is a thoroughly detailed analysis of mind and matter—the *Abhidhamma* is very difficult to understand without expert experience in meditation, which is why it's often inaccurately referred to as metaphysics or philosophy; it's more of a manual than anything else. Together, these teachings constitute the Pali Canon, and is known as the *Tipitaka*, or "Three Baskets," as they were written on palm leaves and kept in baskets.

The Pali Canon is the oldest collection of Buddhist texts we have, and are the scripture of today's Theravada Buddhism. Usually, the word "Theravada" is translated as "doctrine of the elders," (*thera*: elder; *vada*: teaching), but a more thorough and less concise translation, according to Buddhist scholar Glenn Wallis, is "the exposition of the Buddha's doctrine based on the teachings of the firm seniors of the order." Contrary to general understanding, and what I previously thought, Theravada does not mean Early Buddhism, which is a separate category only recently established by the scholarship of the German-born scholar-monk Bhikkhu Analayo, and designates the first few centuries after the Buddha's death. The Theravada tradition as we know it was shaped by later commentators, mostly in Sri Lanka, such as the prolific fifth-century scholar Buddhaghosa, who is sometimes referred to as "Mr. Theravada." Theravada also includes the vast forms of spirit worship, dream interpretation, divination, and other local cultural practices found across the countries of Southeast Asia, many of which would not be considered "Buddhist" at all, and which the Buddha would not likely approve. As the Buddha says in the Tuvatka Sutta, in the Atthakavagga chapter of the Suttanipatta, which is one of the oldest Buddhist scriptures we have, dating back to at least the third century BCE, a bhikkhu "should not employ Atharva spells, or interpret dreams, signs, or constellations. My follower would not decipher animal cries, or practice healing or making women fertile."

The term Early Buddhism designates the time period spanning the Buddha's life and the few hundred years following his death. It includes not only the Pali but also Gandharan and Chinese scriptures, focusing on what's common between them. Early Buddhism is usually looked at from a historical perspective, meaning all supernatural and other nonscientifically perceived elements are dismissed, which explains its popularity in the modern West. But the standard view shared by both Theravada and Early Buddhism is that after the Buddha's death, he is beyond recall, beyond communication. He has ceased to exist, in any form, in any plane, in any realm. But in the Mahayana vision, the Buddha is not really dead. He's still around somewhere, and so there is the possibility of an ongoing revelation. That is, if he's still around, through meditation one could have visions of the Buddha, and one could even receive new teachings from the Buddha. New revelations.

The Mahayana sutras are part of this ongoing revelation. That is, they are "new" revelations given by the Buddha long after he died. And since they are "new" teachings, the *Diamond Sutra*, the *Lotus Sutra*, the *Heart Sutra*, and the *Lankavatara Sutra* were composed only after the Pali Canon was committed to writing, over five hundred years after Gotama the Buddha's death. To non-Mahayanists, they are thus considered apocryphal. In other words, the Mahayana sutras can be understood as profound works of fan fiction.

This may be getting too far into the weeds here, but the notion of previous buddhas visiting meditators is not restricted to the Mahayana world, and I'm particularly fascinated by the case of Ajahn Mun Bhuridatta, an austere Thai Buddhist monk who lived from 1870 to 1949, and is credited with establishing the modern Thai Forest Tradition—of all the Buddhist traditions, I find the Thai Forest to be the most right on, as it not only scrupulously observes the code of discipline, but it also does not try to change the Dhamma to fit into contemporary ideologies. Soon after becoming an arahant, Ajahn Mun claimed that a number of previous buddhas, accompanied by their arahant disciples, came to congratulate him. One night, a certain buddha would come with tens of thousands of his disciples, and the next night a different buddha would come with hundreds of thousands of his own disciples. Only the buddha would express appreciation, while the arahants remained silent. This is strikingly similar to what is described in chapter fifteen of the *Lotus Sutra*, the most popular Mahayana text (and by far the most bizarre text of all Buddhist scriptures).

But according to long-held Theravada beliefs, this situation is impossible. As noted, the claim is that once an arahant dies and achieves parinibbana, they are inaccessible. They are simply extinguished, and cannot be referred to as either existing or not-existing, as they are no longer a subject to refer to. They are not in any of the thirty-one planes of existence, and cannot visit anyone or anything. Therefore, knowing his experience would cause controversy, Mun only shared it with his closest disciples. One of these disciples was Ajahn Maha Boowa Nanasampanno, who reluctantly related this experience in his biography of Mun. When it was published in 1971, twenty years after Mun's death, this claim did indeed cause major controversy. In order to address this issue, Maha Boowa included an appendix with Mun's explanation.

According to Maha Boowa, Mun himself was perplexed by how these deceased buddhas and arahants—having attained nibbana without any remaining physical or mental components of personality—could appear to him in a bodily form. Reading his mind, one of the buddhas explained to him that previous buddhas and arahants who have died could in fact appear in conventional form if they wish to interact with living arahants. Later, when relating this experience to his disciples, Mun also explained that the Dhamma inscribed in the Pali Canon is analogous to the amount of water in a small jar, whereas the Dhamma that is not elucidated in scriptures is comparable to the amount of water contained in all the great oceans. As he was not formally schooled in the Pali Canon, Mun was able to experience what he called "living dhamma," realities that fell outside of what was contained in scripture. Finally, in an end note, Maha Boowa adds that we should "keep in mind the unconditioned nature of nibbana naturally implies that absolutely no conditions or limitations whatsoever can be attributed to nibbana. To believe that, having passed away, the Buddhas and Arahants are completely beyond any possibility of interacting with the world is to place conditions on the Unconditioned."

Even with this explanation, this account rocked the Theravada world, and Maha Boowa received heaps of criticism. In any case, it is delicious food for thought (I'm still trying to wrap my mind around it), as is much of Mun's life story; many of his disciples claim Mun could read their thoughts, and with such developed psychic abilities, Mun also claimed to regularly give teachings to terrestrial and celestial *devas* who visited him in the night, just as the Buddha had done. There are many more fascinating anecdotes from Mun's life that challenge our modern ideas of what is possible, but this detour has taken long enough, and it's time to get back to Kerouac.

Like *On the Road*, *The Dharma Bums* is perhaps most appealing for the way of life it offers. First of all, nobody in the novel has a real job. If they do, it's manual labor. Alvah Goldbrook, for example, a graduate of Columbia, works part-time as a busboy in a cafeteria. (Ginsburg moved to Berkeley with the intention of enrolling in a graduate program, but never did.) Members of the Glass family rebelled against conventional American society, but they remain within social boundaries. They're not dropouts. And they're solidly upper-middle class. Even Larry Darrell survives on a fixed income. Despite looking the part at times, he's no bum. But in *The Dharma Bums*, no one has much money, and no one is constrained by the requirements of a job or a family. The characters live with a minimum amount of responsibility. So what do they do?

Every morning, Ray Smith sits in a rocking chair and reads the *Diamond Sutra*. Then he meditates under a tree. He doesn't say how he meditates, what technique he uses, and that's most likely because he doesn't have one. Though *Siddhartha* first turned me East, and *Franny and Zooey* inspired me to study Buddhism, it was while reading *The Dharma Bums* that I first tried to meditate, sitting on that bank of a Swiss lake. And perhaps like Kerouac and his Ray Smith, I didn't know what I was doing. Close your eyes. Focus on your breathing. Quiet your mind. Yes, but then? It sounds like a plan, but it only gets you so far.

Japhy, too, meditates first thing in the morning before breakfast, and always meditates for a long time in the afternoon. But he's sometimes interrupted, either by friends or girls who want to play "yabyum." Ray doesn't know what yabyum is, and Japhy says he'll show him later. In Tibetan, *Yab-yum* literally means "father-mother." But in the Tantric tradition, *Yab-yum* is meditation through sexual intercourse. And in Buddhist *gompas* all over Himalaya, there are murals and statues of couples with legs wrapped around each other, the male's *linga* firmly implanted in the female's *yoni*.

Ray is first introduced to yabyum at a party, when a twenty-year-old girl called Princess strips and straddles Japhy, who's naked and sitting in full-lotus position. She has her arms around his neck, and they sit silently in intercourse. Ray watches in astonishment. Still in yabyum, Japhy explains, "This is what they do in the temples of Tibet. It's a holy ceremony, it's done just like this in front of chanting priests. People pray and recite Om Mani Padme Hum, which means Amen the Thunderbolt in the Dark Void. I'm the thunderbolt and Princess is the dark void, you see." Ray has feelings for Princess, and he's somewhat mortified by how easy she is. She says, "Oh this is lovely," and then tells Ray to "Come on and try it." He declines, with the lame excuse that he can't sit in full lotus, with both ankles over thighs. Ray then explains to the reader he'd gone through an entire year of celibacy based on the feeling "that lust was the direct cause of birth which was the direct cause of suffering and death." He'd now come to a point where he "regarded lust as offensive and even cruel." His motto was, "pretty girls make graves." This aversion to lust is why he initially refuses to participate in what he calls the "Zen Free Love Lunacy orgies." He also says he's afraid to take his clothes off "in front of more than one person, especially with men around."

All this is quite disingenuous. Sexual promiscuity was certainly a feature of the Beat Generation, as it is with any bohemian movement. Yet despite Kerouac's insistence on writing honestly, there is much he keeps hidden about the group's sexuality, particularly its homosexuality and bisexuality. It's now well known that Allen Ginsburg was gay. In his early years he sought psychiatric help to "cure" him of his sexual preference. After doctors informed him that he was as sane as his analysts, Ginsburg embraced his gayness more openly. But regarding his homosexuality, Ginsburg said Kerouac "completely blanked out on that aspect of me." It's not well known, however, that Ginsburg and Neal Cassady were not only close friends, but lovers. Kerouac ignores this aspect of their relationship in *On the Road*. It also may be a surprise to learn that Kerouac, too, had several homosexual encounters during this time period. This isn't well known because he omitted these experiences in his writings. For example, one night he slept with Gore Vidal in the Chelsea Hotel. In *The Subterraneans*, Vidal features as the character Arial Lavalina, a successful novelist. Once the novel was published in 1958, Vidal confronted Kerouac about why he didn't describe what truly happened during their night together in Chelsea. Kerouac claimed he forgot. When Vidal called his bluff, Kerouac said, "Well, maybe I wanted to forget." Vidal called out Kerouac's image of himself as writing "honest, straightforward, absolutely truthful tell-it-like-it-is literature." Vidal also suggests that Kerouac advanced his writing career by giving homosexual favors. This certainly sheds a different light on Kerouac's sexuality, but we always have to take what Vidal says with a grain of salt.

Despite his bohemian reputation and lifestyle, Kerouac retained conservative conventions. But if he said straight-out that free sex or homosexuality is a sin, from a Catholic perspective, his friends would have laughed at him. So in this orgy scene of *The Dharma Bums*, Ray Smith uses the idea of Buddhist celibacy to justify his prudery. Also, at the time Kerouac was suffering from his chronic phlebitis, as well as an increasing addiction to morphine, which kills sexual desire, so he also may have been covering up his impotence. Even so, after Alvah has a turn with Princess, Ray can't resist. He starts working on her arm, and moves on from there, "with everybody everywhere working on her." Soon, "all the peaceful celibacy of my Buddhism was going down the drain." Explaining away any hint of contradiction or hypocrisy, Japhy later says, "I distrust any kind of Buddhism or *any* kind of philosophy or social system that puts down sex." In other words, since he's not claiming to be a Buddhist, or a follower of any religion or philosophy, he can't be a hypocrite.

Everybody ends up naked, and afterward Ray and Princess take a bath. In the tub, Princess says she's "the old mother of earth." "I'm a Bodhisattva," she declares. Ray realizes she's repeating Japhy's words and that she wants to "be a big Buddhist." But as she's female, the only way she can express it is through promiscuous sex. He's uncomfortable with this, but he reasons that because the free sex has "its traditional roots in the yabyum ceremony of Tibetan Buddhism," everything was fine. That is to say, their sex parties are legitimized through the lens of Tantric Buddhism.

In a section that Gary Snyder later criticized for its sexism, Japhy explains that "the Bodhisattva women of Tibet and parts of ancient India were taken and used as holy concubines in temples and sometimes in ritual caves and would get to lay up a stock of merit." Perhaps not wanting to portray women as passive, he adds, "They meditated too. All of them, men and women, they'd meditate, fast, have balls like this, go back to eating, drinking, talking, hike around, live in viharas in the rainy season and outdoors in the dry." (A *vihara* is the Pali and Sanskrit word for a Buddhist monastery.) He says, "there was no question of what to do about sex which is what I always liked about Oriental religion."

In truth, these "Zen Free Love Lunacy orgies" don't have anything to do with Buddhism, but rather, in Japhy's words, the rejection of America's "suburban ideal and sex repression and general dreary newspaper gray censorship of all our real human values." This rallying against the "suburban ideal" is the heart of the Beat movement, and here there is crossover with Salinger. Echoing Franny's rant, Ray writes that "colleges are nothing but grooming schools for the middle-class non-identity," which we can see "in rows of well-to-do houses with lawns and television sets in each living room with everybody looking at the same thing and thinking the same thing at the same time." And like ten-year-old Teddy, Japhy thinks that being reborn in America is a spiritual disadvantage, saying:

> When I first discovered Buddhism and all I suddenly felt that I had lived in a previous lifetime innumerable ages ago and now because of faults and sins in that lifetime I was being degraded to a more grievous domain of existence and my karma was to be born in America where nobody has any fun or believes in anything, especially freedom.

Freedom. That's what it's really about. Drunken Buddhist sex parties are liberating. Such experiences free one from the "suburban ideal and sex repression and general dreary newspaper gray censorship of all our real human values." It's psychological freedom they're after. Breaking down mental boundaries. This is where Buddhism comes in, because no matter how financially or physically or socially or sexually free we are, we're still slaves to the habit patterns of the mind. But at this point, not all of the Beats are into the Buddha.

Allen Ginsburg's character Alvah is impressed with Japhy. He admits "Japhy Ryder is a great new hero of American culture," with "all the background he has, in Oriental scholarship, Pound, taking peyote and seeing visions, his mountainclimbing and bikkhuing." Peyote? It's not alluded to in *The Dharma Bums*, but Gary Snyder had studied Native American traditions, and presumably took peyote to experience their ritual use of the psychedelic cactus in facilitating spirit quests. A few years earlier, after accidently killing his wife Joan, William Burroughs went to the Amazon in his quest for *yagé*, or ayahuasca, the hallucinogenic vine that provides spiritual revelations, or access to spiritual dimensions. In the 1940s and 1950s, Kerouac and the Beats experimented with both LSD and psilocybin, or magic mushrooms, but these were not yet widely available. At this time, Ginsburg was very much into the drugs, but not into the Buddhism, especially the meditation part. (In 1961, about seven years after these events took place, Ginsberg met Gary Snyder in India, where they were supposed to study religion and meditation, but Ginsburg was basically super high all the time—he even tried to give LSD and mushrooms to the twenty-seven-year-old Dalai Lama!) Alvah asks, "Don't you think it's much more interesting just to be like Japhy and have girls and studies and good times and really be doing something, than all this silly sitting under trees?"

During the mid-fifties, Kerouac had been trying to teach Ginsburg about Buddhism, but without much success. Alvah is always bugged by Ray's "little lectures on Samadhi ecstasy," which is described as "the state you reach when you stop everything and stop your mind and you actually with your eyes closed see a kind of eternal multiswarm of electrical Power of some kind of ululating in place of just pitiful images and forms of objects, which are, after all, imaginary." Unimpressed, Alvah replies, "I'm just going to go on being Alvah Goldbrook and to hell with all this Buddhist bullshit." He gets more "of a satori out of Princess than out of words." Ray tries to explain that Alvah is being "fooled" by his senses. The external world doesn't really exist but only arises through contact with one of the sense doors. Kerouac doesn't use the term, but he's referring to *maya*, the notion that the world is an illusion. "Do you want to go on being fooled every damn minute of your life?" Ray asks. "Yes, that's all I want," Alvah says, expressing a tempting sentiment. Again echoing Teddy, who said people don't want to stop being born and dying all the time, Ray accuses Alvah of only wanting to "run out there and get laid and get beat up and get screwed up and get old and sick and banged around by samsara." He adds: "you fucking eternal meat of comeback you you'll deserve it too." Understandably, Alvah perceives a problem with Ray's approach to his spirituality, just like Zooey found fault with Franny's. "Your Buddhism has made you mean Ray," Alvah says, "and makes you even afraid to take your clothes off for a simple healthy orgy." Something is wrong if there's righteousness, if there's judgment, negativity. Not quite admitting agreement, Ray says he'll find out how Japhy is doing things differently on their upcoming trip to the mountains, and he goes outside to meditate.

Confusing the Buddha for a god, Ray prays "that God, or Tathagata" would give him enough time and enough sense and strength to be able to tell people what he knew. The word "Tathagata" is the epithet with which the Buddha referred to himself; literally meaning "thus gone," it's a difficult word to translate, but according to Bhikkhu Bodhi, "the word means both 'the one who has come thus' (*tatha agata*), that is, who has come into our midst in the same way that the Buddhas of the past have come; and 'the one who has gone thus' (*tatha gata*), that is, who has gone to ultimate peace, nibbana, in the same way that the Buddhas of the past have gone." Even if this is confusing, what's clear is that a tathagata is not God.

Ray thinks that if people knew what he knows, they wouldn't despair so much. But he despairs much in the book, and so something is wrong. And it has to do with what he knows.

Kerouac's confusion can be traced to the first page of *The Dharma Bums*, when he provides his own definitions of the words Buddha and Dharma. The word Buddha means "Awakened One," not "Awakener." And I've never seen Dharma translated as "True Meaning." The Pali word *dhamma*—or *dharma*, in Sanskrit—is one of the trickiest to define, as it has many meanings, each of which evolved over a long period of time. Depending on how it's being used, dhamma can mean: "teaching," "quality," "thought," "morality," "phenomenon," "universal law," "truth," or "religion." As Glenn Wallis points out in his translation of *The Dhammapada*, because of the word's multivalent nature, this sentence makes sense: "The dhamma is the dhamma because of the dhamma." For traditional Indian religion, that sentence would mean: "the religion is the truth because of the universal law." But for Buddhists, it would mean: "the teaching is the proper way of living because of the way things are." But dhamma also means "Way," like the Chinese word "Tao," and it is this meaning that Kerouac has in mind. His bums are following "the Way." And indeed, they are much more like Taoists than Buddhists. In fact, many people today have ideas about Buddhism that more resemble Taoism than the actual teaching of Gotama the Buddha. This confusion is widespread and mainly due to the works of fiction explored in this book. Even Hermann Hesse admitted, "The ending of *Siddhartha* is almost closer to Taoism than to Indian thought."

The basic difference can be understood in the idea of "going with the flow." People tend to think of Buddhists as going with the flow, when the Buddha specifically and explicitly taught his followers to go *against* the flow. *Appamadena sampadetha* were the Buddha's last words: "Strive diligently!" Damn up the stream of consciousness. Stop the ceaseless flow of the mind. Fight against instincts. Don't give in to passions. The point is to uproot passion. And in order to uproot passion, one must go against the inertia of thousands of years of evolutionary biology. Next to the will to live, the sex urge is the strongest desire we have. The Buddha said he knew of nothing that overpowers a man's mind so much as the form of a woman. He said he knew of nothing that overpowers a woman's mind so much as the form of a man. Ray is correct that sexual desire is what binds us to *samsara*, the rounds of life and rebirth. To strive for the liberation of nibbana is to swim against the current of desire. Nibbana is, after all, the extinguishing of desire. The unbinding. The cessation. The blowing out. Whether we want to admit it or not, Buddhism is a life-denying path.

It's perhaps because of this life-denying quality that, soon after attaining nibbana, the Buddha actually decided to keep his discovery to himself. He thought that if he were to teach the Dhamma, others wouldn't understand him, and he'd find their misunderstandings to be "wearying and troublesome." So he didn't want to teach. In stanzas that spontaneously came to him, he said:

> *Enough with teaching the Dhamma*
> *That even I found hard to reach;*
> *For it will never be perceived*
> *By those who live in lust and hate.*
>
> *Those dyed in lust, wrapped in darkness*
> *Will never discern this abstruse Dhamma,*
> *Which goes against the worldly stream,*
> *Subtle, deep, and difficult to see.*

Which goes against the worldly stream. So even the Buddha himself said that practicing his teaching is going against the flow.

He also once gave a discourse called The Stream, which further clarifies that practicing Buddhism is precisely *not* going with the flow, or not *following your bliss*, and also how difficult it is initially to live the Buddha's teachings:

> These four kinds of persons, O monks, are to be found in the world. What four? The person who goes with the stream; one who goes against the stream; one who stands firm; and one who has crossed over and gone to the far shore, a Brahmin who stands on dry land.
>
> Of what nature is the person going with the stream? It is one who indulges his sensual desires and commits wrong deeds.
>
> Of what nature is one who goes against the stream? It is one who does not indulge sensual desire and commit wrong deeds. He lives the holy life, though in painful struggle, with difficulty, sighing, and in tears.

> Of what nature is one who stands firm? It is one who, with the utter destruction of the five lower fetters, is due to be reborn spontaneously (in a celestial realm) and there attain final nibbana, without ever returning from that world.
>
> Of what nature is one who has crossed over and gone to the far shore, a Brahmin who stands on dry land? It is one who with the destruction of the taints, in this very life enters and dwells in the taintless liberation of mind, liberation by wisdom, having realized it for himself by direct knowledge.
>
> These, monks, are the four kinds of persons to be found in the world.

Clearly, the Buddha doesn't advise us to go with the flow. Taoism, on the other hand, is all about going with the flow. The Tao is "the Way," as in the way of nature, or the way of the universe. Unlike the Dhamma, which the Buddha clearly explained in meticulous detail, the Tao is indefinable and incomprehensible: "Looked at but not seen, listened to but not heard, grasped for but not held, formless, soundless, intangible: the Tao resists analysis and defies comprehension." The main Taoist scripture is the *Tao Te Ching*, the Book of the Way. It is ascribed to Lao Tzu, the elusive (and perhaps legendary) contemporary of Confucius. The *Tao Te Ching* is a wonderfully profound guide for a way of thinking, but does not offer specific meditation techniques or instructions on how to live. It teaches a paradoxical truth, seeing beyond the dualities that blind us.

A good way to summarize the teaching is in the concept of "nonaction," or *wei wu wei*, when action happens of its own accord: "Do by notdoing. Act with nonaction. Allow order to arise of itself." A Taoist aims to live in harmony with the Way. They surrender to the energy flows of life. Unresisting, a Taoist lets themselves be pulled this way and that. In surrender, they find stillness. They let go to the current. Taoists make decisions using intuition, not the intellect. In fact, they don't make decisions at all. The decisions have already been made. There is no formal doctrine or moral code in Taoism, but Chuang Tzu, the most famous Taoist teacher after Lao Tzu, offers some guidance:

> The Great Man in his actions will not harm others, but he makes no show of benevolence or charity. He will not move for the sake of profit, but he does not despise the porter at the gate. He will not wrangle for goods or wealth, but he makes no show of refusing or relinquishing them. He will not enlist the help of others in his work, but he makes no show of being self-supporting, and he does not despise the greedy and base. His actions differ from those of the mob, but he makes no show of uniqueness

or eccentricity. He is content to stay behind with the crowd, but he does not despise those who run forward to flatter and fawn. All the titles and stipends of the age are not enough to stir him to exertion; all its penalties and censures are not enough to make him feel shame. He knows that no line can be drawn between right and wrong, no border can be fixed between great and small.

A Buddhist will study hard and try to understand scripture, but for a Taoist there's nothing to understand. A Buddhist strives diligently to achieve nibbana, but for a Taoist there's nothing to achieve. "I confess that there is nothing to teach," says Lao Tzu in the other (possibly spurious) work ascribed to him, the *Hua Hu Ching*: "Simply be aware of the oneness of things." Rather than practice specific meditation techniques, a Taoist connects with a deeper, intuitive part of the mind, and lets things happen. One's body and mind are simply parts of the whole of nature, and so a Taoist will harmonize with the vibrations of their surroundings, and let nature take care of everything on its own. Also, in Taoism, there's no separation between the religious and the mundane; again from the *Hua Hu Ching*: "Chanting is no more holy than listening to the murmur of a stream, counting prayer beads no more sacred than simply breathing, religious robes no more spiritual than work clothes." A Taoist knows that peace comes with the cessation of wanting, but wanting should cease on its own, through surrender to the Tao. So if a Taoist feels like having sex, they have sex. If they feel like getting drunk, they get drunk. If they feel like sleeping, they sleep. If they feel like eating, they eat. Actions are spontaneous, for once one has come in harmony with the Tao, there is "non-action." *Wei wu wei.* Like water flowing downstream toward the sea, Taoists simply go with the flow.

At a certain point, I suppose, a Buddhist does go with a flow, yet only after much practice and development. Eventually, the resistance against the natural flow of desire creates a flow of its own, and the current reverses directions. When this happens, one is called a *sotapanna*, or a "stream-enterer." Becoming "one who has entered the stream" is achieved after a practitioner's first *nibbanic* experience, the first dip in the reality beyond mind and matter. After that, a *sotapanna* fully and experientially understands that there is no substantial personality—that is, they are free from ego delusion. (They also no longer have any doubt or skepticism of the Buddha's teaching, and are free from believing that rites, rituals, rules, or vows can bring liberation.) All a practitioner's effort toward skillful cultivation has created an inertia of current that now leads toward liberation, instead of further bondage. The Buddha explains that "when a noble disciple understands as they really are the origin and passing away, the gratification, the danger, and the escape in the case of these five aggregates subject to clinging [form, feeling, perception, mental fabrications, and consciousness], then that one is called a noble disciple who is a stream-enterer." A stream-enterer has reached a stage where they have purified all past karma that causes rebirth in a lower realm, and will supposedly achieve nibbana within seven births. In other words, they're in the flow of nibbana. Thus, after many years of practice, or even lifetimes of practice, there is a flow that a Buddhist goes with. But at the beginning, and for ordinary people, there's no going with the flow in Buddhism.

Whether Kerouac likes it or not, there's also a strict moral code in the Buddha's teachings. The Buddha emphasized that morality—*sila*—is the foundation of the practice. Without a strong base of moral conduct, there is no meditative concentration—*samadhi*. And without *samadhi*, there cannot be wisdom—*panna*, the experiential understanding of impermanence. Without the strong foundation of morality, the house falls down. Even the slightest breach in moral conduct severely damages the ability to progress on the path. For lay Buddhists, the moral code includes five precepts: abstaining from taking life, taking what is not given, sexual misconduct, speaking falsely, and the use of intoxicants.

This insistence on complete sobriety is difficult for Westerners to accept, much less practice. Because it means not having a glass of wine during dinner or even a toast of champagne at a wedding. Not a sip of beer or a puff of pot. Nothing at all. (Caffeine and nicotine are considered stimulants but not intoxicants; they are discouraged but not prohibited.) Understandably, Zen practitioners who like to drink a little wine prefer to translate this fifth precept as "abstain from the heedlessness caused by distilled and fermented beverages," rather than the usual and absolute "abstain from distilled and fermented beverages that cause heedlessness." Pali is ambiguous in terms of translating syntax, and I admit it can technically be translated either way.

The term "sexual misconduct" is also vague, and the Pali explains it as "not going to another man's wife," or sleeping with any woman under the protection of her father, brother, or another man—times were different then. Generally, today "sexual misconduct" means rape, all forms of non-consensual sex, infidelity, and even includes sex outside of marriage or a lifelong partnership.

On the Sabbath-like *Uposatha* days—the new and full moon of every month, and the two quarter moons in between—devout lay Buddhists also observe three more moral precepts: abstaining from eating after noon, sleeping in a high comfy bed, and from all forms of sensual entertainment, such as music, dancing, and singing. Basically, no partying. They usually spend the day at a local monastery or temple, meditating and chanting, and speaking only when necessary.

But of course, many who consider themselves Buddhists don't observe these moral rules. In Burma—the supposed Land of Dhamma—the national beer brands Mandalay and Myanmar are consumed ubiquitously. Japan is well known for its sake, and the Buddhist Himalayan regions are fond of their home-brewed millet alcohol. Yet if these alcohol-guzzlers were asked what religion they were, they'd answer Buddhist. This is to say, there is a difference between being a cultural Buddhist and a religious Buddhist—scrupulously following the Buddha's teaching, in which observing the moral precepts is as important as scriptural study and meditation. You can be a cultural Buddhist without following the teaching of the religion, because it's a term used for identity, designating someone who was born into a Buddhist culture. It's similar to how over seventy percent of Americans identify themselves as Christian, regardless if they follow the nonviolent, nonjudgmental teachings of Jesus.

In any case, what one calls oneself doesn't matter. The Buddha discovered a law of nature, just like Galileo, Newton, or Einstein. It makes no difference whether one calls oneself a Buddhist or anything else, what matters is if one makes use of the Buddha's teaching, because the Buddha's teaching is a path, not a perspective. It's a prescription, not a faith. You either follow the prescription of the Eightfold Noble Path, or you don't. There's no partly following a prescription. If you take only part of your prescribed medicine, the medicine doesn't work.

The moral requirements become much greater for monks, who must follow 227 rules. (Nuns must follow 311.) Many of these rules seem irrelevant to morality, such as not owning a blanket or rug made of silk, not carrying raw wool for more than forty-eight meters, and not building a hut exceeding 3 x 1.75 meters in size. But many rules of the *Vinaya* deal with the prohibition of sex (including self-sex) and interaction between the sexes, as celibacy is a strict requirement. It's quite strange, then, that Zen priests can marry and have children. Because as the Buddha says in the Tuvataka Sutta, a bhikkhu "should abandon indolence, hypocrisy, laughing, and playfulness, sexual intercourse, and personal ornamentation." In another instance, in regards to what the Buddha refers to as "the coarse practice of sexual intercourse," in the section of the *Vinaya* called the *Patimokka*, he admonishes a monk who broke his vow of celibacy: "Worthless man, it would be better for you to put your penis into the mouth of a black viper than into a woman's vagina. It would be better that your penis be stuck into a pit of burning embers, blazing and glowing, than into a woman's vagina." Pretty harsh. But if the whole point of taking the going forth is to come out of passion, the worst thing a monk can do is feed passion. Sex is putting more fuel on the fire, when the goal is to let the fire burn itself out.

But this doesn't mean that a Buddhist can't enjoy life. It doesn't mean that the Buddha taught his followers to give up pleasure. Enjoyment will be there. Pleasure will be there. Indeed, meditation is a great pleasure. After all, *Pita*—joy, delight, rapture—is one of the seven factors of Enlightenment. *Samadhi* is often synonymous with ecstasy. And practicing *metta-bhavana* (the meditation of loving-kindness) is true bliss. A Buddhist can certainly enjoy wholesome pleasure when it's there. The point is not to crave pleasure, or have attachment to joy.

It's also important to remember that this moral code is not according to dogma or divine mandate. It's not a commandment from God or even a commandment from the Buddha. A practitioner observes the precepts only because they think it's a good thing to do. It is voluntary and based on pragmatism. The act of sex or drinking alcohol is not seen as a wicked sin but simply a hindrance on the path to awakening, because they cause further craving and clinging. It's like eating and brushing your teeth at the same time—it's counterproductive.

Even though the Pali is admittedly ambiguous, the Buddha's moral teachings are clear. The confusion of doctrine and discipline comes from the mutation of Buddhism as it traveled east from India across Asia. Wherever it went, it mixed with the local traditions, taking on cultural characteristics. Even in Burma—arguably the first place outside India to receive the Buddha's teaching, and where it was kept in its most pristine form—popular Buddhism incorporates worship of the indigenous spirits called *nats*. And when Buddhism came to southern China in the first century, it mixed with the indigenous Taoism. On one hand, Buddhism gave Taoism a more formal structure, with a doctrine and discipline, as well as a monastic system. But the resulting Chinese Buddhism hardly resembles what the Buddha taught. As David Hinton writes in *China Root: Taoism, Ch'an, and Original Zen*, between the third and fifth centuries, Buddhism in China was "so transformed by Taoist thought that, aside from a few institutional trappings, it is scarcely recognizable as Buddhism at all." For instance, Taoists had long understood reincarnation as being possible if there were a soul or essential essence to reincarnate. They simply assumed this was also the teaching of the Buddha; his emphasis of *anatta* shows it definitely was not. And just think of the difference between the skinny Indian Buddha statue and the big-bellied Chinese Buddha statue—where did that fat laughing Buddha even come from? Who the heck is he? In the Pali Canon, the Buddha smiles but never laughs. And, as Hesse wrote, he eats like a bird.

From China, the teaching went to Korea and Japan, losing much, and gaining much, along the way. For instance, I mentioned earlier that the Buddha mastered the practice of absorption meditations known as *jhanas*, which were practiced by *samanas* long before the Buddha. In Pali, the word *jhana* means "mental absorption," a form of concentration meditation. The Sanskrit word for *jhana* is "dhyana." In Chinese, *dhyana* translates to "chan," which becomes "seon" in Korean, and "zen" in Japanese. Thus the word *zen* is Japanese for *jhana*. It simply means meditation. Yet the use of the paradoxical riddles called *koans* and the instant-enlightenment concept of *satori*, which are intrinsic to Zen Buddhism, have no place whatsoever in the practice of *jhanas*. The *jhanas* are, after all, specific, clearly defined states of meditative absorption. There are eight *jhanas*, and the Buddha describes the first four like this:

1. Detached from sense-desires, detached from unwholesome mental states, the practitioner enters and remains in the first *jhana*, which is with thinking and pondering, born of detachment, filled with delight and joy.
2. With the subsiding of thinking and pondering, by gaining inner tranquility and oneness of mind, the person enters the second *jhana*, which is without thinking and pondering, born of concentration, filled with delight and joy.
3. With the fading away of delight, remaining imperturbable, mindful, and clearly aware, the person experiences the joy of which the noble ones say, "Happy is the person who dwells with equanimity and mindfulness," and enters the third *jhana*.
4. Having given up pleasure and pain, and with the disappearance of former gladness and sadness, the person enters and remains in the fourth *jhana*, which is beyond pleasure and pain, and purified by equanimity and mindfulness.

Now how did the Buddha's teaching of the *jhanas* go from this to being hit with sticks and asked what's the sound of one hand clapping? As Hinton writes, "In the end, Buddhism is only a scrim on the surface of Ch'an."

Similarly, when Buddhism finally penetrated the Himalayas in the medieval era, it basically formed a light veil over the indigenous shamanism and animism, the fairy and demon worship that has been practiced in the region for centuries. (And we're not talking about nice fairies.) Step into a Vajrayana (Tibetan) Buddhist *gompa* today, and you'll see murals of sword-wielding demons drinking blood from skulls and fornicating with voluptuous consorts, with fire and psychedelic swirls all around. Among the array of bodhisattvas, yidams, dakinis, and dakas, you might find a buddha sitting in lotus posture. But besides sharing the Four Noble Truths and the Eightfold Path, Tibetan Buddhism, like Zen, has little to do with what the Buddha of the Pali Canon actually taught.

Understandably, Kerouac is confused. But how would he know better? Even in the 1950s, there were few reliable books on Buddhism, and more importantly, there were no Buddhist monasteries or meditation centers in the US. (The Buddhist temples in Chinatowns were for Chinese only.) Kerouac couldn't go to a Zen center and learn *zazen*, as I did. He couldn't take a thoroughly guided ten-day course in Vipassana meditation, or a three-month retreat in Insight meditation. Shunryu Suzuki didn't found the San Francisco Zen Center until 1962. Its affiliated mountain center Tassajara, the first Zen training monastery outside of Japan, wasn't established until 1967, the same year that Taizan Maezumi founded the Zen Center of Los Angeles. Jack Kornfield, Joseph Goldstein, and Sharon Salzberg didn't offer a Theravada-rooted meditation retreat at the Insight Meditation Society in Massachusetts until 1976, and didn't open the Bay Area's Spirit Rock until 1988. S. N. Goenka didn't establish Dhamma Dhara, the first Vipassana center in North America, until 1982.

Without such organizations, Kerouac would be unable to make crucial distinctions in theory and, more importantly, wouldn't know if he were practicing meditation properly. Like the old monk Subhadda, who was happy after the Buddha died because he wouldn't have to follow all the rules, Kerouac could pick and choose what he liked, discard what he didn't, and call it Buddhism. But he had the intent, and he had the influence. And for the purposes of this book, that's what's important.

In *The Dharma Bums*, the Beats find freedom not on the road but in nature. After the Zen sex party, Japhy invites Ray to climb the Matterhorn in the Sierra Nevada. They're joined by Henry Morley, a friend of Japhy's who mumbles bits of wisdom. Before they go, Japhy teaches Ray how to pack a rucksack with only the essentials. Dried bulgar and vegetables are better than canned goods, which are heavily weighed down with water. A mixed bag of peanuts and raisins and another of dried apricots and prunes will provide them with energy while hiking. Ray seems impressed. To us, trail mix and light packing isn't anything revolutionary, but perhaps it was for people in America's postwar suburban society, without an established backpacking culture and REI supply stores. Judging by the reactions of people they meet on their way to the mountain, it wasn't common then to go into nature simply to enjoy it. The hunters are especially skeptical. These guys just want to *climb* the mountain? *Weirdos.*

Around these hunters, Japhy reveals some uncharacteristic negativity. "I hate these damn hunters," he says, "all they want to do is level a gun at a helpless sentient being and murder it, for every sentient being or living creature these actual pricks kill they will be reborn a thousand times to suffer the horrors of samsara and damn good for 'em too." In foothill towns along the way to the mountains, our Dharma Bums also see "bluejeaned Elvis Preselys in the road, waiting to beat somebody up." Elvis had just exploded the year these events took place. To most Americans, Elvis was a revolution. But to Kerouac, he represented conformity in another form. This is somewhat surprising, as Elvis's manic energy—his inability to stop moving—is similar to how Neal Cassady is portrayed in *On the Road*. Always fidgeting and shaking. Perhaps by the time he met Gary Snyder, Kerouac was looking for something else. An energy that sprung from spiritual wisdom. Or maybe Cassady and Snyder each provide a distinct aspect of the myth Kerouac wanted to create: the myth of the Beat Generation.

According to Gary Snyder, it is this skill of mythmaking that explains Kerouac's popularity. "Jack was, in a sense, a twentieth-century American mythographer," Snyder said in 1978. "And that's why maybe those novels will stand up, because they will be one of the best statements of the myth of the twentieth century." Snyder understood Kerouac's fascination with him in these terms: "I think Jack saw me, in a funny way, as being another archetypal twentieth-century American of the West, of the anarchist, libertarian, IWW tradition, of a tradition of working outdoors and fitting in already with his fascination with the hobo, railroad bum, working man. I was another dimension on that." In other words, Kerouac saw Snyder in the tradition of Thoreau, Whitman, John Muir, and Jack London. Snyder understood Kerouac's use of Ginsburg in this mythographical way, too: "Allen was the New York radical, Jewish intelligentsia." Snyder adds, "Jack was really skillful in identifying these types, recognizing them as being a particular image that would become part of the mythology of America that he was working at." This insight also explains our culture's fascination with Kerouac, not necessarily as an artist but as a persona. By creating a myth, he himself became mythical.

In *The Dharma Bums*, this mythology of the Beat Generation combines with the mythic image of the Orient to produce a powerful synthesis. For instance, when they stop in a bar before starting their hike, Japhy talks about his plans to go "to Japan and walk all over that hilly country finding ancient little temples hidden and forgotten in the mountains and old sages a hundred and nine years old praying to Kwannon in huts and meditating so much that when they come out of meditation they laugh at everything that moves." It's a vision taken from a Hokusai or Hiroshige painting, the Oriental mystique. And to Ray, Japhy fits right in to the mythical imagery of the Orient; during their climb, Ray observes how

> Japhy, kneeling there studying his star map, leaning forward slightly to peek up through the overhanging gnarled old rock country trees, with his goatee and all, looked, with that mighty grawfaced rock behind him, like, exactly like the vision I had of the old Zen masters of China out in the wilderness. He was leaning forward on his knees, upward looking, as if with a holy sutra in his hands.

It's just like a woodblock painting. By the mid-fifties, movies, too, had made their impact. Once they reach the Matterhorn, Ray says "the wind began to howl like the wind in movies about the Shroud of Tibet." In addition to art and film, popular books also fueled imaginations of Asia, particularly novels like James Hilton's *Lost Horizon* (1933), with its introduction of the fabled Shangri-La. In all cases, the attraction is the archetypical image of Asia. The myth, not the religion. Their friend Morley confirms this when he says, "My Buddhism is nothing but a mild unhappy interest in some of the pictures they've drawn though I must say sometimes Cacoethes strikes a nutty note of Buddhism in his mountainclimbing poems though I'm not much interested in the belief part of it." (Cacoethes is a reference to Reinhold Cacoethes, the character based on Kenneth Rexroth, the poet and translator who introduced Allen Ginsburg to Gary Snyder, and who *TIME* magazine called "the Father of the Beats." This association was much to Rexroth's dismay, as he was a generation older and an already established poet and Zen scholar by the time he hosted the Gallery Six reading. Even so, for a while Rexroth was to the Beats what Gertrude Stein was to the Lost Generation.)

Pictures and poems. This is their Buddhism. And throughout their climb, there are many references to Buddhist art, images, concepts, and culture. At the start, Japhy draws a "magic mandala" on the ground. Ray asks what a mandala is and Japhy responds, "They're the Buddhist designs that are always circles filled with things, the circle representing the void and the things illusions, see. You sometimes see mandalas painted over a Bodhisattva's head and can tell his history from studying it. Tibetan in origin." Certainly, Buddhism has made much of its way into American popular culture through the visual candy of Tibetan mandalas. They fill galleries of our finest museums, and popular media has particularly been interested in those mandalas made of colored sand, ranging from Martin Scorcese's film *Kundun* (1997) to an episode of Netflix's *House of Cards* (2015).

Then there is the poetry, particularly the short Japanese form known as haiku. One of the most memorable scenes of *The Dharma Bums* is when Japhy and Ray compose haiku while hiking. Knowledgeable about the subject, Japhy explains, "a real haiku's gotta be as simple as porridge and yet make you see the real thing, like the greatest haiku of them all probably is the one that goes 'The sparrow hops along the veranda, with wet feet.' By Shiki." Shiki's haiku might not initially impress, but Japhy elaborates on the benefit of the form's minimalism: "You see the wet footprints like a vision in your mind and yet in those few words you also see all the rain that's been falling that day and almost smell the wet pine needles." As a scholar, Japhy is disciplined about their composition, saying, "You can never be too careful about haiku." But Ray wants to make them up spontaneously. "Rocks on the side of the cliff," he calls out, "why don't they tumble down?" Haiku are a simple reflection of reality, and that's why they're appealing. As Ray notes, "Walking in this country you could understand the perfect gems of haikus the Oriental poets had written, never getting drunk in the mountains or anything but just going along as fresh as children writing down what they saw without literary devices or fanciness of expression." It is, in other words, a writing style that matches Kerouac's own.

Even their style of boulder hopping is described with the Zen-Taoist concept of nonaction: "The secret of this kind of climbing," Japhy says, "is like Zen. Don't think. Just dance along." He has in mind Zen archery, when an archer doesn't aim when letting loose an arrow, relying more on intuition than eyesight. (As children, Seymour Glass advises Buddy to shoot his marbles this "Zen" way.)

There are also hints of reincarnation. While hiking, Ray confesses, "There was something inexpressibly broken in my heart as though I'd lived before and walked this trail, under similar circumstances with a fellow Bodhisattva, but maybe on a more important journey." He echoes this a few days later: "That whole afternoon, even more than the other, was filled with old premonitions or memories, as though I'd been there before, scrambling on these rocks, for other purposes more ancient, more serious, more simple." They've done this together before, climbing and composing poems.

Only Japhy makes it to the top of Matterhorn. Beaten by the weather, Ray gives up. But when he sees Japhy running and leaping down the mountain, Ray "suddenly understood everything." Morley responds, "Ah a little satori for Smith today."

Back at camp, Japhy makes a pot of "Chinese tea," and again references *The Book of Tea*, saying, "The first sip is joy, the second gladness, the third is serenity, the fourth madness, the fifth ecstasy." Ray agrees, admitting that with the tea he doesn't mind being away from alcohol. "Now you understand the Oriental passion for tea," Japhy tells him.

At night they meditate, Japhy with his eyes open, slitted as advised in *zazen*. Ray closes his eyes and "fell into deep meditation." He felt "that the mountains were indeed Buddhas and our friends." He also felt "the weird sensation that it was strange that there were only three men in this whole immense valley: the mystic number three. Nirmanakaya, Sambhogakaya, and Dharmakaya." In Mahayana traditions, these "trikayas" or "three bodies" represent both the nature of mind and reality, and were systematized around 300 CE in the Yogacara school, which is considered the most popular and influential of philosophical schools associated with Mahayana in India. Like much of Mahayana Buddhism, these concepts seem far from the historical Buddha's teaching. But in a nutshell, everything we can detect with our senses is nirmanakaya, the field of matter, all the manifestations in time and space. Sambhogakaya is the subtle-spiritual body, the bliss of being in the heavenly realms, through having a continuous mental state of pure love and compassion, altruistic joy and equanimity. Dharmakaya, or truth body, is the principle of enlightenment, taking form in a buddha. It could be my bias against Mahayana, but to me such concepts are as distracting as they are irrelevant, and are another example of Kerouac's unguided grasping and promoting of ideas he doesn't understand.

It's much more beneficial when he talks about Japhy's generosity; charity is a Buddhist concept that anyone can relate to and try to develop. "He was always giving things," Ray says about Japhy, "always practicing what the Buddhists call the Paramita of Dana, the perfection of charity." There are ten *paramitas*, or perfections. Some teachers describe them as ten jars; in order to become fully liberated, a practitioner must fill up each *paramita* jar. *Dana* is charity, or donation, as householders are expected to make charitable donations to monasteries and meditation centers. When Ray says he can't accept Japhy's sneakers, Japhy responds, "Smith you don't realize it's a privilege to practice giving presents to others." It's true, because if you don't practice giving, you can't fill up the jar of *dana*. *Dana* is the first *paramita*. The second is *sila*: proper morality, observing the precepts. The third is *nekkhama*: renunciation, to accept what is given without preference. The fourth is *panna*: wisdom, insight into the impermanent nature of reality. The fifth is *viriya*: energy, vigilance, effort. (Work your butt off!) The sixth is *khanti*: patience, tolerance. (Don't get irritated at the sneezing, coughing, and farting meditators around you.) The seventh is *sacca*: truthfulness, honesty. The eighth is *adhitthana*: strong determination. (I will sit in meditation for a full hour without moving; or in the Buddha's case, I will sit under this tree until I die or achieve *nibbana*.) The ninth *paramita* is *metta*: loving-kindness, having compassionate love for all beings. The tenth is *upekkha*: equanimity, balanced observation without reacting to craving or aversion.

Advancing toward *nibbana* by following the Noble Eightfold Path, a Buddhist meditator works to develop all of these qualities, to fill up the jars of *paramitas*. The *paramitas* show that progress on the path of purification intrinsically depends on one's interactions with others. You can be an advanced meditator who can sustain *samadhi* and access the *jhanas*, but if you're also a jerk who gets easily upset, then you're doing something wrong.

Climbing and being in the mountains is good for Ray Smith. He realizes that more backpacking would be beneficial for him, especially by getting him "away from drinking." It would make him "appreciate a whole new way of living." In a line that could have been spoken by Holden Caulfield, he tells Japhy, "I'm gonna learn all about how to pack rucksacks and what to do and hide in these mountains when I'm sick of civilization."

Japhy suggests Ray work as a fire lookout in the northern Cascades of Washington state. There, living in a hut on top of Desolation Peak, he'd find complete solitude, and live like their Zen Lunatic Dharma Bum hero, Han Shan.

After returning to Berkeley, they buy wine and have another wild party in Alvah and Ray's cottage. As the party progresses, a drunken Ray goes to town, walking down the street "shouting haikus and hoos and satoris at everybody." Late at night, while the poets continue to shout nonsense, Japhy says he's been reading Whitman, mentioning the line *Cheer up slaves, and horrify foreign despots*. In a speech that encompasses the spirit of the book—its theme, its motivation, and its purpose—Japhy explains,

> that's the attitude for the Bard, the Zen lunacy bard of old desert paths, see the whole thing is a world full of rucksack wanderers, Dharma Bums refusing to subscribe to the general demand that they consume production and therefore have to work for the privilege of consuming, all that crap they didn't really want anyway such as refrigerators, TV sets, cars, at least new fancy cars, certain hair oils and deodorants and general junk you finally always see a week later in the garbage anyway, all of the imprisoned in a system of work, produce, consume, work, produce, consume, I see a vision of a great rucksack revolution thousands or even millions of young Americans wandering around with rucksacks, going up to mountains to pray, making children laugh and old men glad, making young girls happy and old girls happier, all of 'em Zen lunatics who go about writing poems that

happen to appear in their heads for no reason and also by being kind and also by strange unexpected acts keep giving visions of eternal freedom to everybody and to all living creatures.

For the Beats, Buddhism, mountain climbing, and partying all have the same overall purpose in mind: freedom from the capitalist system and the rejection of the consumerist lifestyle of postwar America. It's a political message, despite the Beats' reputation for political apathy. Political freedom is the first step, before social freedom and mental freedom. Japhy continues, "Who's to say the cops of America and the Republicans and Democrats are gonna tell everybody what to do?" For an attitude like this, the US government considered Gary Snyder a communist. In 1953, during the height of McCarthyism, he was actually barred from working as a fire lookout for the US Forest Service. In reality, he wasn't a communist but a "Buddhist anarchist," with a long career of advocating the use of civil disobedience, protest, criticism, pacifism, and voluntary poverty, as well as an individual's right to sexual freedom and the right to use drugs. That is, he was an American advocating the American principle of individual freedom. Later in the book, Ray thinks of how Japhy takes food seriously and says, "I wish the whole world was dead serious about food instead of silly rockets and machines and explosives using everybody's food money to blow their heads off anyway." Considering these political messages, *The Dharma Bums* shows that the Beats found validation for their condemnation of the capitalist culture of the West by aligning themselves with the culture of the ancient East. Without the Buddhist context for validation, they were simply bums.

In the midst of this drunken party scene is also where Kerouac first writes about a specific technique of meditation. At one point, Japhy is talking about Hakuin, the influential Japanese Zen Buddhist of the Rinzai School. He says Hakuin was taught to "take deep breaths and then concentrate your mind on a spot one and half inches below your navel until you feel it get like a ball of power and then start breathing from your heels clear up and concentrate saying to yourself that the center just here is Amida's Pure Land, the center of mind." Recognizing the lack of specific instruction in the Beats' Buddhism so far, Alvah Goldbrook says, "That's what I like, see, these actual signposts to something." He wants a technique, a practice. Japhy tells him, "Alvah, the trouble with you is you don't do plenty night zazen especially when it's cold out." But how's one to do zazen if one hasn't been taught zazen?

Before going to the Los Angeles Zen Center to learn zazen more formally, I tried it on my own, based on the instructions I read in Shunryu Suzuki's book *Zen Mind, Beginner's Mind*:

The most important thing in taking the zazen posture is to keep your spine straight. Your ears and your shoulders should be on one line. Relax your shoulders, and push up towards the ceiling with the back of your head. And you should pull your chin in. When your chin is tilted up, you have no strength in your posture; you are probably dreaming. Also to gain strength in your posture, press your diaphragm down towards your *hara*, or lower abdomen. This will help you maintain your physical and mental balance. When you try to keep this posture, at first you may find some difficulty breathing naturally, but when you get accustomed to it you will be able to breathe naturally and deeply.

Your hands should form the "cosmic mudra." If you put your left hand on top of your right, middle joints of your middle fingers together, and touch your thumbs lightly together (as if you held a piece of paper between them), your hands will make a beautiful oval. You should keep this universal mudra with great care, as if you were holding something very precious in your hand. Your hands should be held against your body, with your thumbs at about the height of your navel. Hold your arms freely and easily, and slightly away from your body, as if you held an egg under each arm without breaking it.

You should not be tilted sideways, backwards, or forwards. You should be sitting straight up as if you were supporting the sky with your head. This is not just form or breathing. It expresses the key point of Buddhism. It is a perfect expression of your Buddha nature. If you want true understanding of Buddhism, you should practice this way.

Once you have the posture, you simply concentrate on the breath: "When we practice zazen our mind always follows our breathing." Like the practice of zazen itself, *Zen Mind, Beginner's Mind* is easy to understand. A transcription of Suzuki's talks, the book encourages seekers to simply practice meditation and forget about the intellectualization of concepts, like those found in the *Diamond Sutra* and the *Lotus Sutra* and all those Mahayana sutras. *Zen Mind, Beginner's Mind* is now considered a Buddhist classic. But it wasn't published until 1970, and so the Beats didn't have access to it.

After this wild party, Ray feels like he needs a break from the "lunatic" part of all this bohemianism. He wants to find solitude and pray for all living creatures, which he sees as "the only decent activity left in the world." So he goes with Alvah and Japhy to thrift stores in Oakland and gets himself a rucksack and outdoor gear. He buys a hooded rain poncho to wear over his rucksack, saying it made him "a huge hunchbacked monk," and a molybdenum water bottle, which he says he used "as a canteen for wine more than anything else, and later when I made some money as a canteen for whiskey." He's still confused about how a monk shouldn't be drunk.

After shopping in Oakland, Ray visits a friend named Cody Pomeray. (Cody is such a noncharacter in the book that it would be impossible to guess he's based on Neal Cassady, that this bland Cody is also the wild Dean Moriarty, and that in a few years he'd be driving around Ken Kesey and the Merry Pranksters.) Cody pawns off a troubled girl named Rosie on Ray, and the following incident is based on a real one that deeply disturbed Kerouac. It seems Rosie (whose real name was Natalie Jackson) became paranoid that the cops were going to arrest all the bohemians in North Beach and Greenwich Village and Paris. She's freaking out. Ray tries to teach her about the rucksack revolution and the Dharma, saying her worries are "nothing but bullshit." He tells her, "You're getting these silly convictions and conceptions out of nowhere, don't you realize this life is just a dream? Why don't you just relax and enjoy God? God is *you*, you fool!" But he's not getting through. And he gets the feeling he always gets when trying to explain the Dharma to his friends and family who never listen: "They always wanted me to listen to them, *they* knew, I didn't know anything, I was just a dumb young kid and impractical fool who didn't understand the serious significance of the very important, very real world." Thinking her paranoid worries are very real, Rosie goes up on the roof while everyone is asleep, and tries cutting her wrists with jagged glass from a broken skylight. At dawn, a neighbor finds her and calls the police. When a cop comes up to get her, Rosie jumps off the roof of the six-story building, killing herself.

On one hand, Ray thinks that if she had listened to him, he could have saved her. Her suicide validates his ideas. "Isn't this the time now to start following what I know to be true?" he asks himself. But on the other hand, the fact is that he failed to save her. And his failure motivates him to further develop in Buddhism. He needs to get away in order to do so, and he plans to leave San Francisco the following week.

Before he leaves, Ray meets Japhy in a Chinatown park. It's Sunday morning, and there's a group of African American preachers outside, and a woman is shouting sermons to passersby. Japhy comments that he "doesn't like all that Jesus stuff she's talking about." Ray wonders what's wrong with Jesus. "Didn't Jesus speak of heaven? Isn't heaven Buddha's nirvana?" he asks. Like many Westerners, he's mistakenly trying to understand Buddhism through the Judeo-Christian worldview in which he was raised.

Japhy clarifies that no, the Christian heaven is not at all the Buddha's nirvana. This is just Ray's interpretation. But Ray feels "suppressed by the schism we have about separating Buddhism from Christianity, East from West, what the difference does it make?" There's a big difference, and when

Japhy tries to explain, Ray says, "Words, words, what's in a word? Nirvana by any other name." He's not interested in the accurate use of Buddhist terms, despite the fact that the Buddha spent most of his life meticulously explaining his terms and concepts so that people properly understood the theory and practice. Ray's more interested in doing than understanding. One drunken night, he helped build the new Buddhist temple there in Chinatown, and he's surprised that Japhy is "not interested in the Buddhism of San Francisco Chinatown because it was traditional Buddhism, not the Zen intellectual artistic Buddhism he loved." Ray tries to make him see that "everything was the same." But everything isn't the same, and this tendency to see everything as the same shows the Western inclination toward a universal mysticism—the religion ultimately embraced by both Hermann Hesse and J. D. Salinger. To say "it's all the same" is to show a lack of discernment. And it's by discerning the fine distinctions in theory that makes all the difference in practice.

In any case, Ray says goodbye to Japhy, and then heads three thousand miles across the country to spend Christmas at his sister's house in Rocky Mount, North Carolina.

Alone again, hopping trains and hitchhiking, Ray runs into difficulty. If he were in Asia or Imperial Russia, sleeping outside wouldn't be an issue. Those cultures embrace the mendicant. But in America, there are "sleek, well-paid cops in brand-new cars with all that expensive radio equipment to see that no bhikku slept in his grove tonight." Vagrancy laws are enforced regardless if one considers himself "a religious wanderer."

This deeply bothered Kerouac. Five years later, in a short piece called "The Vanishing American Hobo," published in *Lonesome Traveler* (1960), he wrote: "In America camping is considered a healthy sport for Boy Scouts but a crime for mature men who have made it their vocation.—Poverty is considered a virtue among the monks of civilized nations—in America you spend a night in the calaboose if you're caught short without your vagrancy change." He goes on to say that "Jesus was a strange hobo who walked on water," and "Buddha was also a hobo who paid no attention to other hobos." It's weird to think of the Buddha as a hobo, but technically, he's right; as previously stated, the Pali word *bhikkhu* literally means beggar.

Back in *The Dharma Bums*, Ray knows "a homeless man is in hot water." Outside LA, he's told it's against the law to sleep outside and he responds, "This ain't India, is it." Unable to find a place to camp, he wonders, "Where would I find a quiet grove to meditate in, to live in forever?" Distraught, he has a breakdown and cries. In desperation, his mixing of Buddhism with Christianity becomes more pronounced. "Tonight," he prays, "I sleep tight and long and pray under the stars for the Lord to bring me to Buddhahood after my Buddhawork is done, amen." And as it's Christmas, he adds: "Lord bless you all and merry tender Christmas on all your rooftops and I hope angels squat there the night of the big rich real Star, amen." What the heck is he talking about? Later he thinks, "I am God, I am Buddha, I am imperfect Ray Smith all at the same time, I am empty space, I am all things." Dude's getting out there.

Before going to sleep, he spends "a long time meditating cross-legged," until trucks from the nearby highway disturb him. In the morning, he "meditated first thing and made up a little prayer: 'I bless you, all living things, I bless you in the endless past, I bless you in the endless present, I bless you in the endless future.'" With this prayer, he's ready to start hitchhiking.

After two jaunts into Mexico, a ride on a rig to Ohio, and a bus to North Carolina, Ray finally arrives at his sister's house, where he "would spend all that winter and spring meditating under the trees and finding out by myself the truth of all things." When he gets there, he sees his mother through the window. She's washing dishes. In his mind, his mother is often washing dishes, and now he sees the real image that he often imagines. It's impossible to understand Kerouac without understanding his relationship with his mother, Gabrielle. She raised Jack with strict manners and always wanted him to befriend people of a higher class. She never approved of the girls Jack brought home. Perhaps this is the reason why he was unable to make a romantic relationship work—that is, except for the end of his life, when he, his third wife, and his mother all lived together in the same house. Jack's father Leo died in 1946, and on his deathbed he ordered Jack to take care of his mother. (The gravity of the scene is movingly portrayed toward the end of *The Town and the City*.) Kerouac always felt this burden. His mother's welfare was his responsibility. And because he wasn't successful, he felt guilty for not being able to support her. He always saw her as some Catholic saint and himself as a cross she had to bear. It was his mother's vision of Catholicism that Kerouac could never shake. Its way of looking at the world in terms of good and evil, of right and wrong, of heaven and hell. For instance, it's why he could never accept the bisexual side of himself, much less his friends. Once *On the Road* was published and he came into money, he bought Gabrielle a house, first on Long Island and then in Florida. He lived with her for the rest of his life. He put his funds in her control, and she gave him a weekly five dollar allowance, mothering him through his forties. And here when Ray Smith arrives at his sister's house, he sees his mother as an everyday saint washing dishes in a white tiled sink.

Watching his mother, Ray wonders why Japhy gets so mad about "white tiled sinks and 'kitchen machinery.'" To Ray, "people have good hearts whether or not they live like Dharma Bums. Compassion is the heart of Buddhism." It's the truth, but his family doesn't understand the truth he tries to share with them over the winter. They think he's pretty strange for going off into the pine woods behind the house and sitting cross-legged on a bed of straw most of the day. They don't understand why he insists on sleeping on the back porch rather than in the house. His brother-in-law resents Ray's loafing. When Ray refuses to go on Sunday drives with the family, he hears them talking about him. They were arguing about "the futility of my Buddhism," he says, and asking each other, "What's the matter with him anyway?" He mostly keeps company with dogs and cats, listening to birds and frogs. In the woods he dubs "Twin Tree Grove," he sits near "Buddha Creek" and jots down epiphanies, composes prayers and poems, "practicing Dhyana under the cloudy moon."

He shares these thoughts with his family, particularly the idea of the emptiness of things. But his mother and sister admonish him: "You and your Buddha, why don't you stick to the religion you were born with?" He tries to explain Buddhism not as a religion, as a perception imposed on reality, but as the revelation of how reality actually is: "Things are empty because they appear, don't they, you see them, but they're made up of atoms that can't be measured or weighed or taken hold of." Even "the dumb scientists know" that "things are just empty arrangements of something that seems solid appearing in the space, they ain't either big or small, near or far, true or false, they're ghosts pure and simple." He tries to further explain the idea of emptiness, but his brother-in-law says, "Even if it's true I still don't care." And so Ray retreats to his woods. Alone, he thinks, "I'm empty and awake." And because he believes he's empty and awake, that there's no difference between him and anything else, and that he's become the same as everything else, he thinks, "I've become a Buddha."

He can't wait to tell Japhy when he gets back to California.

During the winter, Ray receives word he's been accepted as a fire lookout for the US Forest Service on Desolation Peak. His plan is to head back to San Francisco and then continue up to Washington and the Cascades, where he'll stay all summer in complete solitude. But before he leaves Carolina, he has a few interesting experiences.

First, he begins to experience "what is called 'Samapatti,' which in Sanskrit means Transcendental Visits." He sees "visions of flowers, pink walls of them." And he also sees "an ancient vision of Dipankara Buddha who was the Buddha who never said anything, Dipankara as a vast snowy Pyramid Buddha with bushy wild black eyebrows like John L. Lewis and a terrible stare." As the historical Gotama Buddha stated several times, he was simply the most recent in a long line of buddhas. Unlike Christ, a buddha isn't unique in history. There have been countless buddhas throughout the eons of the past, and there will be countless buddhas through the eons of the future. Dipankara is a buddha from the past, considered the fourth of twenty-eight known buddhas. Dipankara is especially important because he prophesized to a young Brahmin that he would become a buddha called Shakyamuni. This young Brahmin is the first known incarnation of Gotama, according to the Jataka tales, which are the stories of the Buddha's past lives.

Only after the Buddha's teaching has been forgotten and lost to the world will the next buddha appear. All forms of Buddhism agree that this buddha will be Maitreya. Many Buddhists already pay homage to Maitreya Buddha, even though he won't appear for thousands of years. Some believe that it's impossible for anyone to attain nibbana until Maitreya Buddha appears, but most think it's just very difficult until then. Later in the book, Ray tells Japhy that a lot of people say Christ is Maitreya. He reasons, "Maitreya means 'Love' in Sanskrit and that's all Christ talked about was love." Japhy responds, "Oh, don't start preaching Christianity to me! I can just see you on your deathbed kissing the cross like some old Karamazov or like our old friend Dwight Goddard who spent his life as a Buddhist and suddenly returned to Christianity in his last days." How accurate a prediction.

Like Larry Darrell, Hesse's Siddhartha, and Salinger's Teddy, Ray Smith's meditation bears fruit in the form of psychic powers. For days, his mother has been coughing, with her nose running and throat burning. So Ray decides to go into a deep trance and hypnotize himself, to investigate the cause of his mother's illness. In his trance, he sees a bottle of "Heet" rubbing medicine, and on top of that, "superimposed like a movie fade-in," he sees a distinct picture of little white flowers. He comes out of the trance and goes inside, gathers the white bachelor's buttons that his sister had arranged all over the house, and puts them outside. Then he takes some "Heet" from the medicine cabinet and tells his mother to rub it on her neck. The next day, her cough was gone. She had an unknown allergy to the flowers.

During this experience, Ray realizes "perfectly clearly that people get sick by utilizing physical opportunities to punish themselves because of their self-regulating God nature, or Buddha nature, or Allah nature, or any name you want to give God, and everything worked automatically that way." That is, physical sickness has psychological causes—what we now call psychosomatic conditions. Ray claims this was his "first and last 'miracle,'" because he's afraid of "getting too interested in this and becoming vain." And also because he "was a little scared too, of all the responsibility."

With these delusions of grandeur—of becoming a Buddha and a worker of miracles—he leaves his family in North Carolina and heads on the road again.

Back in California, Ray lives with Japhy in a three-room shack in Corte Madera, in Marin County. The shack sits behind the house of Japhy's friend, Sean Monahan. Ray sees Monahan as a "lay brother" of the Dharma Bums, as he has a wife, children, and a job—he's a carpenter. On his days off, Monahan meditates and studies the Buddhist sutras, brews pots of tea, and takes naps. Monahan's character is based on Locke McCorkle, perhaps most well-known for being the author of *How to Make Love: The Spiritual Nature of Sex*. McCorkle studied with Alan Watts at the American Academy of Asian Studies, and he's the one who'd later say that though Kerouac's "intuitions were right," he "made up his Buddhism" and "didn't know a lot about it, didn't have a lot of training in it."

Philip Whalen was another poet who performed at the Gallery Six reading, and he's the character Warren Coughlin in *The Dharma Bums*. Whalen, who later became an actual Zen monk, said Kerouac "was quite incapable of sitting for more than a few minutes at a time," partly because his knees were ruined from playing football, and so "he never learned how to sit in that sort of proper meditation position." Whalen thinks Kerouac's "interest in Buddhism was pretty much literary, and the idea that people were actually trying to do it was interesting to him as exhibitions of their character." And here we have the crux of the book's confusion: the self-proclaimed spokesman for Buddhism actually knew little about Buddhism.

Japhy senses this and has changed somewhat over the winter. He doesn't want to hear about the realizations Ray had while meditating in the Carolina woods. "It's just a lot of words," Japhy says. He's shaved off his goatee, and Ray tells him he no longer looks like "a happy little sage." Japhy responds, "I ain't a happy little sage no mo." He's "getting tired of battin around like this," thinking that after he comes back from the monastery in Japan he'd have had his fill of Zen. He even wants to get married. "Maybe I'll be rich and work and make a lot of money and live in a big house," he says. Then a minute later he asks, "Who wants to enslave himself to a lot of all that, though?" It's clear he's feeling depressed, struggling as Ray had struggled during the winter.

But in the morning, Japhy bangs on a frying pan and chants, "Buddham saranam gocchami . . . Dhamman saranam gocchami . . . Sangham saranam gocchami." This chant is the taking refuge in the Triple Gem. It's chanted in thousands of monasteries and meditation centers every morning. *Buddham saranam gocchami.* I take refuge in the Buddha. (Not the person, but the quality of Enlightenment.) *Dhamman saranam gocchami.* I take refuge in the Dhamma, the universal law—the truth. *Sangham saranam gocchami.* I take refuge in the Sangha, the community of monks and nuns—"the church," as Japhy explains. During this chant, Ray realizes the "number one Dharma Bum of them all" is back.

Over breakfast, Japhy shares lore about koans, sudden enlightenments, and the first Zen patriarch Kasyapa. Out and about all day, Japhy says, "My Buddhism is activity." In contrast, Ray loafs around, writing haikus, practicing "do-nothing." He says Japhy's meditations were by the clock, first thing in the morning, in the mid-afternoon, and then before going to bed. But only for three minutes at a time. He and Japhy "were two strange dissimilar monks on the same path."

The time comes for the "monks" to prepare for two big parties, the latter to celebrate Japhy's departure for Japan. The parties are wild, and Ray is thrilled "to meet so many Buddhists after that harsh road hitchhiking." Of these Buddhists, there's Bud Diefendorf, who had "started out as a physicist at the University of Chicago and then gone from that to philosophy and finally now to philosophy's dreadful murderer, B u d d h a." In real life, Bud Diefendorf is Claude Dalenberg. Like Locke McCorkle, Dalenburg got turned on to Zen from a talk by Alan Watts, and like Philip Whalen, he was later ordained as a Zen monk by Shunryu Suzuki. Watts himself attends the party, as the character Arthur Whane, who's dressed in necktie and suit. During the party, Ray approaches Whane and asks, "Well, what is Buddhism? Is it fantastic imagination magic of the lightning flash, is it plays, dreams, not even plays, dreams?" If Kerouac really asked this question, you could imagine Watts must have been thinking, *What the . . . .* But in the novel, Whane answers, "No, to me Buddhism is getting to know as many people as possible." It's as ridiculous an explanation as any I've heard, but Kerouac seems to really have dug it, as he mentions the phrase again in his book *Desolation Angels.* The generational divide is clear when Alvah Goldbrook and George (based on Ginsburg's companion, Peter Orlovsky) strip naked and have a "serious conversation about world affairs" with the well-dressed Whane and Cacoethes.

Throughout the party, Ray struggles with lust. While girls get naked and dance around, he sits with his eyes closed and listens to the music, saying, "I was really sincerely keeping lust out of my mind by main force and gritting of my teeth." Bud feels that in some previous lifetime he and Ray "were monks in some monastery in Tibet where the girls danced for us before yabyum." Ray agrees, adding they "were the old monks who weren't interested in sex any more but Sean and Japhy and Whitey were the young monks and were still full of the fire of evil and still had a lot to learn." Secretly, he and Bud sneak glances at the naked flesh and lick their lips. Craving arises with the sight of flesh—there's nothing we can do about it. This is why real monks live in monasteries and not shacks where they throw bohemian parties and have orgies.

While he curls up alone in his sleeping bag, Ray admits he felt lonely seeing everybody paired off and having a good time. He also longs for Japhy's sister, who comes to the party with her fiancé. Japhy has an oddly close relationship with his sister and is jealous of her engagement. He gives the fiancé a hard time, even though the guy had just returned from being a serviceman in Burma. The guy tries to talk about Burma, but can't get a word in edgewise. That's a shame. Burma is the Land of Dhamma, and the fiancé could have told them about Burmese Buddhism, which at the time was transforming the Buddhist world—in the early twentieth century, the Burmese monk Ledi Sayadaw launched the modern Vipassana movement, which is essentially a Buddhist Protestantism, in that it bypassed centuries of tradition and encouraged both monastics and laypeople, including women, to meditate and study scripture, on their own. This Burmese Buddhism is adamant about observing the moral precepts and is generally much more faithful to the historical Buddha's teaching than the Taoist-flavored Zen and Tantric-infused Tibetan forms that the Beats popularized. But the great value of Burmese Buddhism wasn't recognized until the 1960s, when Westerners began going to Burma to learn Vipassana meditation from Sayagyi U Ba Khin and Mahasi Sayadaw. So, Japhy's jealousy could be seen as a missed opportunity. For instance, knowing about the morally strict Burmese Buddhism just might have helped Kerouac avoid his alcohol-fueled demise.

Speaking of, a few days after the party, Japhy and Ray get in an argument about alcohol. They're supposed to attend a lecture at Berkeley's Buddhist Center. But Ray buys a bottle of port on the way and just wants to "drink in alleys." Japhy gets upset, reminding Ray that people are expecting to hear him read his poems. He also says Cacoethes criticized Ray for drinking too much. (There was an actual incident around that time, when Kenneth Rexroth kicked Kerouac out of his house. Rexroth held a *salon* at his home once a week, and one day Ginsburg took along Kerouac, who was a little drunk and laughing loudly. According to Ginsburg, "Rexroth got upset Jack was going to wake his baby—his daughter—and got mad at him, called him a son of a bitch, and ordered him out." Afterward, Rexroth withdrew his support of the Beats.) But Ray doesn't care if he's drinking too much. "There's wisdom in wine, goddam it!" he shouts. He drains the bottle, and buys another. Sad and disappointed, Japhy asks, "How do you expect to become a good bhikku or even a Bodhisattva Mahasattva always getting drunk like that?" He's really worried, thinking Ray will "end up lying in the street in the rain, dead drunk." But Ray just keeps on drinking and refuses to go with Japhy. Alone for two hours, Ray hangs around and drinks until he becomes dizzy and sad.

In real life, this was right before Kerouac's drinking habit became a disease. He had the sober summer of 1956 as a fire lookout, which was followed by his trip to Morocco and Europe (documented in *Desolation Angels*). But when he returned, *On the Road* was published and he began to drown himself in alcohol. Whenever he hung out with friends in San Francisco or New York, he'd get so drunk he'd just pass out. He loved to drink cheap, sweet Tokay wine. On road trips, he'd demand to stop in bars. Friends said he wasn't fun to be around. They tried to get him to stop drinking. They didn't have much success. With so much alcohol in his system, Kerouac began to fill out, losing his looks and even the grace of his movements. He became bloated and irritable. The novel *Big Sur* captures the alcoholism, the deterioration of his mind, and his full transition back to Catholicism—rather than having visions of Buddha, he has visions of "The Cross." Those events took place in 1960, and from there his demise took less than a decade. A daily bottle of Tokay turned to a daily bottle of brandy. If he didn't drink, he'd break out in the sweats. First came "wet brain" and then the cirrhosis. And maybe, just maybe, something could have been different if his Zen lunatic models didn't validate his drinking. Because when Japhy comes back from the Buddhist Society, he's drunk too. Everyone at the lecture was drinking raw white sake out of teacups. They "all got drunk and discussed pranja," Japhy says, "all those crazy Japanese saints!" And so Japhy tells Ray "You were right! It doesn't make any difference!"

But it does. Oh, it does.

Before Japhy sets sail for Japan, he and Ray have one last hike, this time through Muir Woods, just north of the Golden Gate Bridge. As they hike, Japhy asks what Ray thinks about death. "When we die," he answers, "we go straight to nirvana heaven and that's that." Death is a reward, he thinks. Japhy comments, "but supposing you're reborn in the lower hells and have hot redhot balls of iron shoved down your throat by devils." Ray doesn't think the notion of Buddhist hell "is anything but a dream cooked up by some hysterical monks who didn't understand Buddha's peace under the Bo tree." Yet in the Devaduta Sutta, the Buddha describes the punishments of hell in vivid detail, and there's plenty of torture by red-hot irons. After the description, the Buddha clarifies, "Bhikkhus, I tell you this is not something I heard from another recluse or brahman. I tell you this as something that I have actually known, seen, and discovered by myself." So Ray is wrong again.

Though the Pali word *niraya* is usually translated as "hell," its literal meaning is "to go down." It's a place where negative fruits of karma are born and then purged and is therefore more like purgatory. Instead of "hell," with its Christian connotations, a better translation of *niraya* is "the lower world." Despite the torture with red-hot irons, *niraya* isn't the Christian hell. First of all, unlike Christianity, with its dualism of heaven and hell, there are many heavenly and hellish realms in Buddhism; *niraya* is the lowest plane of existence. More importantly, no one is sent to *niraya* by divine judgment or for punishment; beings end up in "the lower world" based on their own unwholesome actions. Immoral actions bring you down, just like a stone sinks in water. It's a law of nature. But the biggest difference is that *niraya* isn't permanent. After one works off their karma in *niraya*, they are reborn in another realm. Same goes for heaven. It takes eons, but even gods get old, decay, die, and are born in another realm, depending on their actions. In Buddhism, nothing is eternal. Not even the afterlife.

From topics of hell and death, Ray and Japhy move on to clothes, and how Japhy will dress in robes while in the monastery: "old T'ang Dynasty style things long black floppy with huge droopy sleeves and funny pleats, make you feel real Oriental." Japhy looks forward to "little tucked-away temples down rocky trails, cold mossy ancient places where frogs croak, and inside small statues and hanging buttery lamps and gold lotuses and paintings and ancient incense-soaked smells and lacquer chests with statues." Again, the mythical images of the Orient. In an insightful line, Ray responds, "Alvah says that while guys like us are all excited about being real Orientals and wearing robes, actual Orientals over there are reading surrealism and Charles Darwin and mad about Western business suits."

As Japan was over a decade into its American occupation, this was true. But rather than see themselves as silly, Japhy understands the cultural-copying as an inevitable cultural-synthesis: "East'll meet West anyway. Think what a great world revolution will take place when East meets West finally, and it'll be guys like us that can start the thing." Again an accurate prediction. Gary Snyder and Jack Kerouac did play a part in the influx of Eastern spirituality into Western culture. It's partly because of them that the once exotic words dharma and karma, zen and nirvana are now part of everyday language, and that thousands of people have learned to meditate in the dozens of meditation centers now scattered across the country. What's more, Japhy foreshadows the spirit of the following decade's hippie movement. He and Ray "ain't out to bust anybody's skull, or cut someone's throat in an economic way," because they've dedicated themselves "to prayer for all sentient beings." And "who knows, the world might wake up and burst out into a beautiful flower of Dharma everywhere." It's all there: Peace, love, and flower power.

Ironically, Kerouac loathed the hippies. (As he makes clear during his embarrassing appearance on *Firing Line*, the public affairs show hosted by the conservative William F. Buckley). Dr. Frankenstein, too, loathed his creation. And just because of the look of it.

Winding down, Japhy Ryder leaves for Japan on June 17, 1956. The next morning, Ray Smith heads north. He hitchhikes to the redwoods of northern California, to Eugene, to Seattle, and finally to the Marblemount Ranger Station in the Skagit Valley. Once he arrives, Ray realizes he "wasn't a free bhikku any more." He was now a government employee and has to spend a week in Fire School.

Afterward, a ranger named Happy the Muleskinner—or as Japhy called him "Happy the Packer"—leads Ray on an old gold miners' trail through the Upper Skagit. On the way, Ray says all he wants is to be left alone all summer. Happy responds, "You're sayin that now but you'll change your tune soon enough. They all talk brave. But then you get to talking to yourself. That ain't so bad but don't start *answerin* yourself, son."

This line reminds me of that time I took a weekend off from volunteering at the meditation center near Dharamsala and went off on my own to sleep in a cave in the Himalayas. Dharamsala is actually further down the mountain than people might think. It's an Indian town, full of Hindus. Higher up the mountain is McLeod Gange, where the Dalai Lama and the Tibetan refugee community live. That's where all the tourists go. The Vipassana center is a bit further up the mountain, in a village called Dharamkot. There's nothing above the village, and so you can just walk into the high Himalayas. A few hours on a steep trail of stone steps takes you through thick forest and up to a cluster of tea-shop tents known as Triund, where goat herders and hikers can buy food and supplies and, obviously, tea.

From Triund, I continued up and up until I was above the tree line. There was one more tea-tent, and then the path disappeared into a steppe-like terrain of grass and boulders, cliffs rising high on either side, waterfalls rushing down everywhere. A Japanese friend had drawn me a rough map of how to get to the caves, but really I had no idea where I was going. Eventually, I came to a river of ice—the glacier my Japanese friend had told me to cross. She said the caves were just on the other side. I crossed the glacier, but I couldn't see any caves. It started to rain. And a thick fog was coming quick up the mountain. So I nestled in an overhang next to a waterfall. I had a panoramic view of the glacier, the jagged rocky snowy peaks high above, and a sea of lower mountains all around, their tips poking through the fog like islands in the ocean. And then the fog swept over everything, and I couldn't see anything.

I meditated for an hour and when I opened my eyes, the rain had stopped and the fog was gone. So I left my bag and hiked around the mountain through waist-high wild flowers. At first, all was glorious and I was kissing the flowers and feeling freer than ever. Nobody was around for miles and miles. I kept exploring, looking for the caves, but there wasn't a path and eventually I lost the way back to my overhang. Then the fog rolled back and I couldn't see anything again. Only a few feet of visibility in each direction, and then nothing but gray. I'd slowly wind my way down a ridge, only to come to a cliff. I'd go back and try to find another way down. But I was lost. I started repeating the mantra, "Lord Jesus, have mercy on me. Lord Jesus, have mercy on me!" Then I started talking out loud to myself. "Okay, Randy, just keep cool. All you have to do is go down. You'll eventually hit the glacier. You'll be able to find the overhang from there." Only a few hours of solitude, and I was already talking to myself! Then I started asking myself questions. "What did you get yourself into? Why did you even come up here? What the hell did you think you were doing?" I asked, "Can't you just keep cool?" And then I answered myself, "Yes I'll keep cool if you just shut up for a while!"

So there we go. I was answering myself, just like Happy warned Ray not to do.

After hours of hiking, Happy and Ray reach six and a half thousand feet. They come to Desolation Peak and the "funny little peaked almost Chinese cabin among little pointy firs and boulders standing on a bald rock top surrounded by snowbanks and patches of wet grass with tiny flowers." It's dark and dismal, cold and wet, with pelting hail. Inside, the cabin is a mess of dust, chewed magazines, and "black balls of rat turd." Outside, all they can see is fog. Happy says it will be clear in the morning, but Ray thinks of what Han Shan wrote on Cold Mountain—the fog never went away. He cleans and they cook and sleep. In the morning, Happy leaves Ray in complete solitude. "Here indeed was the Great Truth Cloud, Dharmamega, the ultimate goal." Finally, he's above it all.

Some of the most beautiful passages in the book occur in the following twelve pages, where Kerouac's prose really sings. Similar to when Ray was away staying with his family during the winter, there is much plotless, contemplative writing here. But now, as it's free from nonsensical Buddhist ramblings and delusions of grandeur, it's not ridiculous. Many lines are poignant, even profound. The descriptions of nature are particularly delicious. During the day, he's surrounded by "hundreds of miles of pure snow-covered rocks and virgin lakes and high timber, and below, instead of the world," he sees "a sea of marshmallow clouds flat as a roof and extending miles and miles in every direction." At sunset, the "mountains were covered with pink snow, the clouds were distant and frilly and like ancient remote cities of Buddhaland splendor." At night, he sees the Northern Lights "reflecting all the ice of the North Pole from the other side of the world." In his diary he writes, "Oh I'm happy!"

In a piece in *Lonesome Traveler* called "Alone on a Mountaintop," Kerouac wrote about this solitary experience in nature as a necessity: "No man should go through life without once experiencing healthy, even bored solitude in the wilderness, finding himself depending solely on himself and thereby learning his true and hidden strength.—Learning, for instance, to eat when he's hungry and sleep when he's sleepy." He's a Taoist through and through.

Though Ray keeps a journal, he doesn't write any fiction during the summer. Instead, he rolls cigarettes and makes coffee, saying, "Time for hot coffee and a cigarette, boys," addressing his "imaginary bhikkus." He gets mad at himself when he spoils a flapjack or slips in the snowfield while getting water. He keeps a look out on the horizon for smoke, and he chops wood. He thinks of things he wants to tell Japhy. Before bedtime, he stands on his head, and thinks of how the world is always upside down. In the moonlight, he meditates facing west, "wishing there were a Personal God in all this impersonal matter." And here is the turning point in the sequence of his books—the Legend of Duluoz—and in his life. He makes his turn from the Buddha back to God.

In *Desolation Angels*, which begins at the end of *The Dharma Bums* and was taken directly from the journal he kept as a fire lookout, Kerouac paints a less rosy picture of his time on the mountain. Alone in absolute solitude, he thought he'd "come face to face with God or Tathagata and find out once and for all what is the meaning of all this existence and suffering and going to and fro in vain." Instead, he came face to face with himself: "no liquor, no drugs, no chance of faking it but face to face with ole Hateful Dulouz Me and many's the time I thought I die, suspire of boredom, or jump off the mountain." Later passages reveal how much he suffered from loneliness and boredom, how desperate he was for company. How obsessed he was with food. How he craved alcohol. This summer was maybe the last time he was sober. His experience on Desolation Peak was perhaps the peak of his life. In a way, he was never happy again.

At the end of his job, after two months of solitude, Ray says he "learned all." And like Larry Darrell, Siddhartha, and Franny Glass, Ray Smith has his awakening. On the last day in his hut, he gazes down at the rosy reflections of celestial vapor on the lake and says, "God, I love you." He gazes up to the sky and says, "I have fallen in love with you, God. Take care of us all, one way or the other." And before he goes down the trail and back to the world, he kneels to say a little prayer to the camp, as Japhy used to do. "Thank you, shack."

As Ray Smith walks down the path from Desolation Peak, he leaves behind the path taught by the Buddha. But simply by picking up the teachings and diving into them, by living the life of a Dharma Bum and writing about it, Jack Kerouac led so many others to the Buddha's path. And so maybe he really was a bodhisattva after all.

Postscript

THE STORY OF HOW Eastern religion and Buddhism in particular came to saturate Western culture has another story than the one I just told—a prequel, as it were. Because before the famous writers came a bunch of relatively unknown archeologists and academics who provided the raw data that later inspired the artists whose names we know.

It may be difficult for us to believe, but up until the nineteenth century it wasn't only Westerners who had little idea what Buddhism actually was, but Indians too. Centuries of systematic Brahmanic and then Mughal oppression of Buddhist practice and culture had left ancient stupas, temples, and other Buddhist sites decrepit, overgrown, lost. It took curious Europeans trying to figure it out that allowed the teachings of the Buddha to become known again in the land of his birth, as well as the Western world. Much of this story is covered in Charles Allen's book *The Buddha and the Sahibs*, which I'll summarize here.

The first Westerner to come in contact with any form of Buddhism might have been the Italian Jesuit missionary Matteo Ricci, who journeyed to China between 1582 and 1610. The syncretic Buddhism being practiced there, as it accommodated Taoist and Confucian elements, led him to believe that Buddhism was a form of Pythagoreanism brought from Greece, by way of India, as Pythagoras was the most famous proponent of reincarnation in the ancient West.

Buddhism's first messenger to the British Isles was Robert Cox, a "rough and tough sea-dog" who in 1680 wrote letters about his twenty-year stay in Ceylon. About monks he wrote: "They are debarred from laying their hands to any manner of work; and may not marry or touch women, nor eat but one meal a day . . . nor must they drink wine." Well, he got the precepts down, it seems.

A hundred years later, in 1780, Charles Wilkins became the first man to decipher an ancient Sanskrit inscription. This moment was, Allen writes, as if "a huge corpus of information hitherto unknown and unquantified has suddenly became accessible—as if a door had been opened to a great library piled high with unread books, but one without a shelving system." This decipher led to the conception of the Asiatic Society in 1783, headed by William "Oriental" Jones, who published the first Sanskrit translations of Buddhist texts: the Sakuntala, by fourth-century poet Kalidasa, and the Hitopadesa, a collection of Buddhist morality fables. In 1794, these translations hit Europe, and German Romantics in particular, with Goethe, Schopenhauer, von Herder, Schiller, Schubert, and the Schlegels eating them up.

The first scholarly account of Burmese Buddhism was Dr. Francis Buchanan's *On the Religion and Literature of the Burmans*, which came out in 1799 and effectively launched the field we now call Buddhist studies. Buchanan was the first to get down matters ranging from the philosophical—"when we say that *Godama* obtained the *Niban*, this is to be understood as a state exempt from the four following evils: conception, old age, sickness, and death. Nothing in this world, nor any place, can give us an idea of the *Niban*: But the exemption of the above mentioned evils, and the possession of perfect safety, are the only things of which it consists"—to the historical—"In his eightieth year Godama had died of dysentery, brought on by an excess in eating pork."

In 1802, Buchanan discovered "a second form of Buddhism" in Kathmandu. This was, of course, what we know as Tibetan or Vajrayana Buddhism. Soon Csoma de Koros produced the books *Tibetan Grammar* and *Tibetan English Dictionary* and translated the first Vajrayana sutra into English.

In the early 1820s, George Turner learned Pali from a Sri Lankan Buddhist monk, becoming the first Westerner to learn the language. He was the first to start translating the Mahavamsa, or Great Chronicle, but he abandoned the project when Sir Alexander Johnson published his own translation in 1824.

The year 1824 was also when James Alexander discovered the Ajanta caves.

The Theravada-Mahayana divide was first understood in 1836. It was only in this year that the Indian origins of Buddhism and the main biographical facts of the Buddha's life were established beyond doubt. (Previously, it was thought the Buddha might have lived in Sri Lanka; some even suspected he was African, due to his tight, curly hair.)

In 1844, Eugéne Burnouf's *Introduction á L'Historie du Buddhism Indien* was the first comprehensive account of Indian Buddhist history and Buddhist doctrine. Burnouf's work clarified Romantic projections by "presenting Buddhism as it really was: a profoundly unsettling view of the human condition that offered an equally disturbing means of release of that condition."

The *Dhammapada* was first translated in 1855, by the Danish scholar Viggo Fautsball, who soon followed with translations of the Jataka Tales.

In 1857, Max Muller published his article "Buddhism and Buddhist Pilgrims," sparking a controversy about the nature of nirvana that lasted for years.

In 1881, Thomas William Rhys Davids founded the Pali Text Society. This marks a shift to a more positive attitude toward Buddhism in the West, mainly due to understanding it as an Eastern Protestantism, thereby finding favor in Germany, Britain, and the US. This attitude depended on readings of Pali rather than Sanskrit sources, and thus on the Theravada rather than the Mahayana tradition of Buddhism. The main vehicle for this shift was Rhys Davids's book *Buddhism: Being a Sketch of the Life and Teachings of Gautama, the Buddha*.

This book, along with Muller's translation of the *Dhammapada*, provided the source material for Edwin Arnold's poem "The Light of Asia," which was published in 1879 and became "the chief instrument by which Buddhism was brought into the Western mainstream." In the process, Allen adds, it also helped to westernize Buddhism. From here, *The Dharma Bums* was inevitable.

In 1890, Anagarika Dharmapala discovered a treatise on meditation in a Sinhalese monastery, which Rhys Davids translated as "The Manual of a Mystic." This revived the practice of meditation throughout Ceylon, Burma, and Siam, where it had "died out entirely."

Up until the nineteenth century, Hindu sannyasins kept the ruined temple and relics at Bodhgaya without having any idea what Buddhism was, or why the site was important. Burmese pilgrims eventually told them that the Buddha achieved enlightenment at that spot. The first international Buddhist organization, the Maha Bodhi Society, was founded in 1891, with the prime aim of the protection of Mahabodhi Temple at Bodhgaya. The thirteenth Dalia Lama was its first president. Its director was the American Colonel Henry Olcott (the first Westerner, along with Madame Blavatsky, to officially take refuge and the five precepts, as well as the designer of the international Buddhist flag), and its secretary was Anagarika Dharmapala.

In 1897, Dr. Lawrence Augustine Waddell, a Scot, published "The Buddhism of Tibet, or Lamaism." After journeying to Tibet, Waddell wrote Lamaism was "a priestly mixture of Shivaite mysticism, magic, and Indo-Tibetan demonolatry, overlaid by a thin varnish of Mahayana Buddhism ... beneath which the sinister growth of poly-demonish superstition darkly appears." Yikes.

Moving into the twentieth century, we get closer to the works of fiction explored in this book, which would require more of a popular boost than these academic writings and translations. In the *Wheel Publication* no. 42/43, "Early Westerns Buddhists," Francis Story puts together extracts of important articles from *The Buddhist Review*, between 1909 through 1914. Story begins by saying that after Arnold's "The Light of Asia" there grew an interest in Eastern philosophy that was more than academic. The first European Buddhists, feeling the mounting pressures of world war, took to writing pieces of journalism aimed—unlike the scholars previously described, who wrote to discover and explain what Buddhism is—to inject some sanity into their society by spreading Buddhist philosophy to mainstream newspaper readers in Britain and the US.

This led to the founding of *The Buddhist Review* in 1909. Its editor, J. E. Elam, introduced its first issue by explaining "Buddhism is a friend of all, enemy of none." He's referring to the lack of hostility Buddhism has with traditional religions of the West, but also to the new religion of psychology, in which "Buddhism moves at ease, confident of its knowledge, confident of its logic, to state clearly, fully and conclusively its solutions of those problems which have vexed the minds of men from time immemorial."

Also in the first issue was an article by Caroline Rhys Davids, "Buddhism and Ethics," in which she established that early Buddhism and modern science share belief in a universal law of causation. E. J. Mills continued to support this theme in the same issue with the article, aptly titled "Buddhism and Science," which specified Buddhism's embrace of evolution, as *On the Origin of Species* was still very much on everyone's minds. In the same issue, another scientific writer, Ernest R. Carlos, explained reincarnation in "Transmigration in East and West," writing that reincarnation "furnishes the answer to problems which religious dogma cannot deal with, and which material science is not ready to face." It's difficult to imagine Maugham, Hesse, and Salinger building their mental castles of reincarnation without first laying such foundations by reading such articles.

In the July–September issue of 1910, Alexandra David cemented the practical relevancy of Buddhist philosophy with the article "Buddhism and Social Problems," in which she addresses social inequalities and industrial exploitation. In the 1912 article "The Value of Buddhism to the Western Mind," Victor E. Kroemer wrote, "Buddhism shows the purpose of all existence, the object of our life here, and the goal to which all is tending." As if that weren't bold enough, he continued: "In Buddhism, in whatever form it ultimately comes to the West, lies the solution of all the social problems, all the unrest, that exist in the Western World." Directing Buddhism to international matters at hand, Marr Murray wrote "The Basis of Peace," an essay that proposed Buddhist morality will prevent world war, as Buddhism is a religion—no, the only religion—that "will *make all* men good and *keep* them good." Indeed, for him, "Buddhism with its Noble Eightfold Path alone holds out any hope to the world."

It didn't work; as we know, the Great War began two years later. But it was after the war that Hesse and Maugham first found Eastern religion, inspiring them to write about an ancient Indian sage named Siddhartha and a disillusioned World War I pilot named Larry Darrell. Hesse and Maugham must have shared the same desire to help spread peace by spreading the wisdom of Eastern religion, and like Salinger and Kerouac, they knew this wisdom ultimately comes from meditation. I'm sure they'd all agree with the author of the last article Story includes in his collection, "The Fruits of Meditation" by a mysterious C. R. J., who wrote:

> Some prejudiced travellers in Buddhist countries have seen monks seated in meditation and have seized the occasion to attribute to them laziness. But this meditation is useful, profitable. The feverish West groans for the lack of it. Without the slightest verbal inaccuracy it can be asserted that time is infinitely more profitably employed in meditation than in a hundred forms of activity directed to non-utilitarian ends, including the making of scientific instruments of warfare and battleships, which activity will cease when right meditation has shown the superiority of tranquility.

In fact, time employed in meditation is infinitely more profitable than any other activity at all, including reading and writing. With that in mind, I'll take a break from doing both and go meditate.

Sources

INTRODUCTION

THE QUESTIONS THAT A young Somerset Maugham asked himself during a trip to Capri and which I quoted twice in the Introduction are from his essay "Early Travels," originally collected in the book *The Partial View,* and later collected in the book I found them in, *The Skeptical Romancer: Selected Travel Writings,* edited and introduced by Pico Iyer (Everyman's Library, New York: Alfred A. Knopf, 2009).

The Susan Sontag quote is from the documentary on her, *Regarding Susan Sontag* directed by Nancy D. Kates (HBO Films, 2014).

Quotes from Arthur Schopenhauer about the Upanishads and Buddhism are found in John James Clarke's *Oriental Enlightenment: The Encounter Between Asian and Western Thought* (Oxfordshire: Routledge, 1997), pages 68 and 77, and from *Richard Wagner and Buddhism* by Urs App (University Media, 2011), page 17.

The quote from Henry David Thoreau's *Walden: or, Life in the Woods* is from chapter 16, "The Pond in Winter"; in my Signet Classic edition (with an afterward by Perry Miller, New York: The New American Library of World Literature, 1960), on pages 198–99.

Quotes from Friedrich Nietzsche about Buddhism are taken from *The Portable Nietzsche,* selected and translated with an Introduction, Prefaces, and Notes by Walter Kaufman (New York: Penguin, 1976; originally 1954), from the excerpt of *The Antichrist,* starting page 565.

CHAPTER 1: THE RAZOR'S EDGE

All quotations from *The Razor's Edge* by W. Somerset Maugham are taken from the Penguin Classics edition, with an Introduction by Anthony Curtis (New York: Penguin, 1944; reprint 1992).

Quotes from Maugham's travel writings are taken from his books *The Skeptical Romancer: Selected Travel Writings*, edited by Pico Iyer (Everyman's Library, New York: Alfred A. Knopf, 2009), including the quotes from his essays "Buddha," originally collected in *The Gentleman in the Parlour*, and "India," originally collected in *A Writer's Notebook* (1949). For material related to his experiences with his guru Sri Ramana Maharshi, I relied on his essay "The Saint" from the collection *Points of View* (London: Mandarin Paperback, 1996; originally William Heinemann Ltd, 1958).

For biographical information about Maugham in this chapter, I relied on *The Secret Lives of Somerset Maugham* by Selena Hastings (New York: Random House, 2009).

The Buddha's explanations about the lengths of an eon are taken from Samyutta Nikaya 15.5, A Mountain, and 15.8, The River Ganges, and can be found on pages 38–39 of *In the Buddha's Words: An Anthology of Discourses from the Pali Canon*, edited and introduced by Bhikkhu Bodhi, Foreword by the Dalai Lama (Boston: Wisdom Publications, 2005).

The story of Patacara is adapted from *The Great Disciples of the Buddha: Their Lives, Their Works, Their Legacy*, by Nyanaponika Thera and Hellmuth Hecker, edited with an Introduction by Bhikkhu Bodhi (Boston: Wisdom Publications, 2003).

CHAPTER 2: SIDDHARTHA

All quotations from *Siddhartha* by Hermann Hesse are taken from the New Directions edition, translated by Hilda Rosner (New York: Bantam Books/New Directions, 1951; reprint 1971; original 1922).

The quotes from Hesse's *The Glass Bead Game* are translated by Richard Winston and Clara Winston and are from the Picador edition (New York: Picador/Henry Holt and Company, 1969; reprint 1990).

I also relied on Hesse's book of essays *Wandering*, translated by James Wright (New York: Farrar, Straus & Giroux, 1972 original 1920); and *Autobiographical Writings*, translated by Denver Lindley (New York: Farrar, Straus & Giroux, 1971; original 1945).

Quotations from Hesse's letters are taken from *Soul of the Age: Selected Letters of Herman Hesse 1891–1962*, edited by Theodore Ziolkoski, translated by Mark Harman (New York: Noonday Press/Farrar, Straus & Giroux, 1991).

For biographical information about Hesse in this chapter, I relied on *Hermann Hesse* by Edwin F. Casebeer (New York: Warner Paperback Library, 1972) and *Herman Hesse: A Pilgrim of Crisis* by Ralph Freedman (New York: Pantheon, 1978).

For most translations of Buddhist scripture in this chapter, I relied on *In the Buddha's Words: An Anthology of Discourses from the Pali Canon*, edited and introduced by Bhikkhu Bodhi, foreword by the Dalai Lama (Boston: Wisdom Publications, 2005). The Buddha's description of his emaciation is from the Longer Discourses to Saccaka or Maha-Saccaka Sutta, and can be found on page 63–64. The Noble Eightfold Path can be found on pages 239–40. The part about how past karma creates present-life circumstances is from the Shorter Exposition on Kamma or Culakammavibhanga Sutta, and can be found on page 166. Bhikkhu Bodhi's explanation of nibbana is found on page 5. Sariputta's description of nibbana is found on page 364. The Buddha's note that the dhamma is unattainable by mere reasoning is found on page 69.

Translations of verses from the Dhammapada are by Glenn Wallis, from his *The Dhammapada: Verses on the Way; A New Translation of the Teachings of the Buddha, with a Guide to Reading the Text*, the Modern Library edition (New York: Random House, 2004). Wallis's idea about the Buddha being a literary protagonist is from his *A Critique of Western Buddhism* (New York: Bloomsbury Academic, 2019), page 183.

The translation of verses from Ambapali's poem is by Charles Hallisey from his *Therigatha: Poems of the First Buddhist Women* (Murty Classical Library of India, Cambridge: Harvard University Press, 2015), in which I also found the information about the royal concubines of the future Buddha before he set forth on his quest for enlightenment.

The story of Sirima is adapted from *A Treasury of Buddhist Stories from the Dhammapada Commentary*, translated from the Pali by Eugene Watson Burlingame, selected and revised by Bhikkhu Kantipalo (Kandy, Sri Lanka: Buddhist Publication Society, 1996).

The story of Anathapindika is adapted from *The Great Disciples of the Buddha: Their Lives, Their Works, Their Legacy*, by Nyanaponika Thera and Hellmuth Hecker, edited with an introduction by Bhikkhu Bodhi (Boston: Wisdom Publications, 2003).

For the story of the Buddha's death due to eating "hog's mincemeat," what the bad monk Subhadda said that caused Mahakassapa to call the First Council, and Ananda's strive for awakening after the Buddha's death, I relied on *The Life of the Buddha* by Bhikkhu Nanamoli (Kandy, Sri Lanka: Buddhist Publication Society, 1972; reprint BPS Pariyatti Edition, 2001).

For other Buddhist scriptural references, in this chapter and elsewhere, I also relied on *Numerical Discourses of the Buddha: An Anthology of Suttas from the Anguttara Nikaya,* translated and edited by Nyanaponika Thera and Bhikkhu Bodhi (Altamira Press, Rowman & Littlefield, Walnut Creek; first published, Kandy, Sri Lanka: Buddhist Publication Society, 1999), and *The Suttanipata: An Ancient Collection of the Buddha's Discourses Together with Its Commentaries,* translated by Bhikkhu Bodhi (Boston: Wisdom Publications, 2017).

Nyanatiloka Mahathera's explanations of the dynamics of rebirth are from his essay "Karma and Rebirth" (The Wheel Publications Issue 9, Kandy, Sri Lanka: Buddhist Publication Society, 1964).

CHAPTER 3: FRANNY AND ZOOEY

All quotations from *Franny and Zooey* are taken from the Little, Brown and Company paperback edition (New York, 1961).

Quotations from the story "Teddy" are taken from *For Esmé—With Love and Squalor* (London: Penguin Books, 1953; originally *Nine Stories,* New York: Little, Brown and Company, 1953).

For all biographical information in this chapter, I relied on *J.D. Salinger: A Life,* by Kenneth Slawenski (New York: Random House, 2010).

All quotations from *The Way of a Pilgrim* and *The Pilgrim Continues His Way* are from the edition translated by R. M. French and with a foreword by Huston Smith (New York: HarperCollins, 1965).

Quotations from *The Philokalia* are from Faber and Faber edition of the complete text, compiled by St. Nikodimos of the Holy Mountain and St. Makarios of Corinth, translated from the Greek and edited by G. E. H. Palmer, Philip Sherrard, Kallistos Ware, with the assistance of the holy Transfiguration Monastery (Boston: Faber and Faber, 1979).

CHAPTER 4: THE DHARMA BUMS

All quotations from *The Dharma Bums* are taken from the Penguin Books edition (New York, 1976; originally published by Viking Press, 1958).

Quotations from *Lonesome Traveler* are from the Grove Press edition (New York, 1988; first edition 1960), and quotes from *Desolation Angels* are from the Riverhead Books edition (New York, 1985; originally 1965).

SOURCES

For all biographical information in this chapter, I relied on Barry Gifford and Lee Lawrence's *Jack's Book: An Oral Biography of Jack Kerouac* (New York: St. Martin's Press, 1978).

The quotations from *The Book of Tea* by Okakura Kakuzo are taken from the edition published by Tuttle Publishing (Boston, 1956).

For the explanation on the difference between Mahayana and Theravada Buddhism, I relied on *Buddhist Thought: A Complete Introduction to the Indian Tradition* by Paul Williams (Oxfordshire: Routledge, 2000), mostly pages 96–111. Charles Hallisey also helped me understand this complicated issue. Bhikkhu Bodhi's explanation of a bodhisatta is found on page 44 of *In the Buddha's Words*. The Buddha's verse about not neglecting one's own goal is from stanza 166 of the Dhammapada, translation by Glenn Wallis, from his *The Dhammapada: Verses on the Way: A New Translation of the Teachings of the Buddha with a Guide to Reading the Text*, the Modern Library edition (New York: Random House, 2004). Translation of the excerpt from the Tuvatka Sutta, about the prohibition of divination, is taken from Bhikkhu Bodhi's *The Suttanipata: An Ancient Collection of the Buddha's Discourses Together with Its Commentaries* (Boston: Wisdom Publications, 2017) pages 313–14. For the accounts of Ajahn Mun's experiences being visited by past buddhas, I relied on *Venerable Acariya Mun Bhuridatta Thera: A Spiritual Biography* by Acariya Maha Boowa Nanasampanno, translated by Bhikkhu Dick Silaratano (Lexington, VA: Forest Dhamma Books, 2010); for full explanation of the account of the visitations of the deceased buddhas and arahants, see pages 170–76 and 451–54.

The note about Allen Ginsberg in India is found in Deborah Baker's *A Blue Hand: The Tragicomic, Mind-Altering Odyssey of Allen Ginsburg, a Holy Fool, a Rebel Muse, a Dharma Bum, and His Prickly Bride in India* (New York: Penguin, 2008).

Bhikkhu Bodhi's definition of the word *tathagatha* is found on page 44 of *In the Buddha's Words*.

For explanations between Buddhism and Taoism, I relied on Anguttara Nikaya 3:68 for the parts about men and women, and Anguttara Nikaya 4:5 for the discourse on the Stream, both found in *Anguttara Nikaya Anthology: An Anthology of Discourses from the Anguttara Nikaya*, selected and translated from the Pali by Nyanaponika Thera and Bhikkhu Bodhi (Kandy, Sri Lanka: Buddhist Publication Society, 2007), and Ariyapariyesana Sutta I 167–73, for the Buddha not wanting to teach after achieving nibbana, translation by Bhikkhu Bodhi, *In the Buddha's Words*, page 70. All quotes from the *Tao te Ching* are from Brian Brown Walker's *The Tao te Ching of Lao Tzu* (New York: St. Martin's Press, 1996); the definition of Tao is from chapter 14; non-action is from chapter 3. For quotes of Chaung Tzu, I relied on

Burton Watson's *Chuang Tzu: Basic Writings* (New York: Columbia University Press, 1996). For quotations from the Hua Hu Ching, I relied on Brian Walker's *Hua Hu Ching: The Teachings of Lao Tzu* (Livingstone, MT: Clark City Press, 1992), chapters 8 and 47; though this edition appears to be out of print and I see there's a newer edition, titled *Hua Hu Ching: The Secret Teachings of Lao Tzu*, published by HarperOne, 2009). The translation of the four *jhanas* is from Glenn Wallis's notes in *The Dhammapada*, page 156. For the Taoist roots of Zen, I relied on David Hinton's *China Root: Taoism, Ch'an, and Original Zen* (Boulder, CO: Shambhala, 2020) pages 6–7.

The story of Ledi Sayadaw launching the Burmese Vipassana movement is told in Erik Braun's *The Birth of Insight: Meditation, Modern Buddhism & The Burmese Monk Ledi Sayadaw* (Chicago: University of Chicago, 2013).

POSTSCRIPT

For the prequel story told in this section, I relied on *The Buddha and the Sahibs* by Charles Allen (London: John Murray, 2018).

Acknowledgments

FIRST, A HUGE THANK you to my editor at Cascade Books, Charles Collier; I'll be forever grateful to you for believing in this book. Also thank you to Kyle Lundburg for your beautiful cover design, and to Matt Wimer, George Callihan, Savanah Landerholm, Chelsea Lobey, and everyone else at Cascade and Wipf & Stock.

Thank you to Robert Meagher for graciously pointing me in Cascade's direction.

Thank you to Robert Wilson and Bruce Falconer at *The American Scholar* for publishing an excerpt of this book, adapted as the essay "Kerouac at 100," and to Lilly Greenblatt at *Lion's Roar* for publishing another excerpt, adapted as the essay "Siddhartha's 100th Birthday."

Thank you to my teachers at Harvard who helped me, either directly or indirectly, to complete this book: Stephanie Paulsell, Beatrice Chrystall, Greg Harris, and especially to Charles Hallisey, who taught me to unknow what I thought I knew, so that I could maybe know something.

Thank you to my other teachers who have shaped my understanding of the Buddha's teaching: S. N. Goenka (of blessed memory), Thanissaro Bhikkhu, Bhikkhu Bodhi, and Bhikkhu Analayo.

Thank you to the Vieira family, for first turning me toward the East.

Thank you to my parents, Sue and Michael Rosenthal, without whose support this book would not exist. My gratitude is inexpressible.

Finally, thank you to my wife, Linda, for being my number one fan, as I am hers. *Te amo.*

About the Author

RANDY ROSENTHAL IS THE author of the novels *Dear Burma* and *The Messiah of Shangri-La*. He has a Master in Theological Studies from Harvard Divinity School, an MFA in Creative Writing from the City College of New York, and a BA in History from UCLA. His work has appeared in *The New York Times*, *The Washington Post*, *The Los Angeles Times*, *Los Angeles Review of Books*, *The Boston Globe*, *The Jerusalem Post*, *The Minneapolis Star Tribune*, *The American Scholar*, *The Paris Review Daily*, *Lion's Roar*, *Buddhadharma*, *Tricycle*, *Harvard Divinity Bulletin*, and several other publications. He teaches writing courses for Harvard University and lives in Boston.

www.ingramcontent.com/pod-product-compliance
Lightning Source LLC
Chambersburg PA
CBHW030110170426
43198CB00009B/570